War Wounded:

Let the Healing Begin

I0161243

Basil B. Clark

WALDENHOUSE PUBLISHERS
Walden, Tennessee

War Wounded is an enjoyable and heartfelt collection of poems embodying an array of emotions. Basil pours out his poetic soul to reveal what I feel are the emotions that many of us experience, yet find it challenging to convey. Whether "War," "Nature," "Family," or "Love," this is a pleasant read with a flavor for all tastes. Enjoy!

Vincent Ivan Phipps, Motivational Speaker, and, Author of Beyond the Poems: Explanations Behind My Inspirations, and Spooky-nooga (Ghost Stories from Chattanooga, TN)

Basil Clark writes of the frailty of humankind with the compassion of one who has hoped, endured, and is overcoming. His empathy for the hurting and descriptions of recovery reveal an understanding from which all of us can learn. By joining his own experiences with the interviews of others he presents a multi-layered exposition on recovery for damaged people.

Basil's use of poetry between the poignant memories of pain and hurt serve as a buffer to balance the empathic feelings of the reader.

Paul M. Stackhouse, Jr. Lexington, KY

Basil Clark has compiled a moving and insightful collection of testimonials, personal stories, and reflective poetry that can change the lives of many people struggling with physical and emotional scars. As a theatre artist and registered nurse, I know the importance of "healing arts" whether it is performance art, visual art, or the written word. This is an important collection of prose, poetry, and shared experiences that will provide insight and comfort to patients as well as caregivers, and be a powerful resource not only to veterans of war, but all those struggling to overcome their physical and emotional "battle scars."

Lauren Brooke Stewart, Artistic and Technical Director Artists Collaborative Theatre Inc., Elkhorn City, KY

In reading through *War Wounded: Let the Healing Begin*, I'm struck anew by the tenacity of the human spirit to triumph over adversity. I admire the determination of these people to choose to find good in the midst of suffering instead of being totally defeated by the circumstances. I pray that readers of this book join those featured in the book on the pathway to peace and healing.

Paula Kempton, Littleton, CO

As a soldier for 21 years, a husband and a father, I was deeply moved. In reading *War Wounded: Let the Healing Begin*, I often felt Basil was speaking directly to me. Through this marvelous collection of stories, poems, observations and life lessons, he was able to touch on all facets of my life. As I read I felt a whirlwind of emotions that brought back so many memories both painful and happy. I also came to realize that even the painful memories have their place, as does learning to cope with them. Healing is the part of life that doesn't come with instructions. I truly feel this book serves as a guide along the healing path. Regardless of your walk in life, this book contains stories that will touch the hearts and souls of all. "Thanks Basil."

Todd McLean, Lieutenant Colonel (Retired)

So many people struggle daily with demons that go unseen by passersby -- memories and disquieting feelings that refuse to leave even as we move farther and farther from the traumatic, emotional events that triggered them. Basil Clark has stepped bravely into the world of the quietly suffering, and returned with a valuable tool that will help those who are on the long healing path.

Tom Shealey, former Executive Editor, Backpacker magazine
Sr. Communications Specialist/Worldwide Marketing
and Communications - UNISYS

We all have areas in our lives that need healing; whether from a tragic event, or the daily struggles that continue to build; the wounds and scars of life find a way to enter. For most of us, we are happy to cover those wounds with a bandage, and then try to ignore them as we wrestle along our daily paths. My father did not do that. In *War Wounded: Let the Healing Begin*, he offers direction on how to treat our wounds and experience true healing, and on how to overcome the tragic events and hurts and pains of life, and use them to influence and help others.

Rodney Clark, Superintendent, Wesleyan Christian School, Bartlesville, OK

Having served in Vietnam with Basil Clark, I know firsthand of many of the traumas he experienced during infantry combat against the North Vietnamese and Viet Cong, and of his acts of personal heroism that saved American lives. Now in *War Wounded: Let the Healing Begin*, Basil uses the framework of his own life experiences and his amazing artistry with words to relate the stories of other Americans who have also survived devastating traumas, and somehow carried on to find useful and even happy lives. This is an incredible volume, not to be overlooked. With its publication Basil Clark is now elevated in my mind from American Hero to National Treasure.

Gary DeRigne, former Staff Sergeant, U.S. Army: Author, Speaker, and Veterans' Advocate

I just love this book! Basil takes the reader on a journey through life, sharing from personal experiences and from the lives of people he met. We live in a wild world, where bad things happen to people. But the things that hit you may not crush you. And even if they crush you, there's gold to be found in the deepest places. This book is beautiful in its honesty and life-tested wisdom. These are not words from a scholar throwing out clever remarks from behind his desk. Through every page of this book the seasoned, thorough wisdom of Basil strengthens the reader's heart. The message of the book is so profound that prose alone can by no means capture the depth. It's the warriors' poetry, gentle in its strength and straightforward in its musing on things unseen, that make me want to read and reread this book.

Henk Stoorvogel, The Netherlands; author, pastor and founder of the 4th Musketeer www.the4thmusketeer.com

War Wounded: Let the Healing Begin is a book that can add to an already existing ministry of healing. Basil Clark has compiled gripping poetry and stories of pain, suffering and loss that lead to conclusions of healing, restoration, peace and grace.

William J. Baird III, Attorney, WestCare Kentucky Chairman

Basil Clark articulates the very understandable trauma which war can inflict on its participants, and then relates that trauma to more ordinary events that any of us may be subject to which can also affect our lives in ways not unlike the effects of war. His poetry injects a poignant element to his message, and I found his use of acrostics unique and moving.

Paul E. Patton, Governor of Kentucky (1995-2003)

For many people, life is – or becomes – a battlefield, a place as full of fear, conflict, confusion and tragedy as some seared landscape across which people are shooting at each other. Those who have been scarred by illness, addiction, loss, loneliness, and all the other shrapnel of the human condition are often, and appropriately, referred to as the walking wounded.

In his book *War Wounded: Let the Healing Begin* Basil Clark, himself a veteran of both literal and spiritual battle, examines case histories of walking wounded who made it to the triage station and are now convalescing. Reminding us that "There is a place beyond the war," Clark demonstrates, through interviews and observation, how his subjects made it through the fire, and by extension, how the rest of us can as well. There is nothing Pollyanna-ish here; only testimony of simple faith and courage, practically applied. That in itself makes *War Wounded* a valuable survival manual.

Roger Waring McCredie F.S.A. (Scot.), Asheville, NC

I grew up enthralled with my father's stories from the Vietnam War. As a young kid I remember thinking it was really cool that my dad had those experiences which made for some fascinating storytelling in our home. As I grew older and learned more about the world – including the human psyche – my admiration grew for my father as I realized what a difficult chapter in history he had lived through and yet somehow managed to become a more compassionate and thoughtful person.

War Wounded is his personal journey through a particular hell on earth and how he found redemption despite such a difficult path being placed before him. However, though it is deeply personal and transparent, it is written as a guidepost for others who are walking a tough road and are desperate for signs of hope.

Winston Churchill once said, "If you're going through hell, keep going." Though not shying away from the cruel realities of life, the message of this book is essentially one of hope that no matter where you find yourself in life, there is a way to move forward focused on the future while reconciling and finding healing for the past.

Ralph Clark, Pastor, Oakdale Free Methodist Church; Dean of Students, Oakdale Christian Academy; Father of four boys; Proud owner of one very large dog :-D

Throughout the scriptures people are called to "hear" and to "remember." Basil Clark has provided a beautiful story which empowers others to be healed through remembering their own stories in light of hearing the journey of others.

This book is a masterful job of weaving Basil's story and the story of so many others into a healing narrative which will impact you on many levels. I have personally been enriched and grown through walking in the stories of God's behind the scenes work in the lives of so many. Just like in the story of Esther, although God is not always mentioned in all the accounts, God is working and God has used Basil "for such a time as this" to help others who are limping forward. This book is a must read for all who are seeking support for inner healing and are searching for a companion in the journey.

Rev. Rob Musick, University Chaplain, University of Pikeville,
Pikeville, KY

Basil Clark has captured the essence of recovering from life's traumatic events. As a former soldier who has experienced multiple battle traumas, Basil has an insight that few mental health care professionals have.

As John Keegan, in his seminal work on battle, *The Face of Battle* reminded us when he said: "What battles have in common is human. ... it is always a study of solidarity and usually also of disintegration – for it is towards the disintegration of human groups that battle is directed," we know that those who participate in battle have their humanity forever changed. Life then becomes a struggle to reinvent ourselves. Patricia P. Driscoll and Celia Straus demonstrate this clearly in the soldiers' descriptions of their war experiences in Iraq and Afghanistan that culminated in life-altering injuries to the brain and psyche, along with the equally dramatic stories of their recoveries: *Hidden Battles on Unseen Fronts.* A common result of traumatic events leaves one questioning their selves--their identity as a person--for the event(s) have substantially altered you. The old person is gone but what does the new person look like? "I know what I used to be..." but ... "What am I now?" "Who am I now?" This loss of self-identity can be devastating. *Let the Healing Begin* offers a path to follow toward the goal of establishing the new self. It gives hope to not only the injured but also to those who live around them.

Jonathan B. "JON" Dodson, Colonel, United States Army Retired,
Former Platoon Leader and Company Commander,
Company D, 1st Battalion, 12th Cavalry, Viet Nam

War Wounded:
Let the Healing Begin

IN MEMORY

"Doc" Hurley	Jose
Brian Morrow	Lt. Conner
Larry Parr	Gary Johnson
Bob Hawkins	Rodney Evans
Tommy Fowler	Cpt. Reaume
Sam Waddell *	* Suicide (1982)

Watercolor by Basil B. Clark

In our diversity of experiences we find just how much we have in common.

Poems from *Poetic Healing; A Vietnam Veteran's Journey from a Communication Perspective* (Mark Huglen, Basil B. Clark) used with permission of Parlor Press, Publisher, and indicated by P/H.) Photographs by Basil B. Clark unless otherwise acknowledged.

DEDICATION

Ralph E. Clark Sr.

To my Dad, Ralph E. Clark Sr. [b. 1922] One of my favorite recollections from my childhood is of the Sunday afternoon walks on the railroad tracks near our house that he would take us kids on. The tracks may be older now [so am I] but those memories are still fresh and pleasant pictures in my mind.

Tracks of Yesteryears
[picture by B. Clark, 2008]

CONTENTS

FOREWORD

I was in college during the Vietnam War, waiting to be called into service for my country. The war wasn't popular on the college campus; but many felt that we needed to be there. Freedom was the key word that was bantered about; freedom from tyranny; freedom from oppression; freedom to live the American dream. But, I wasn't crazy about the idea of going to a far off area to free a people who I didn't know and didn't feel they really cared about our presence in the first place.

I remember my draft physical examination. The day was early and warm. I was called in to the Draft Center, along with a few hundred other individuals. It was a strange mix of individuals of varying colors, backgrounds, and even accents. We were there to be evaluated for fitness of service. Many were hoping to be found unfit for service. We were told to bring any documentation of any problems, whether mental, social, or physical, which would be a factor in the determination of suitability. I brought mine.

I had asthma as a child and my physician noted it in a one line, terse, letter to "Whom It May Concern." It stated that I had a "history of asthma and urticarial (hives) of unknown etiology." I sailed through the mental and physical examination, realizing that the suitable candidates were to be inducted into the Marine Corp. During the blood draw, I remember the person in front of me, arguing with the Paramedic. Because of his mockery, the Paramedic grabbed my hand, aggressively piercing my finger with a lancet for blood. As I bled for the requisite test, I continued to actively bleed, marking on all of my military paperwork that I was there.

I was to be a lean, mean, fighting machine! However, at the last examination station where physicians were reviewing the total data of the day, a grumpy, elderly physician reviewed my papers. After what seemed to be an extremely long time of scrutiny, he popped his head out of the mass of papers and sullenly asked what I was going to do now that I was out of the military. His immediate question was to why my physician hadn't cured me of my hives. I wasn't expecting his question, as I stammered for a response.

One has to wonder why these moments in one's life are truly life-changing experiences. I had to return home only to tell my family that I wasn't suitable for military service. I was to be given a Draft Classification 4-F, meaning

I was not able to participate in any part of the military. It really meant that my soon-to-be wife would be more likely to serve than me. I jokingly would tell her "women and children first." Adding to my poignant news, I was also to tell my future father-in-law that I was not suitable for military service. Since he was the past State Commander of the American Legion, it was difficult for him to understand how I was not suitable for military service but was suitable to marry his daughter.

My moment of bittersweet encounters of that day was one of the reasons why I decided to enter medical school. After a series of life experiences, I was led through a circuitous route towards medicine. My clinical activities in Family Medicine traversed my encounters with numerous men and women of all venues of life. Many were individuals who were called to military duty, while I was not. I remember feeling the duplicity of confused feelings, realizing that these individuals were able to serve while I was not; still, I wasn't crazy about the idea of being a Marine in Southeast Asia. In fact, there was a sense of jubilation that I could take my toothbrush and razor home after that physical examination, realizing that I was to be safe at home, while others would be going in my place.

But, in my clinical practice as a family physician, I met numerous individuals who were the Vets of all of the military excursions from WWI, WWII, Korea, Viet Nam, Grenada, and other actions less known. I experienced the interactions of those who made it home without the outward signs of injury. But, I also experienced those with physical and mental injuries of war. Having a minimal amount of training in post-war trauma, whether it was of a physical nature, lost limbs, eyes, etc., or whether it was of a mental nature with post-traumatic stress disorders, I muddled through my care with these individuals, hoping to provide the best that I could. It really didn't make any difference where they served or how they were injured; I knew they were injured. And, as I worked with them, I realized I needed to let their restoration begin, wherever they were in their healing process.

Ironically, there are those who were not in a military conflict, but have experienced many internal wars in life. Those who have had a history of child abuse, bullying, spousal abuse, even substance abuse, are individuals who are undergoing the need for healing. I met with many of those wounded individuals on a daily basis, noting that, while they may not have the readily visible external scars caused by bullets or shrapnel, they are ones who have internal scars, dealing with their subjective memories of life. These are the scars that cosmetics cannot cover or eliminate. They are forever internal with a need for healing to begin.

Basil Clark has amassed a compendium of stories of individuals who were injured in war. Not just the military conflicts of the past, but the wars associated with the walk of life. He has walked with people in physical and emotional pain, cried with people as they told their life stories, and listened to those who are injured from the war of life. It is in this journal that he has let the healing begin. Allow this to bring healing to your war.

William T. Betz, DO, MBA, FACOFP dist
Senior Associate Dean for Osteopathic Medical Education
Chair, Department of Family Medicine
University of Pikeville – Kentucky College of Osteopathic Medicine

ACKNOWLEDGMENTS

First and foremost, my gratitude and love to Cora Larson-Clark, my wife, my life, and my main proofreader.

In addition, Doug Lange has proofread and given feedback.

Rob Musick, Chaplain, University of Pikeville; Thank you so much for listening to me during some "high point moments," and, some "lower point moments." I truly appreciate you.

Tom Hess, Academic Dean for supporting and recommending my Sabbatical request.

The University of Pikeville, the Faculty Executive Committee, and the Board of Trustees, for approving my Sabbatical.

David Blakesley and Parlor Press for permission to reprint some of my poems from *Poetic Healing: A Vietnam Veteran's Journey from a Communication Perspective.*

For those who shared their stories for chapters, or parts thereof, in the book: Retired SFC Jacob Goble, Sam Waddell, Greg Hicks, Cora Larson-Clark, Ronnie Hylton, Kelly and Shawne Wells, Jeff and Lynn Waldroup, Elisha Taylor, Dr. David A. Smith, Dr. Mary Beth Webb, Mark Rogers, Ralph E. Clark, Brandon Teasley, Doug Lange, Retired Lieutenant Col. Todd McLean, and Paul and Linda Shirk.

Also for sharing their stories, but for a variety of reasons wish to remain unnamed: the young woman in Chapter Nineteen, the four inmates in the WestCare Substance Abuse Program, and others whose names are withheld when mentioned throughout other chapters.

James Riley and Elgin Ward, colleagues: for feedback.

To Allyson Gibson: for use of her e-mail to me.

To Troy Radtke: for use of the picture of him playing ball with Nicholas.

To Ralph C. Clark: for use of the picture of the bear coming onto his back porch.

PROLOGUE

On September 16th, 1969, my platoon leader, Jon Dodson (LT for Lieutenant), took me aside and said he needed to talk with me about something. He said that if in the course of combat anything happened to him or Gary (the platoon sergeant) that he wanted me to be the squad leader who took over. He said he had also mentioned it to the company commander, who agreed with him. I told LT Dodson I would comply with his unlikely-to-be-fulfilled wishes, and he said that was good and he just felt like he needed to get that settled.

The next evening, September 17th, soon after we settled into a perimeter for the night, we came under attack. The firefight lasted some 45 minutes, and included my going out after some fellow squad members on OP (Observation Post) who were pinned down in crossfire. After things settled down and the firing stopped, we checked over our situation and found we had two members of our platoon who were injured and needed evacuation. You might see where I'm going here; yes; LT Dodson and Gary DeRigne, the platoon sergeant.

Before the attack, since foxholes were already dug, Observation Posts set out, and something "off the C-ration menu" consumed, some of us in my squad were just sitting around the foxhole playing cards. That was when gunfire opened up and we became engaged in the firefight. I realized we had three members out in front of the perimeter on observation and, as mentioned in the preceding paragraph, I grabbed my rifle, called for my squad to stop firing (so it would only be a one-way traffic of bullets) and went out to bring my men back to safety. After we got back, and my squad again rejoined the rest of the company in fighting, I looked down and realized I was still clenching cards in my hand. I dropped them and told the guy next to me I didn't think they were a winning hand anyway.

One thing I think we can take away from this is there will be things that occur, that may even cause some form of inner wounding, but there is still life to live, and things to get accomplished. And many actions may well be things that must be done immediately (without running them past a committee.) We may still carry the "inner-wounding-cards" with us, but as we are occupied with the healing process, and other positive activities, we can reduce their influence over us.

Scattered throughout the chapters in this book you will meet some "card-carriers": the couple who lost two children to Cystic Fibrosis; a veteran returning from Iraq for a fishing trip with his dad, only to learn of his father's death as he stepped off the plane; the couple bound together more intimately than most; the woman learning how to live again after a stroke at the age of twenty-three; the young woman who at the age of fifteen was waiting on her father to pick her up from school, who then learned her father had just been killed in a car accident; the veteran still questioning the battle in Afghanistan over a 5-ton truck that didn't run, but left American soldiers injured, some scarred for life; the now-successful pharmacist who was fifteen when his father committed suicide in the next room; the young woman whose abusive (now ex) boyfriend almost killed her; the woman with COPD who might appear "anti-social" to some of her friends, but doesn't feel like elaborating on the instructions her doctor has given her – to avoid crowded areas; the university professor who grew up so poor his house had the earth for a bathroom floor; these, and others.

The preceding are all people who are still functioning quite well in life, but there are still some cards that will always remain "clenched in their minds." They all have found the restoration device that works for them; theirs may not be what works for someone else, but they may inspire others to continue to search for their own path on what sometimes is a "long road home," to borrow the expression used by the Iraq veteran who finds peace in fishing and walks in the woods with his dog.

Furthermore, with the exception of the young, wheelchair-bound Mennonite farmer, and the woman who suffered a stroke at a young age, these are people whose "cards" are not visible. There are volumes to be written commending those with the physical, emotional, and other "observable woundings" who daily overcome the odds to live life to their fullest possible capacity. Probably *Left for Dead; A Second Life After Vietnam*, by Jon Hovde and Maureen Anderson, is one of the better recountings of this type of struggle as Jon moved beyond the obstacles of losing an arm and a leg to live a productive life.

The pages of *War Wounded: Let the Healing Begin* focus more on those with the unseen set-backs. These people are all around us.

Many commented to me something like, "But compared to some, I have it pretty good." I have come to realize over time that the difficulties of our "subjective inner woundings" on a "ten-scale" may well be "minus 2" (or - at times "minus 20") compared to what many others go through. Nonetheless, there are also times where, to us, it still may feel like a 10.

And even if one doesn't identify with the need for inner healing over some traumatic event or circumstance, we all can gain from becoming more aware of the fact that we are surrounded by many "wounded warriors"; I have not "searched far and wide" for these stories, some of them come from people who are now, or have been, associated with the University of Pikeville. Others I ran across in my "daily life routine." These stories are all around us, and contain people who appreciate our understanding, and maybe even our empathy.

War Wounded: Let the Healing Begin

Wars come in a myriad of shapes
And sizes, and frequently the lingering scars
Remain unseen, in our minds. So,

What are some
Of the ways we
Usually receive wounds and other
Not so nice
Damages from?
Experiences come in
Diverse manners;

Lots of different events,
Even sometimes from
The things others didn't

Think were such a big deal.
Harassment and other forms of
Emotional abuse all

Have their places on the list too. By the way,
Everyone has some form of "woundedness."
A part of what goes along with this
Life, it seems,
Is that there is
No one exempt from
Getting hurt somehow.

But there is also hope for
Everyone. There are ways to
Grapple with the past and look
Into the future and find
New ways to forge ahead.

INTRODUCTION

There is a place beyond the war.

Not just the wars that depleted our national treasures of young men and women, and forced families to live in an at least subconscious fear of a knock at the door by the pastor, chaplain, or other military representative. For those of us now living in the United States, these wars took place during World War II, Korea, Vietnam, Kuwait, Afghanistan, and Iraq.

However, there are other, individual battles people often fight, many times not even close to a battle zone or in a "declared war," but nonetheless, these are still battles. These other conflicts also leave their marks; oppressive attitudes; illnesses that hinder; physical, sexual, and emotional abuse; self-sufficiency; a sundry of addictions; traumatic events; rejection; bullying; victims of natural disasters; random acts of violence and loneliness; to name a few. These battles are usually very subjective, and the end results can be just as devastating as real bullets, shrapnel, IED's, or other weapons.

Now, one might ask why self-sufficiency is listed as a hidden handicap, and that is because, from my experience, perspective, and observations, it too, has an effect on our intrapersonal communication ("self-talk"/thoughts) which in return affects our interpersonal communication and relationships. Self-sufficiency can be good; it may also be not-so-good.

So all these handicaps, along with other hidden things not listed, have impact on our lives and affect our relationships with others.

While a student at Eastern Kentucky University I was talking with one of my professors in his 50's about a basketball game my sons had recently played in (they were still in grade school at the time.)

He said he was glad to see I enjoyed their games and that I seemed to enjoy doing things with them. Then he became real serious and told me that his father had only gone to one of his games when he was a young boy. My professor said that at one point in the game, the ball was passed to him, the floor was clear, and he took off running and made a basket – on the opposing team's end of the floor. He said his father stood up in the stands, hollered out, "You stupid idiot!" stomped out of the gym, and never attended another of his games.

As he related this I could still see the pain on his face and hear it in his voice. Some 40+ years later he was still affected by that one incident, which actually was a microscopic definition of his relationship with his father.

Living beyond the war does not mean it is totally eliminated. The saying, "What happens in Vegas, stays in Vegas" does not apply to inner woundings. Try as we like, these things don't stay in Iraq, Afghanistan, Vietnam, the funeral parlor, the doctor's office, the playground, and other places where the traumatic events occurred. Some things will never fully leave us, nor should they. As humans we aren't constructed this way, and to forget some things could be a disservice as we want to learn from the negatives so we won't repeat them.

Of course, for each of us, if the "wounding" is bothering us, at that time it may well be a 10 on a scale of 1 to 10. I say the above to set the stage for the following: at one time or other we may look at someone else and say either, "So what's his problem? He ought to deal with what I deal with," or, "Okay. Let me deal with my situation; I really don't have it 'near as bad' as she does."

I recently read *The Long Walk* by Slavomir Rawicz (an escapee from a Soviet prison camp in Siberia.) I was, and am, bowled over particularly by two things; the depths of evil that can exist in this world, and, at the same time, just how much humans can endure in a fight for survival as they are physically, emotionally, and spiritually wounded again and again.

For over 40 years now I have had a loud, continual ringing in the ears (severe tinnitus.) The only time I don't hear it is when asleep, and even then, it sometimes awakens me and makes it difficult to get back to sleep. But, if asleep, I do have to eventually awaken "normally" to go on with my life. Oh, and there is another time I don't hear it; if I place my head about a foot away from a loud, whistling teapot, but, I don't particularly like the close-up sound of a whistling teapot (like I said, I have my own version, thank you very much.)

However, the continual ringing is not that much different, and definitely no worse, than memories of abuse, or a traumatic event or severe loss, thoughts regarding an illness or injury, or feelings of loneliness or rejection, or perhaps just a sense that you are living in a fog. All are subjective.

Subjective Things ^{P/H}

If I were set in a wheelchair and hit a big old bump
And slipped a little on my side and fell out on my rump,
Some aid would soon be with me,
For evident problems would show,
And seeing me lying flat on my rear,
Others would quickly know I needed help.

But my handicap is subjective,
So even if it lays me low,
And batters and beats me all about
No one will ever know unless I tell them.

But who wants to share in a defect?
And who really cares how it beats?
For subjective things are the hardest to share,
And the easiest to cause defeats.

So this book is about the subjective wars, whether the wounds come from a military war, or whether the wounds are of another, personal nature.

My "poetic healing" did not end the ringing just as your healing will not eliminate certain memories or other subjective pains, but it does allow me to cope and function in a way that can reach out to others. And that involves not just reaching out to help others (important as that is), but also allowing others to help me.

I am not a psychologist, so I am probably the wrong person to ask, "So, tell me, just how does the healing begin?" All I know is that at various times in the years after Vietnam I felt an overwhelming urge at times to write; about the ringing, the war, pain, loneliness, sanity (or lack thereof), God, death, etc. But there were other times I didn't write, but still felt the need to have an activity I could focus on. For example, for an almost two-year period, I worked on model cars almost every evening, eventually having a collection of almost 40 NASCAR race cars.

I think it's fair to say that we probably can't "trademark and sell" the process for healing; each person has to search for his or her own way. I am sharing with you some things that worked for me, and some poetry that I believe many can identify with (I know this to be true from comments I have received from people who have read my poems in *Poetic Healing*.)

Poetry
My poetry comes out of a pen.
Yours may be in
The bounce of a basketball,
Hiking, decorating a cake,
Working on a Habitat for Humanity house,
Reading, teaching Sunday School,
Or anything else that brings relief,
A certain sense of structure, and place.

My prayer for this book is found in Proverbs 15:4a, "The tongue that brings healing is a tree of life." I also subscribe to the "Teacher's Prayer" I heard somewhere, "Lord, if I can't help anyone today, please don't let me hurt anyone."

In an appendix I'll recount the process of some events that occurred over 40 years ago, and a recent re-creation of some of those events (on-stage at the University of Minnesota, Crookston Campus), and, oh how the perspectives have changed. I can honestly say, that if a "poetic healing" had not taken place in my life, I would either not be here, due to suicide (conscious or subconscious), or, if still existing, most likely it would be in an alcoholic or drug-filled haze.

You'll notice several poems that are marked [P/H], and then another "acrostic version" comes right after it. In a place where that occurs, I just decided to see if I could get the same idea to fit its title. I guess this is another phase I am going through in the on-going struggle to maintain "poetic healing."

After almost all interviews where the person's real name is given, I also wrote an acrostic poem using their name; again, another phase.

Different World

Do you hear what
I hear running through my
Frightened mind? The screams of
Fears that always, ever,
Each new day will still
Repeat the same old song.
Ever wonder why I
Nod and smile, then turn so you can't see the
Tears in my heart. The fears are

Whistling their invulnerable, little
On-going tunes.
Reverberating their way through
Lonely
Days and nights.

Disclaimers

Many things these days have disclaimers, so I might as well join the trend.

As Advisor

Let me give you two examples of the benefits of following my advice.

(1) My youngest son did not follow my advice when it came to where I thought he should complete college (Pikeville College, of course), and it turns out that he made the correct decision for his life and where he is now; married with four great kids, and, Superintendent of Wesleyan Christian School, Bartlesville, OK.

(2) My oldest son did follow my advice. He wanted to quit Berea College after one year and go to a college in Michigan. I talked him out of it. The next year he met the woman he married and has had four wonderful children with, and my urging is a huge factor in him being in the good place that he is right now; also, he is Pastor, and Dean of Students at Oakdale Christian Academy, Jackson, KY. So with my sons I'm at 50%. You figure the odds; take my advice at your own risk.

As Counselor

I'm not. There are many competent, professional counselors around, and their advice should be sought.

As Theologian

I'm not. I know what some things mean to me, and I can only speak to those perspectives.

So, What Do I Know?

My favorite line I've ever had in a play was as DOC in West Side Story when I got to say, "What do I know; I'm the Village Idiot." So, keep in mind that this book is written by someone who:

(**1st**) dropped out of high school – twice – before

(**2nd**) getting his GED and then later, a Bachelors, and two Masters Degrees.

Disclaimers

Don't you know that
In everything we do
Someone will think we are
Claiming this or that, so
Lest you misunderstand,
Allow me to make clarification;
In my life, there have been
Many instances which have been the
Exception, not necessarily
Rules that somehow
Sum me up (true for all of us.)

Part One:
Looking From the Inside, Out

1

Life Unfolds; or Turning Points, Etc.

Turning points in our lives

I have done the following exercise with Interpersonal Communication classes. The point is to discuss the direction a person seems to be heading – I tell them for simplicity, make the events happen to a male. I have them fill out three negative things that could happen to this person growing up; Things have to be within the years of 0 (can include with mother prior to birth) to 30.

I collect them up and then read from cards I have made up prior to the exercise - it looks like I am reading to the class from their selections – we stop as I am reading them to speculate on possible directions of this kid/young adult.

Things I select to read to them:
1. Mother attempted suicide while pregnant with him.
2. In the 8th grade served a week long "in school suspension" for breaking into the school shop area during a basketball game.
3. In the 9th grade received about 100 after school detentions.
4. Dropped out of high school (twice.)
5. Ran away from home and lived with relatives 75 miles away.
6. Arrested for public drunkenness at the age of 17.
7. Killed a man at the age of 20.
8. Age 21 arrested for drinking while driving.
9. Age 29 fired from job as coal truck driver for rolling coal truck twice in two weeks.
10. Now in his 60's, makes his University interpersonal communic-tion class do a silly assignment like this.

The first thing I point out to them is that #7 (killing a man) occurred while in the Infantry in Vietnam (I don't want them worried); the second thing discussed is that we are affected and shaped by our past, but we do not have to be chained to, or by, it.

If I have learned anything in life, it is that turning points in our life (1) are usually not recognized while going through them – only later can we gain perspective; (2) often, a major turning point in our life (for our, or someone else's, good) is something we wouldn't, or don't, choose to do; we only see the "good" later; and (3) as a result of the first two, I believe my life is more than a biological accident waiting to happen; there is a plan and a purpose unfolding.

Let me give some examples.

(1) Events Beyond Our Control

After Vietnam, while at Ft. Hood, Texas, I decided to re-enlist for six years, and started off my stint with three years in Germany. At the time, I was giving serious consideration to making the military a career. While in Germany, in early October 1972, my unit had to send several troops on a six-day field problem as a part of a larger Battalion exercise. It worked out that about one in five from the Company had to go, and I was one of the unfortunate ones (or so I thought at the time) to be assigned for this duty. The main problem I had with going was that the exercise came right in the middle of a four-day weekend, and during one of these, a soldier could get a four-day pass, and see several places in Europe (via the Autobahn, I was stationed about five hours from the Bavarian Alps, within seven hours of Austria, less than eight hours from Holland and Belgium, you get the idea.)

So I did everything I could to get out of this duty (except refuse to go – I wasn't particularly partial to court-martials), but to no avail. So out I went. While on the exercise I ran into a Captain I knew from Vietnam, Cpt. Jan Beer, who, after we caught up on the past couple years, asked me if I was interested in teaching at the First Armored Division Non-Commissioned Officer Academy located at Katterbach, near Ansbach, GY. I told Cpt. Beer that I was interested; however, I had applied earlier in the year, presented the required sample class, and was turned down. He then said, "Why don't you apply again; I'm the Officer in charge of training and education in the Division now, and the Academy falls under my jurisdiction."

So I applied again, gave another sample class, and, lo and behold, was accepted. Cpt. Beer always said that I got the job on my own merits, but I think I know "the rest of the story."

I got out of the military after 8 ½ years, and started college. The main problem I had was I couldn't really make up my mind what I wanted to major in. I started in Elementary Education, later switched to Biology and Chemistry (major mistake for me), and so I found myself at the age of thirty, with 87 college hours, switching my major for the third time. The only problem was I still wasn't sure what I wanted to do "when I grew up." After thinking about it, and recalling how much I had enjoyed teaching at the NCO Academy in Germany, I decided to major in Speech and Theatre. I have taught Speech and Theatre for almost twenty-five years at two different colleges, and realize it is my niche. And I have told students the story, stressing that my standing behind the lectern was a direct result of that field problem in Germany that I tried so hard to avoid.

Turning Points

There are things that occur on our journey through life, that are
Usually not recognized at the time as a real big deal.
However, as we later look back, sometimes we see that
They were something of major significance.
So, I have come to the conclusion that major turning points

In our lives are not usually seen as such (at the time.)
Also, I have observed many things that really
Worked out for my good were not something that, at the time,
I would have chosen to do (some I even tried to avoid doing.)
Didn't change the end results – they were good for me.

In addition, as I look back over my life I have to echo
(Or at least paraphrase) the words of our 20th President,
James A. Garfield. "My life seems to have been a series of
Accidents, most of them favorable to me."

Turning Points II

Tried a few times to get out of something
Until the futility of it came crashing down,
Really getting my attention.
Now I know I have to strengthen my
Inner being and prepare.
Not for the worst, but for what I must
Go through. I know now that

Peering back through my personal history I can
Only conclude that many difficult things turned out to be
In my own best interest,
Not that they were particularly
Timely, or enjoyable, (although)
Surely I must admit, some were.

Another element coming into play which could fit the "events beyond our control" category is we might never be able to calculate how we may impact someone else's life by doing at times "what needs to be done – when it needs to be done." Recently, one of my daughters-in-law, Becky Clark, was at a pool when a young girl started to drown. Becky dove into the pool, fully dressed, and rescued the girl. She wasn't thinking of the I-phone in her pocket. Of course, it was ruined, which meant all photos, videos, and so forth were permanently lost. But can we imagine if Becky had gone through a "ten-point checklist"; I-phone out – check; shoes off – check; make sure no dollar bills in pocket – check; etc.? The drowning girl's future might not have been. Becky is a heroine in my opinion, because she did what needed to be done – when it needed to be done; aware of what really mattered.

The Phases ^{PH}
My mind sometimes moves in hazes
When I think of various phases
I've been through so far
To get me where I am.
If I were allowed to make one change
Of anything I could rearrange
I don't believe I would change one thing
For who knows what that consequence would bring.
And at least I know where I am now
And what I'm doing.

(2) In 2000 I was reading a Backpacker Magazine

and there was an article on "The Long Trail" in Vermont, a trail that runs from the Massachusetts border to the Canadian border following the Green

Mountain Range. From the minute I read it, I knew I wanted to do it, so in November 2000; I started to train for a hike the following summer. I started the hike the end of May 2001, and every evening I jotted notes into a journal about things I had been thinking about, or just observations I had made during the day.

One day I was hiking along a ridge line along the Crittendon Reservoir. The trail was following a mountain range, and the foliage was thick enough that you could only occasionally catch glimpses of blue through the leaves; the water below. There was a spot near the southern end of the reservoir where I was able to get a "barely-a-glimpse-shot" of the reservoir, and, then, over an hour later, at the northern end I was able to get another picture.

I jotted down something that at the time I did not realize the full significance of:
"only two places in over an hour where pictures could be taken → notes for Two Little; Too Short (draft book) → twofold 1. take the pictures while you can → 2. sometimes only catch a glimpse of the larger picture → doesn't mean the larger picture isn't there, waiting to "unfold."

The Vermont Long Trail

I trained for over six months for the 270 mile
Backpack trip of the Vermont Long Trail.
Harmon Hill in a late May snow storm was pretty,
Stratton Pond in early morning fog, beautiful.
Killington Mountain, where you could see into
Several states, and Canada, was fantastic, and the
Later sunset at Cooper Lodge surpassed the earlier view.

Really enjoyed the meal in Clarendon, one mile down
A highway the trail crossed, at the Whistle Stop Restaurant.
One hundred fifty miles into the hike, due to unforeseen circumstances,
Headed back to Kentucky; had to abort the backpacking trip.
Went home and battled some "lows" over a "mission unfulfilled."
However, something that helped, hiking it solo, I knew my sons
Were proud of their dad for taking on the challenge.

And that (sorry, Robert Frost) "has made all the difference."

I only backpacked the lower 150 miles before returning earlier than initially planned to Kentucky. I was a little frustrated with myself that I had not completed the entire trail, however, about a week after getting back, I noticed an article in the paper about a local theatre person, Stephanie Richards, who was going to direct the play, *The Kentucky Cycle*, the next summer (2002), and asking for people to show up for a read-through. I went to it and later auditioned and was cast in two roles in the play. It was a continuing learning experience for me, and I think I may have learned more about directing and acting in that whole experience than I did while studying those areas in college.

(3) I have developed and perform

several character monologues, and several years ago (2002 or 2003 I believe) was asked to act out my President James A. Garfield character at a Civil War Symposium being held in Pikeville, Kentucky.

In 2007 I received a phone call from John Justice of Pikeville, and he asked if I could meet with him and his cousin Rusty Justice in a couple days as they were working on a project they wanted to talk to me about. I agreed, and two days later we met at the Pike County Heritage Center. John informed me that the Pike County Coal Education Development and Resources (CEDAR) was working with the Challenger Learning Center of Hazard (Kentucky) to develop a DVD for a 4th grade curriculum centered on comparisons of the trip of exploration by Dr. Thomas Walker into Kentucky and a future trip of exploration to Mars, and, the things that were considered when establishing coal camps and things that will have to be considered when establishing Mars colonies. This included answering questions about "Why go?," "What do we expect to find?," "How do we get there?" etc.

John told me that someone who had seen me perform the President Garfield character monologue a few years earlier had recommended they try and get in touch with me to see if I would be interested in (for pay) writing the script and playing the part of Dr. Thomas Walker in the DVD. It turned out to be a challenging, fun, and rewarding experience as we developed and brought to fruition, *Mars Invasion 2030; From Coal Camp to Space Camp.*

One Thing Leads

It's amazing how in life
One thing leads to another.
We do something here, and
It gets noticed by someone there,
Who in turn mentions it to
Someone else, and it opens the
Door for the next step. As I
Look back over the journeys
Of my life, I am made aware,
There were no accidents.

(4) In 2008, I was going to Vermont

to spend a couple days with my Aunt Beverly, go hiking on about a fifteen mile portion of the Long Trail, see Aunt Bev again for another day, and then return home by way of Seneca Rocks and Dolly Sods Wilderness in West Virginia for a couple more days hiking in Dolly Sods.

I really enjoyed the time I spent with my aunt, and when I eventually hit the Long Trail, I decided to climb the rock steps up to where I could spend a night on Harmon Hill, a beautiful spot where you can look over Bennington, Vermont.

As the pictures below show, the sunset and the next morning's view of fog covering the town below were spectacular.

But as I looked over Bennington, I started to reflect on my plans for the Vermont trip; couple days with Aunt Bev, couple days hiking. I decided to

go back and spend more time with her as it seemed she had really enjoyed my visit, and I realized time spent with her was far more important than any time on the Long Trail, or hiking in the Dolly Sods Wilderness.

She was a bit surprised, but also, pleased when I showed back up at her door. I asked her what she wanted to do, and she mentioned a cousin, Elsie, about an hour away in New Hampshire that she had not been able to see for several months. We made the visit, and in a several-months-later phone conversation with Aunt Bev, I was reinforced in being glad we had, as it was the last time she saw her ninety-three year old cousin before Elsie passed away.

Their Last Visit

The bottom line is, we make choices, and sometimes little choices in our life may have a major impact on someone else's life. And as I wrote in the last part of the poem *One Thing Leads*, "*As I look back over the journeys of my life, I am made aware that there were no accidents.*"

No Accidents

In theatre we talk about the main goal
Of a play, and how every character makes his/her
Choices under the "umbrella" of the Super Objective.

I'd like to think I have a little more free will in life,
But sometimes when I see the way things work out,
I ask myself if I'm not playing things out under Someone's umbrella.

I have heard it said before (can't recall source) "Play each play as if it's the most important play of the game, because it just might be." The older I get, or, putting it another way, the more I can look back and review the game of life, the more I think the above quote really is a profound statement.

And in regards to "playing the plays" of the game, sometimes it becomes easy to dwell on the negative days or times, and think that "the game" isn't going all that well. It may seem that the negatives are outweighing the positives. I urge you to take the time to think of five things going well for you. As I tell my students when I have this on their first "Who Are You?" assignment, force yourself to come up with them (positives), even if you have to "fudge."

2

Turn It Off, Please;
and Other Subjective Things

Turn It Off, Please *(First written, 1982; updated 2010)*

It sounds like an alarm as I stir into half-consciousness, roll over on my belly, and start to reach for my cell to look at the time; 3:26 AM. It's not an alarm, but the usual. Aggravation often begins to settle in, but I can usually push it away with a sigh and turn my now alert efforts toward getting comfortable, and trying to get back to sleep. All else is quiet at this hour except for the persistent ringing. I try to relax and hope for sleep, for during the past forty plus years, during sleep is the only time I don't hear it.

I have tinnitus, along with several million other Americans. According to the American Tinnitus Association (ATA), I am in the category of several million Americans who have the severe form.

Tinnitus is defined as "A subjective ringing, rushing, or buzzing sound in the ears, not caused by any external stimulus."

The causes are varied, including nerve damage due to exposure to loud noises whether as a one-time incident or over an extended period of time; or a reaction to some medicines; psychological reasons; and others. The Veterans Administration (VA) and other doctors said tests indicated that mine was a result of nerve damage.

Some people have recurring dreams; others have links to recurring memories.

April 26, 1969. First Air Cavalry. 1st Battalion, 12th Cavalry, Delta Company. 3rd Squad, 3rd Platoon was assigned the mission of relieving another squad at their overnight ambush site some 20 kilometers N/NE of Quan Loi, south of the infamous "Fishhook." The area had numerous well-used trails, and already different units in our company had been in contact and minor firefights with small parties of North Vietnamese Army (NVA) soldiers.

Replacement time was set for 8 AM. Cautiously, we picked our way through the moderate jungle undergrowth and upon arrival at the ambush site that bordered a well-used trail, set about the various tasks involved in change-over. This included planting and camouflaging several claymore mines. Upon completion of the changeover, Andy, a fellow Infantryman from Puerto Rico, and I were lying down in our assigned position when another soldier on the left flank whispered, "Someone's coming!"

Eerie silence fell. An NVA soldier walked warily into our kill zone and stopped directly in front of a hidden claymore mine. Andy and I hugged the ground as he stared straight at our position, an inquisitive look on his face (we wondered later if Andy's darker skin had him confused.) The detonator to the claymore mine nearest the NVA was in the hands of Mike, our squad leader, who was in the next position over. As the NVA raised his AK-47, Mike squeezed the detonator. The mine exploded, the soldier fell with a cry, and other mines exploded from other positions.

Andy and I waited a few seconds and then cautiously rose and moved toward the body. The squad leader ordered men to pull security for us. We soon had the body stripped and a fruitless document search completed.

"We need to check the trail and look for blood," Mike said. "Sam thinks he heard talking before the ambush. Andy, you and Sam go up that way. Clark, you and Bill go down the trail."

Apprehensively, Bill and I started in the direction the NVA had appeared from, moving without sound, fingers on our triggers. The well-traveled trail turned to the right past a large dirt mound. Due to the undergrowth on either side, we could not see around the bend. Carefully we stepped around and saw the body of another NVA. My heart was in my throat as Bill and I edged forward. When we were about six feet from him, he started to move.

"Look out!" Bill hollered. "He's still alive! Look out!"

My instant reaction was fear and pent-up hatred, bitterness, and revenges all reaching a peak. My mind flashed to an earlier image of war, Jose, leaning against a tree, dead instantly from two bullet wounds in his forehead. As I brought my rifle on line with the NVA soldier and flipped the safety from single shot to automatic, I muttered, "You rotten son-of-a . . . You have one comin' for Jose."

Bill was also aiming at the soldier, and a split second later we both pummeled twenty rounds into him.

If a dream, this would be a good place to end it and awaken. However, the actual nightmare of April 26, 1969, continues. The instant the firing started there was an explosion from the body. My first thought was that a concealed NVA soldier had tossed a grenade at us. "This is it," I thought. "Dad and Mom will get the news. This is it. I'm dead."

"I am hit!" Bill hollered. "What the hell happened?"

I began to realize the explosion had come from the body itself and yelled, "I think he had grenades, and we hit one!"

"My leg! Oh God, my leg!" Bill moaned. A chunk of shrapnel the size of a quarter had lodged in the shin, and he was bleeding profusely.

I knelt to where Bill had sat down, quickly scanning the area for signs of any other enemy. "It doesn't look too serious," I said. "Kind of a mess, though."

"Are you guys okay?" Mike and a couple others in our squad rushed toward us.

"Bill's been hit. Shrapnel from a grenade."

"What happened?"

"Guess he was carrying grenades, and we hit one." I said again.

As Mike and others started to care for Bill, I moved to where the lifeless body lay grotesquely on the trail. In a daze I reached down and turned the soldier over. Yes, the explosion had been from a grenade, or grenades, under him. I was aware of a loud ringing in my ears, and it seemed to mix with the jumbled assortment of thoughts tumbling through my mind. It seemed as if I was in some sort of dream encounter. I asked myself, "Why did you shoot him?" Continuing to stare at the ripped body, I shrugged and answered myself. "Dunno . . . scared . . . Jose . . . won't know . . . wonder . . . what if his mother could see him now . . . will anyone notify her . . . who gave me the right to . . .?" Then the justification, "Ah, the hell with it! That's what we're here for. He wouldn't have worried about me! Chalk it up for Jose . . . Yeah . . . one for Jose."

I turned to see if there was anything I could do to help Bill, but Mike already had the bleeding controlled. Because I had slight shrapnel in my left shoulder, I was "medevaced" with Bill, who had gone into near shock. Later, while getting a tetanus shot, I asked a medic about the persisting ringing in my ears.

His reply was, "After hearing loud noises, sometimes there's ringing for a while, but it usually goes away. 'Course if there has been some nerve damage, then it may be a more permanent thing. You'll just have to wait and see. Guess that's just one of the hazards of being an Infantryman."

Three years later in a dispensary in Germany where I had just finished another hearing test, I was told (for about the fifth time), "Well, you don't hear too bad for an Infantryman, and there's nothing we can do about the ringing."

In October, 1976, after eight and a half years' service, I was processing out of the Army at Fort Benning, Georgia. The examining physician asked about my hearing loss and informed me that I should have been given a "profile" right after Vietnam that would have excluded me from further exposure to loud noises such as rifle-firing and other Infantry related activities. On the physician's referral, a later appointment at a VA hospital resulted in my being awarded ten percent compensation.

In October, 1979, I had a severe head cold that landed me in bed for nearly a week. The head congestion amplified the ringing, and with my "enforced" lack of activity, there was little to keep my mind from being aware of it constantly. After a few days I was extremely depressed and started to feel like no one really cared. People around me couldn't hear what I was listening to, had no awareness of what was bothering me. I was allowing the ringing to remind me of fourteen months of some questionable actions in the Infantry in Vietnam and at the same time felt little or no purpose for my existence. I wrote a very negative eight-page summary entitled "Sowing Reaping" that included the following:

> "Ringing-constant ever ringing. They call it tinnitus.
> Ringing in ears due to ear damage. Got to live with it.
> Collect a little compensation. Put the past behind and live today.
> What makes that hardest to do is that constant ringing.
> A continued reminder of April 26, 1969."

I decided I couldn't listen to it any longer. I felt like jamming something into my ears--anything for relief. I figured that if I didn't hear it in my sleep, then I wouldn't when I was dead either. Ignorant of the effects of aspirin, I took twenty and lay back down. I remember how peacefully I went to sleep only to awaken later feeling terrible. Obviously, I hadn't taken a lethal dose.

The ringing seemed even louder. It was, as I later found out, that too many aspirin can cause a temporary ringing in the ears.

What I did find out that October afternoon was I really didn't want to die. I continued to have low moments over the continual ringing, but I came to believe that the reasons for fighting the depression were stronger than those for giving in to it.

Sometime later a friend who was aware of the disability gave me an article about tinnitus he had saved from Parade magazine. As I read it, I realized for the first time that there were literally thousands of others feeling the same depression, moments of unexplained tension, irritability and difficulty sleeping because of tinnitus.

The article mentioned tinnitus maskers, devices that "fed" a rushing noise into the ear and, in many cases; this masked or covered the sound of the tinnitus. It gave the address of the American Tinnitus Association (ATA) in Portland, Oregon, to which I wrote and received a complete listing of VA hospitals that had "tinnitus clinics."

Due to my school schedule at Eastern Kentucky University, I had to delay an appointment in St. Louis for nearly a year. That year was both the best and worst in reference to the tinnitus.

Tinnitus is aggravated by lack of sleep, and the 1981-82 semesters at EKU definitely increased the level at which I was hearing the ringing. My two young sons had become accustomed to the "habit" of eating, so, in order to keep groceries on the table, I worked midnight to 8 AM four nights a week at a nearby service station. As a theatre student, I was involved in five productions, all of which had evening rehearsals. I carried a full undergraduate load each semester and tried to be a father to two boys I seldom saw. The ringing actually assisted in that it helped me stay awake during times of near exhaustion, but physically, I went through one of the worst times of my life. Nevertheless, in a state of continually being tired and constantly being reminded of an undesirable incident from my past, a major turning point in my attitude occurred. I was seriously searching for more than trite, neatly memorized answers to the purpose for living. I remember reading a "Dear Abby" column titled "With such examples we can overcome," which briefly described many people who had struggled and succeeded against the odds of a variety of disabilities and adversities. Chided about getting my own attitude into perspective, I really began to see this "disability" as somehow linked to an overall plan for my life.

Because of a different attitude toward my situation, I found myself with a new sense of understanding toward others who had to cope with feelings similar to mine. I wept after newscast announcements about any veteran committing suicide; there were a few in the news at the time, and I wished there was some way to communicate a message of understanding and extended hope. This desire started to become a reality in my life.

In 1982, enrolling as a graduate student in Theatre at the University of Kentucky, I decided to take a course in play-writing, which led to a roughly autobiographical play using Vietnam and tinnitus as symbols of wrestling with whatever obstacle a person needed to overcome. At the completion of the semester our class had readings of our rough drafts. I learned how the rough draft came to be so named. I had poured a lot of myself into the script, and it had been a type of healing process, but dramatically it lacked much. The next semester my professor, Dr. Linda Burson, was patient and gracious enough to guide me through an independent play-writing study where the play was cut, chopped, revised, restructured, and eventually much improved.

The completion of *Starkle, Starkle, Little Twink*, the play in Appendix "B," saw an end to a period marked by a purging of my soul. Night after night for almost a year ('82-'83), primarily between the hours of 10 PM and 3 AM, I had alternately wept, drank, cursed, and prayed. And I won. For the first time in my life, I was beginning to see the effects of a negative background being blended together with current efforts for a good net result. The desire to fight against my past--and my God--faded. My boys listened as I read through the play to its final message of perseverance, hope, and reconciliation.

Ralph spoke first, "Dad, if I could have anything I wished for, first of all I'd wish that you never had the ringing." I thanked him and pointed out I really believed my play could be helpful to someone else, and that it had come about as a "round-about result" of the ringing.

Starkle. Starkle, Little Twink was later included in the book, *Poetic Healing: A Vietnam Veteran's Journey from a Communication Perspective* (Huglen, Clark, Parlor Press, 2005.) In 2009 I was asked by the University of Minnesota, Crookston Campus to participate in the premier production of the play. I served as the guest playwright and also played the part of DAN. In

Appendix "B" I will go into some detail about the differences in perspective while re-living onstage, some events from 40 years earlier.

Meanwhile, let me list some positives of this internal, infernal ringing.

For one, I believe I can better understand the depression and hopelessness felt by those considering or actually committing suicide. I am also learning the importance of perseverance. There is a greater awareness that we all have obstacles and a commonality in our struggles to win.

Most importantly, I now believe in a purpose for my life in which all things can work together for good as I seek and submit myself to the Author of that purpose. I now find hope and peace in the writings of the Apostle Paul to the Romans, that "the creation itself will be liberated from its bondage to decay and brought into the glorious freedom of the children of God," (Romans 8:21.) As do many others, I live with a constant reminder of just how long a war can go on, but I also have hope for the good that is occurring in the here and now, even on the nights when I wake up and listen to the alarm that isn't going off.

I'm also more aware of how other "hidden illnesses" can affect behavior, for example, cancers one may not want to talk about, or other traumatic events that happen in life. Someone might struggle with a breathing-related illness that affects how much he or she can, or wants to, participate in outdoor activities, which may leave others with questions of "Why don't you want to do this?"

Or what about the child who has been subjected to bullying? As seen in some recent situations, bullying is no longer limited to school playgrounds or after-school walks home, but has found its way onto Facebook, into cell phone text messages, and other technological tools. Memories of these abuses can torment one for weeks, months, or, even years, afterward. Part of the problem with these subjective areas is trying to figure out how to, as the title of this chapter states, "Turn It Off."

Now, in my case, some writing in this book refers to tinnitus and war memories, but it really has equal application for all of the areas so many wrestle with. Loneliness has no limitations as far as subjective battles go.

A POINT OF ORDER, the thing that may seem to be projected in some of these writings is that it is better to try and go it alone; I do **not** want that message to come across. The point is, those struggling with some form of inner woundedness may feel, or have felt, some of these things, and may well identify with them. Part of the healing process should be to seek competent and professional help, part has to come from involvement with something beyond yourself, and part from whatever ordered form (writing, painting, basketball, hiking, etc.) you choose as an "escape hatch."

I have a couple thoughts regarding being involved. In days past, there were a lot more things done involving "hands on" work; quilting, wood carving, canning, furniture making, to name a few. I'm willing to "bet a small portion of the farm" on the concept that a lot of inner healing took place for people who worked and reflected in the process.

There are places where I refer to scriptural writings in this book; because I choose to draw some of my knowledge, wisdom, and thought-provokers from these sources. I try to treat life as a wonder, often times with a big question mark. I subscribe to what Einstein said, "There are only two ways to live your life. One is as though nothing is a miracle. The other is as if everything is." I believe scriptural writing helps me in my living out the belief that everything is a miracle.

In an ancient writing, the *Apocrypha*, Wisdom of Sirach 3:14, we are told to seek wisdom. "Learn where wisdom is, where strength is, where understanding is, so that you may at the same time learn where length of days and life are, where there is light for the eyes, and peace."

And we might note that education, and wisdom, while they may go hand in hand, are not synonymous; education might have let me know that twenty aspirin were not enough to kill me; wisdom would have told me not to even try it in the first place.

I find it interesting in Exodus 14:14 where Moses was answering the people of Israel when they were fearful and complaining at one point, saying, "The Lord will fight for you; you only need to be still." But, verse 15 goes on with the response of the Lord back to him, "Then the Lord said to Moses, 'Why are you crying out to me? Tell the Israelites to move on.'" In other words, do something!

So, the question is what to do, and how to get inspired. Inspiration comes in many forms, sometimes even adversity. There are times in life we might not have been somewhere or gone through a certain situation if the choice had been left to us, but, as a result, there may be things we can now do that we would not have been able to do under any other circumstances.

Again, using a Biblical example, when Queen Esther had the opportunity to speak up in defense of her people, she replied to her adopted father, Mordecai, that she would be putting her life at risk if she went before the king, Xerxes, without being summoned. Mordecai replied in Esther 4:14b with the following, ."... And who knows but that you have come to the royal position for such a time as this?"

So, the question may well be, **are you where you are because you may be able to better relate to and help someone else at a later point?** Food for thought; that's all.

3
Tinnitus; Ring, Ring, Ring

The following is my very subjective definition of tinnitus. It was written on 4/26/2009 – my "40th anniversary" of when I was first aware of ringing in the ears.

"I guess by its very nature the term 'subjective' is just that, 'subjective'. I don't know what I wanted or expected on what I call "Uncle Tinn's anniversary"; I felt like I wanted to talk, but didn't know what to say; how do you deal with what you've pretty much had to deal with – the continual aggravating reminder that 40 years earlier on today's date you shot and killed a wounded man and there really wasn't much other choice – but that doesn't change things."

"And the fact is there are some things that – because they are subjective – each person has to work out alone – not any guilt or remorse – but how to still continue to deal with the pain (that is not physical – although a noise has a certain psychological pain to it – but it's not all psychological either because there is a certain physical aspect attached.)"

"How do you talk about something when you don't know what to say? There really is a certain 'aloneness' that must be, when circled by a 'fence of noise'. You don't just tell it to 'Be quiet,' or 'will it' to quit, and sometimes you can just settle down and go to sleep, but other times there is not enough exhaustion present to overcome the noise, and then what? Just listen, or do something else?"

Something becoming clearer to me on a regular basis is my tinnitus has similarities to dealing with memories from abuse or some other trauma. Re-read the preceding paragraph and apply it to any situation listed in the Introduction: wars that depleted our national treasures of young men and women; physical, sexual, and emotional abuse; bullying for any reason; oppressive attitudes; illnesses; self-sufficiency; addictions; traumatic events; rejection; and loneliness, to name a few. Again, let me re-emphasize, for every "tinnitus" poem, substitute the tinnitus with "your noise."

Tinnitus

Tinnitus: The hardest physical affliction for a person to live with is severe, constant pain. The next hardest thing is considered to be severe, constant dizziness. The third is severe, constant tinnitus.

-- The American Tinnitus Association

tin-ni-tus\`ti-ni-tus s\n.(*L, ringing, tinnitus, fr. tinnitus pp. of tinnere, to ring, of omit. origin*): a sensation of noise (as a ringing or roaring) that is purely subjective.

-- Webster's New Collegiate Dictionary

Most of this chapter is a series of poems about tinnitus.

Sitting In the Silence?

Nonexistent silence – therefore, not
Interrupted by birds
Unaware that their
Chirping imposes on
Nonexistent peace.

Silence?

Silence is non-existent, therefore, not
Interrupted by
Loudly chirping birds
Entirely unaware that their
Noise
Constantly imposes on a non-
Existent peace
? (What's that you say)?

Noise

Never ending circle of noise,
Often accompanied by depression and fear,
Is a continual reminder that
Sometimes wars last longer than we
Ever thought they would.

Again, the "circle of noise" or "wars" can be of any nature, some with drastically different circumstances, and yet they have similarities to the ones I am writing about. This cannot be emphasized enough: your battles are different – and yet, maybe not so different – than someone else's.

It Won't Stay in Bed

It's rather depressing sometimes to wake up and
The first thing to
Grab my attention
Is
The loud ringing, and,
The awareness that
I can't leave it there in the bed;
It must, and will,
Shadow me all day.

If I Can Just Stand It [P/H]

Been up and around for about an hour,
The noises have stuck close by.
They never offer a moment's relief
And probably won't stop 'til I die.
But other sounds offer distractions,
Especially that little bird's cheep,
And if I can just stand it for sixteen more hours,
Then maybe, just maybe, I'll sleep.

I became aware that one of my students also had tinnitus, and so I gave her a copy of *Poetic Healing*. Sometime later I received an e-mail from her; the following is a portion of it.

"I have really enjoyed your book; I can relate to your poetry so well. Even though we have our tinnitus through different circumstances, I am amazed at how much I see what you've been through, I have experienced too. Like your poem 'If I Can Just Stand It', I have days that I say this as I just try to bear through a silent class or a quiet library visit. As you mention birds as your distraction, I often find myself outside, especially during the autumn time of year. I find an escape through the rustle of leaves when the wind blows in the tops of the trees. The leaves make a white noise kind of rattle and that is my most desired distraction ... and again, thank you for the book. I find myself reading it more and more, and feel more of a connection with it."

(Allyson D. Gibson)

Tinnitus Acrostics

The following poems were all written years ago, but still retain their "freshness and relevancy." The only difference is now I know I "can take it."

Tinnitus[P/H]

The noise started gently but then
Increased in intensity that
Never seemed to regress but rather
Needed more and more attention and
I started to become obsessed with
This intruder into my sanity
Until the intruder took priority and
Seemed to turn all else away.

Tinnitus II[P/H]

The sound in my ears
Is something I can
Never quite accept.
Never welcome in.
If it hangs around
Too much longer
Unwelcome
Something's got to give.

Tinnitus III ^{P/H}

The noises screaming constantly
In my ears are of such a
Nature that I fear that the
Naked truth is that
I may eventually have
Two choices: whether to listen
Until the day I die, or to
Somehow move that day forward.

Exhaustion

Every night pure
X-haustion greets me. Hey, I'm glad to
Have this friend so that
A good night's sleep will come.
Unless, of course, I'm not
So tired it doesn't over-ride
The tinnitus. Then
I know I'm in for a long
One. Short on sleep, but plenty of
Noise to go around.

Lying in the Darkness   *8/12/12   2:32 A.M.*

Lying in the darkness, noise screaming in ears;
Earlier did Sudoku, Crossword,
Then read Backpacker.
Took a couple trips in my mind,
Pulled a few from my memories;
Felt the urge to turn on the light and
Write this down, so now once again I can
Turn off the light and
Lie in the darkness, noise screaming in ears.

I am struck by the paradox sometimes of how something can be there – and not there.

Absent Silence

Absent silence
Bothers me
Sometimes, and
Every so often,
No more than once or
Twice every five minutes or

So, I want to strike out at it. However,
I find my tormentor, my
Longtime companion, is quite
Evasive. He will
Not let me pin him down while he
Circles and rings on.
Enough, I say, enough!

Quagmire

Quietness?
Unless you're kidding –
A little inside joke?
Good one. Got me.
Maybe next time
I'll get it. Next time?
Reincarnation? Oh no.
Eventually I've got to break out of this.

Another paradox lies in the fact that with tinnitus (and many other things) we say, "I can't take this any more," but we do.

Tinnitus 2012

You would think that after forty-three years
Of listening to it, one would get used to it,
Just let it pass.

Doesn't happen,
I guess in part because it's such
A pain in the ears (and elsewhere.)

Shrill Sounds

Shrill sounds severing silence.
Hard knocks slamming sanities
Ruthlessly
Into corners,
Letting free wars burn through my mind and
Letting them take control, take command.

So, what to do?
Oh, I can fight,
Until I realize it's
No more than a losing battle.
Damned if I'm quitting!
So look out noise, I'm still in the game!

To My Constant Companion 12/07/08
(My "Tinnsynatical" Friend)

It has been almost forty years, and still you're here,
Obviously can't read or you'd have known you were unwelcome years ago.
Even though you stay by closer than a friend,
I'm still not quite able to call you one,
Although you have taught me a lot,
And have been right here with me through a lot of tough times,
Hanging right in there even when others let me down, or, just forgot.

However, and there's always a however, or is that a "but?"
And I guess for you I'll use "butt,"
However, I still don't like this incessant ringing, buzzing buffoonery,
And I'd say a lot worse, but there may be kids in the room,
(Or even reading this),
And I don't want them repeating the words I'd like to direct your way,
And (or butt), I also hope and pray they never get to meet you firsthand.

Tinnitus (July 2012)

This on-going noise
Is definitely
Not my favorite thing;
Never-ending, and some times
It's worse
Than other times
Until I die, I guess I need to still accept
Saying, "Hello, Uncle Tinn."

Pain

Perhaps someday I'll share
And tell what's bothering
Inside. Hard to explain the
Noise factor.

The next three poems all are to the acrostic "Forget This," written some four years earlier with a different "F-word." However, in early 2013, for purposes of this book, I made the decision to re-write them as "Forget" This.

Forget This

Funny how the ringing goes
On and on and on.
Rambling through each day with me.
Getting on my nerves sometimes.
Extremely stupid, or it would know
That I don't want it to stay.

Tinnitus doesn't
Heed my wishes at all.
Insolent, arrogant, and
Shrill.

Forget This II

Frankly, there are days,
Or weeks, or months –
Ringing goes on and on and on,
Grating on my nerves.
Ever, always, have to remind myself you are temporary,
That cessation is in sight, someday. Still, you

Try to get me down.
Hell no!
I'm not going to let you!
Stop thinking you're the victor.

Forget This III

Finding there may be relief
On the horizon, how do I
Reach for it when the
Grating noise overwhelms.
Enough is enough, but, I am
Thankful for God's patience, waiting for me

To comprehend that
His Amazing Grace helps me to live with the
Infernal ringing that doesn't want to
Stop.

So, the noise is still there. And one can ask, "So, if over thirty years ago, in 1979, you said you couldn't take it, couldn't go on anymore, tried suicide, what happened?"

And the answer is, "I'm not totally sure, but I do know that friends, writing, hiking, writing, gardening, writing, cooking, writing, the Veterans Administration, and God, were all factors in the healing process – which still continues. There are still days where I feel like I can't take it anymore, but I do, because I know I can. That may be simplistic on my part, but it works for me. By the way, did I mention that writing has helped me?"

Two AM

Two AM, noise level testing.
Teapots whistling their ways
Through my mind.
Why this destiny?

I'll find peace in the
Morning during daily Bible readings,
Reflection, prayer, and Communion;
Meanwhile, it's two AM and
No let-up in sight.

One thing irritating with the tinnitus is that sometimes it jumps several decibel levels for whatever unbeknownst reasons. This increase may last anywhere from a few minutes to a few hours. Sometimes it just as suddenly drops back to a lower level, sometimes the decibels slowly decrease.

This …, Too, Shall Pass (2012)

I guess the only difference
After forty-three years of listening to this
Is that now I know that
After a while, anytime from
A few minutes to a couple days,
This level, too, shall pass.

Sometimes the tinnitus used
To aggravate so much that I
Felt like I couldn't go on.
Now I know I can.
So now it still aggravates, but
This level, too, shall pass.

So down the road,
(Probably not another forty-three years –
Although I could live to be 106),
On days (or nights) that it is overwhelming
And beating me about, I'll still remember,
This life, too, shall pass.

There Still Are Times

There still are times when I just want to black out into some state
Where there is no noise whistling through my mind,
Making me want to scream that I can't take it anymore,
But I know I can.

I know I can
Because for over forty years now I have, in a variety of states;
Some better than others, none of them happy with the sound.
So, what happened?

What happened?
I'm not totally sure. But I do know there has been a healing process in play
That has been assisted by writing, family, friends, God, gardening, hiking,
Not all at once, and not necessarily in that order.

So, referring to an earlier statement in this chapter, perhaps we all may discover that our battles are different – and yet, maybe not so different – than someone else's.

4

War; We Have to Pay Our Toll

Honest and sincere people can, and probably will, disagree over the following statement, "War is a necessary evil." I truly wish we could settle dividing issues without battles, but in order to do that, everyone would have to agree to compromise and negotiate, and so on. The reality of life is, "I doubt it." And many (not all) who say they would never pick up arms would sing a different song if they, or loved ones, or friends, were in imminent danger of attack, or had been attacked. I honestly believe there have been many times we (any one/ any nation, anywhere) went to war too quickly without exhausting alternative methods of solving an issue, but the bottom line is, you cannot negotiate with someone who refuses to do so, so I repeat my (possibly flawed) statement, "War is a necessary evil."

Some of the following poems may sound like they were written by a Pacifist, although they weren't (and that is not meant in any way to disapprove of those who oppose wars due to conscience.) The poems were written during various periods of reflection, questioning, and healing. They put into writing part of the "toll" we have to pay.

Toll Booths (first stanza written 2010)

In order to get onto the toll road,
We have to stop and get our ticket,
Then journey on our way. Then
At the end we pay our toll. The same
Applies to wars.

What toll the wars when one stops to think.   (from P/H)
In spite of so-called glory, underneath
There is a stink that perpetrates into a soul
And will not let it go.
When one stops to think, they have to pay their toll.

Black Wall P/H

Black wall, near the Mall,
Fifty-eight thousand names in all.
Hope you make folks stop and think
Just how much a war can stink.

Black Wall II

Blackened angles edging a
Long sidewalk, listing
A myriad of names of those who never
Came back alive. We want them to
Know we will never forget.

Wonder sometimes what their lives would be like if
All of them had
Lived. I'm sure many would have flourished and others would have
Languished, in a variety of ways, just like those of us who did make it back.

Reflections soon after visiting the Vietnam Memorial, May 1985

I wrote the following on May 4, 1985 about the loss of four people from my unit during a time when the bulk of my writings were dealing with Vietnam and, for me, all that went along with that.

RODNEY EVANS

I guess the hardest one may have been Rodney Evans. When he was carried past me that July day in 1969, I was numb inside. I had cried earlier for others, but there were no tears to call forth for Rodney, just a dull pain in the bottom of my stomach. So, a while back, when I stood at the black wall with his name etched in it, along with some 58,000 others, I was able to do what I could not some sixteen years earlier. Ironically, my ten year old son Rodney (Rocky) held my hand and kept patting it to comfort me.

The standard joke between Rodney Evans and me was that if one of us got killed, the survivor should have the other's wristwatch. But it wasn't a joke as the stretcher carrying his lifeless body passed by me. But it had made for lighter moments in a scramble for survival in a race that Rodney didn't win.

"DOC" HURLEY

"Doc" Hurley should perhaps be the most difficult because of the circumstances, but I think he isn't because I try to forget. There has always been a question in my mind as to whether or not I could have done any more for him. On January 1st, 1969, he was wounded from shrapnel, when a fresh volley of gunfire opened up, and I joined others in diving for cover in a foxhole. It was my 8th day with the unit and my 4th day in the field; I was total FNG (aka f*#@ng new guy.) Later, "Doc" was dead, from a bullet in the heart. Whether it was there before we dove away from him or not, I don't know. I do know we left him alive and came back to a dead man. I had nightmares about him for a while, and it doesn't matter that for actions taken a little later to go out under gunfire and bring in a friend who was pinned down, I was awarded a Bronze Star for Valor. The fact is, I don't know that I did all I could have done to possibly save "Doc's" life.

JOSE

When the Viet Cong first opened fire on January 1st, 1969, Tucker and I came running back to the perimeter from the observation post we had just gone out to in order to avoid getting caught in crossfire. Jose was my first exposure to a casualty of war. He had been fixing a "C-ration" meal while sitting by a tree. When I saw him he was still leaning against the tree, eyes glazed over in fresh death, a look of shock still on his face, and blood slowly oozing from two bullet holes in his forehead. Because I was so new to the unit, I hardly knew Jose, but I know I'll never forget him.

As mentioned, the first firefight I was in occurred on January 1, 1969 during a supposed New Year's Day truce, and, the first casualty I saw was Jose, someone I had only known for a few days. He had only a few short weeks left on his tour of duty.

Jose ^{P/H}

Jose was propped against a tree,
His eyes were glazed in death.
He never felt the bullets
In his forehead take his breath.

Souvenirs (?) ^{P/H}

Jose just happened to locate
Himself down in the wrong spot,
Not aware that his forehead was
Soon to become the final
Resting place for two bullets,
Although someone at the morgue
May have fished them out
Before bagging him up and
Saved them for souvenirs.

Jose II

Just minding his own business, thinking
Over the past year, only a few
Short weeks until time to go home
(Except the bullets ruined his thought patterns.)

Jose III

Just that quick.
Only a matter of
Seconds. Someone else
Erased him, took him out.

Some Reason ^{P/H}

The Viet Cong from the house had fled.
At least the ones that were not dead.
It was a killing season and
I was there for some reason,
Even if to only watch the flow
Of blood from Jose's forehead,
Watch it go, and with it, take his life.

In *Fiddler on the Roof*, because of what the Russians had done to their Jewish community, someone says that the Bible calls for "an eye for an eye; a tooth for a tooth." The Rabbi responds that soon everyone would be eyeless and toothless. The fact is, ideas of vengeance may seem sweet, but the satisfaction is short-lived and may well raise a new set of questions.

Vengeance

Venom spilling out,
Every bullet counting,
No misses.
Guess you could say
Even
A decapitated head could
Not stop the pain, or anger;
Could not say we had avenged
Enough for Jose and "Doc" Hurley.

BRIAN MORROW

Brian Morrow, assigned to my unit from an Artillery unit, was a difficult loss because of the crazy friendship we had, bound by similar "don't give a damn" attitudes. We both dared Death to take us if he could, and tried to flaunt ourselves in his face. Sometimes we found our conversations headed in the direction of Delta Company, 2/7th First Air Cav. D 2/7th's nickname was "No-DEROS Delta" because they had gone months without anyone leaving on a normal DEROS – Date of expected return from overseas. During that particular time period, everyone had either been killed, or wounded, or re-enlisted to get out of the field. People "joked" that Custer's ghost rode with the unit.

Brian and I decided we wanted to extend our tour in Vietnam for six months and go to "No-DEROS" to see if we could "beat the odds." We signed extension papers on October 26, 1969. We would have thirty days leave in December back in the States, and then in early January start our tour with "No-DEROS." On October 31st our current unit was getting ready to move to a new location and so several personnel went on an aerial reconnaissance flight in a Huey helicopter. Because he was the assigned Artilleryman, Brian was a part of the group. During the recon flight the helicopter was shot at and hit, and then crashed, killing everyone on board. I was actually a little irritated because Brian had "copped out on me" by getting killed, but mostly sad and empty over the loss of a crazy friend. I guess we had both figured that if one went, we both would. So, along with dealing with the departure of a close friend, I was suddenly facing the prospect of six months with "No-DEROS" alone – or at least without my "don't give a damn" friend. I had the nickname "Crazy Horse," but I wasn't that crazy. I went to my platoon leader and requested that after I took my leave in December, I be allowed to return to my current First Air Cavalry unit. This request was granted.

The following two poems are my tribute to Brian.

Brian Morrow (2010)

Because we both had those
Recurring moments where
It was evident we didn't give
A damn, our Vietnam friendship was
Nourished. Then one day,

"Marble-eyed," we decided to extend
Our tours for six months and try to survive the
Rare odds offered by D 2/7th, "No-DEROS."
Ran into a problem, of sorts,
Or should I say, encountered a chopper crash. I
Wish you were still here, Brian, growing old like me.

Brian P/H (written 1985)

Damned, damned if I can get you off my mind.
I never meant to leave you far behind.
We planned on spending six more months together
Until you up and took that chopper ride.
Brian, can't you die in peace?
Why must you be tossed about?
Sixteen years have come and gone
And still you're on my mind.

Signed extension papers on October 26th.
Six more months to beat the bush we thought.
But on October 31st you left me far behind.
When you up and took that fatal chopper ride.

Brian, can't you die in peace?
Why must you be tossed about?

Damned, damn we were proud of being Cav.
Wore that horse and line with lots of pride.
Now all that's left is a slide or two of you
Before you up and took that chopper ride.

Sixteen years have come and gone
And still you're on my mind.

I know you didn't leave alone, eleven
Others went, and stone of black
Holds their names too. Alongside you
They died in a fatal chopper ride.

Brian, can't you die in peace?
Why must you be tossed about?

Damn, damn, you're only memory.
But one I find I just can't lay aside.
I cried and ached again beside that blackened wall,
Because you up and took that fatal ride.

Brian, can't you die in peace?
Why must you be tossed about?
Sixteen years have come and gone
And still you're on my mind.

The following poem was written while reflecting about the first situation where I knew for a fact my bullets were a part of taking the life of the NVA soldier referred to in Chapter Two. I think my thoughts may have flashed to his mother because they had, just moments before, gone to mine, thinking she would be receiving news of my demise. Fate dealt different cards, and I seriously doubt if his mother ever found out what happened.

Questions P/H

I dazedly stared at his young face and wondered,
What if his mother'd seen what I'd just done?
True, she was nothing but a North Vietnamese,
But still she must have loved this one, her son.

But if he'd seen me first, before I saw him,
I'm sure he would have done the same as I.
And war does not have place for contemplating, so,
Who cares about him? Go on, make him die.

Past

Peering at the names along the blackened
Angle as I
Search and make an attempt
To connect with peace.

Soldier at an Early Age is one of the earliest poems I wrote when the "inks of war" started flowing through my pen. It remains a favorite.

Soldier at an Early Age P/H

I was introduced to "soldier"
At a very early age.
I found it in the hymnal
As in church I turned to page
Three-eighty-five.
Please stand.

So I sang about the onwards and
The Christian soldiers more,
Who with Jesus as their guardian
Went marching off to war;
The cross.
In front.

And my momma always said
When she talked of God's great love
That a Christian must be tough
Like a soldier, for above;
For God.
Drill Sgt.

And the music made in church
Somehow left out all the strife.
And it even failed to mention
How a soldier takes the life
Of someone
Else.

So the natural thing to do
At the age of sweet eighteen,
Was to enlist Infantry
Join the First Air Cavalry team.
I became
A soldier.

And I don't quite think that Jesus
In His wildest crazy dream
Thought it right the day I killed a
Vietnamese, 'bout fifteen;
Or maybe
Fourteen.

But I often pause to reflect,
And I often wonder why;
Why the song of Christian soldiers
Left out how it was to die,
Or watch
It happen.

And I still don't find much comfort
In approaching middle age
In the well-worn, aged hymnal
As I turn in it to page
Three-eighty-five.
Please stand.

Crossfire is when you are being shot at from both sides, which of course, increases your chances of being hit. The 1969 crossfires referenced in the following poem were in combat, but for many in situations of abuse or oppression, or other subjective situations, the crossfires are just as real, and just as dangerous.

The first combat crossfire referred to happened on January 1, 1969 when our position was hit during a supposed New Year's Day Truce. The night before we heard movement, that at times, sounded like people climbing trees. Daylight in the thick jungle area revealed nothing, and then around 8 AM, all hell broke loose with enemy soldiers firing at our perimeter. The firefight lasted for around 45 minutes, and just a few minutes into it I noticed a very white, very frightened-looking face peering our direction from several feet beyond our perimeter. Paul, from our squad, had been outside the perimeter when the attack started. He hit the ground and just lay still.

Afterward, he said that a little after the shooting started he heard firing from right behind him so he just lay there trying not to move, hoping whoever was back there would think he was already dead; we later found several spent shell casings eight to ten feet behind where Paul had been lying – obviously it worked for him. A few minutes after he heard those shots was when I noticed him. I hollered to my squad leader I was going to get Paul. The squad leader said he was going, and I said something to him to the effect of, "F*#@ you, you're already hit; I'm going." I low-crawled out to where Paul was, and then we low-crawled back in together. Ironically, there were ten people in our squad and eight of them were injured. The only two not injured were Paul and I, the only two from the squad out in the crossfires during the firefight.

The second crossfire referenced occurred on September 17, 1969, mentioned in the prologue. Our unit had already dug in for the evening, and, as the squad leader, I had already sent the people assigned observation post to their positions. Awaiting darkness, the rest of us were reading, writing letters home, or playing cards; I was part of the latter. Shortly before dusk NVA soldiers opened fire on our positions, and we all hit the foxholes. As mortar rounds and B-40 rockets hit and exploded on our perimeter I tried to contact the observation post by radio but couldn't. They also were not responding to our hollering, asking if they were all right, so I yelled to my squad to stop firing and then low-crawled out to their position and told the three men to follow me back in. Even though my squad was not firing, other squads were, and with bullets from the Viet Cong flying in, and shrapnel from the mortars and rockets flying around, it was close enough for me to call it crossfire.

Crossfires P/H

Crossfires ain't no fun,
If you've ever been in one,
You know these words are true,
Know what I'm going through.

Hey, Paul, we got caught in the crossfire,
New Year's Day, 1969.
GI's shooting out, Viet Cong shooting in,
We were in the middle, hoping to survive.

Again, in the middle, hoping to survive,
September, 1969.
Friends pinned down, still very much alive.
Went out to bring them back to a friendly line.

Many of us came back to the friendly lines.
Our war was done we thought, we were still alive.
Memories hang on, still we hear the dying.
Still in the crossfires, trying to survive.

And, again, for many in situations of abuse, or oppression, or other
subjective situations, the crossfires are just as real, and just as dangerous.

Larry Parr (died 4/26/69)

Larry made his family proud
As he stood tall in his uniform,
Returning on leave, taking a
Rest from Infantry training before a new
Year; a different direction, Vietnam.

Perhaps it would have been
A different time if they had all
Realized just how close he
Really was from the bullet that took his life.

```
$$$$    $    $$$$     $$              RRRRRRRRR
 $$$$  $$  $$$$      $$$              RRRRRRRRR
 $$$$$$$$$$$$        $$ $$            RRRR   RR
  $$$$$$$$$         $$$$$$$           RRRR RR
    $$$$$$        $$$$$$$$$$          RRRRRRRR
    $$ $$      $$            $$  RRRR      RRR
     $ $      $$             $$  RRRR         RR
```

We know there are logical flaws in the statement, "The good die young."
Putting that aside though, I suppose this could be good news for some of us
(as we take a toast to longevity.)

The Good Die Young [P/H]

The good die young, the old man said,
As he leaned back on the bench.
And if that's so, I sealed my fate
In the war, in the trench.

I thought that I was pretty good,
That's even the reason why
I was willing to take a chance on life
And for others' freedoms die.

But long after noble causes drain out
From minds that are tossing around,
The horrors and pains start to find and bring out
The evil that's lurking way down.

And soon one can wish for another to die,
Seeking to snuff out the life,
And squelch down deep any thoughts of if
He had any kids or a wife.

And he wasn't killed for freedom or peace,
But anger within sought him out.
For his kind had done this to my kind,
And so I continued the bout.

I started to relish the killing,
And put away all questions why.
If the good die young, the old man sighed,
I may never have to die.

The following was not written at 2 AM as you might think is implied. In fact, I was sitting at the kitchen table when the washing machine was in a spin cycle and went out of balance. The "thump – thump – thump" of the machine triggered feelings from years earlier. The booby-traps; they lie in wait all around.

Still Asking P/H

What is it about 2 AM
That lets things roll around?
It may be just a flashback
To a dying friend or explosion sound,
Or just the question asking . . . asking . . . still asking, asking, Why?

I can be doing almost anything,
I can even be asleep,
When sometimes things come tumbling back
And touch my mind and spirit deep
And scrape my heart a little.

Vietnam's many years gone by
So far into my past.
Yet more and more I still can see
Just how long wars can last
And bring back, bring back memories.

And sometimes unexpected things
Can be the trigger on aimed gun
That shoots out memories and pains
At 2 AM or even one . . .
And still the questions why . . . why . . . still asking, asking, Why?

I think that the above is so pertinent in any situation of inner wounding. The triggers? Someone that looks like the loved one lost, has the same name, passing by a store in the mall that sells baby clothes, or sports equipment, a song, a sunny day, a rainy day; all these and more can be the trigger on aimed gun that brings back the questions; Why? What if? Who? And on and on.

Of course, another way of looking at this is, the same human part of us can be triggered by all of the above and more, to fall into pleasant memories, a smile, a place of deep peace inside. I believe we as humans are designed to live, and sometimes flounder, in a world of paradoxes.

Homesickness

For whatever reasons, I did not experience homesickness as a boy growing up. However, as earlier mentioned, at about 8 AM on New Year's Day, 1969, I received my first taste of combat and saw two killed, thirteen wounded from my platoon of twenty-five. Later that evening, squatting down, I was getting ready to fix a C-ration meal, seriously doubting I'd live through this entire year in Vietnam. The events that had occurred earlier that day, plus simple arithmetic, did not foretell a hopeful future.

I pulled a heat tab from my pack so I could have a hot meal, and stamped on the side of the package was, "Van Brodes' Milling Co., Clinton, Mass." Those words slammed me in the gut! Just one mile from home, and my father walked there every day to work!

Another thing we are prone to do as humans, is compare. Our culture is quite different from some others when we think of the ages at which young people are recruited for war. During one of our combat operations we were working with a CIDG unit (Civilian Irregular Defense Group.) In some respects, I guess you could loosely compare them to our National Guard. As they were getting off the helicopters at our cleared-out landing spot in the jungle, I was stuck by how young some of them looked. I choked up when one of them "put me in mind" of my brother Danny, who was thirteen at the time. I got philosophical again years later when my oldest son, Ralph, was thirteen, and I was reflecting on the fact that the soldier referred to in the poem "Questions" didn't appear to be all that much older.

My Oldest Son P/H (1986)

My oldest son is approaching the age
Of a Viet Cong I killed one day.
But my oldest son is still quite young
An age where there should be time for play.

Babykiller

The following two poems were written based on something that happened in 1969. I was returning home on leave, traveling in uniform, and walking from the airport to the bus station in Boston, Massachusetts. There was a group of war protesters, and some followed me down the street hollering, "Babykiller!"

Babykiller P/H

"Babykiller" was the word yelled at me.
Several years later I still can't be free.
I didn't kill no babies. Let me clarify, I mean,
The youngest guy I know I killed was at least fifteen.

Babykiller II P/H

Walking in my uniform
When I heard him say,
"Hey, there, Babykiller."
Kind of marred my day.
I didn't stop to answer,
I didn't want to bother.
I didn't kill no babies,
Though several lost their father.

Dear Vet P/H (written 1993)

I received the following note in a child's handwriting tucked in with my medicine from the VA Medical Center. It said,

> *"Dear Vet,*
> *We love you for fighting for our country.*
> *Love, Joe."*

It is the first time since
I've been home that I've
Received a thank-you note
For going to Vietnam.

When I returned 23 years ago,
In uniform,
Someone did follow me down the street
Hollering "Babykiller!"

Then I was angry and confused.
Tonight I cried.

There are so many occasions in life where we are doing something with a group, and when that particular event is over, we all go our separate ways with all the usual promises made; "let's have a reunion," "I'll write," and so forth. Returning from a mission trip to Mexico with students while at Lees College, or at the cast party at Eastern Kentucky University after *Blue Kangaroo* come to mind. But, for the most part, we don't follow through.

I think a couple factors come into play which make the reuniting even more difficult with combat veterans. First, we disperse to more widespread localities, and second, for a long time after, we try to forget some of the events. But there are still the times of wondering, where are they? What are they doing these days, if even still alive? I mean, there were some good times, too. Like sitting around on a firebase where it was relatively secure (compared to the jungle) singing songs (*Blowing in the Wind*, and such) while Jonathan Wild played the guitar. So, who's where? Sometimes you can reconnect, sometimes not.

Ten Together ^{P/H}

Once upon a Vietnam evening
Some little time ago,
There were ten together
And after a while,
It didn't seem like that at all.

Ten Together II

There was a time when I could count ten together,
Every day, day after day, just doing what
None of us really wanted to do.

Then came some rotations out of the 'Nam,
Or the firefights that
Grated on our
Emotions and
Taught us that although
'Heaven' may have spared some of us, still,
Especially after a while,
Really, it didn't seem like that at all.

The next series of poems are to the acrostic FORGET WARS. As with the "Tinnitus poems" of the same style, they once started out differently.

Frank, Carson, and Kevin

Frank did a good job as a soldier,
Or, at least until the bullet hit his chest.
(Really set him reeling backwards.)
Guess Carson did okay, he only lost one leg
(Except it cramped his running style.)
Then Kevin died (even though medics did their best.)

Wasted lives it seems
Are ever in my dreams.
Remembering brings pain,
Sends inner rain.

I have discovered that anything works when you feel the need to write. I was visiting with one of my sons almost four years ago (2009) and spent the night in the grandsons' bedroom. I couldn't sleep, and had stuff jostling around in my mind. Knowing that in the morning I wouldn't remember most of it the way it was at the moment, I decided to get out of bed and write. The problem was that I only had a pen, no paper nearby, and I didn't want to turn on any lights or cause any disturbance. I realized there was a place that had plenty of paper, and the following four poems were initially written on that available product.

Toilet Paper

Found I couldn't sleep
Or even begin to
Relax unless I wrote. Got a pen.
Good grief, can't find paper – wait –
Eureka!
Toilet paper.

Why not go to the bathroom
And get some off the
Roll (two ply?) Only writing about crap
Stuff anyway. Two ply's fine.

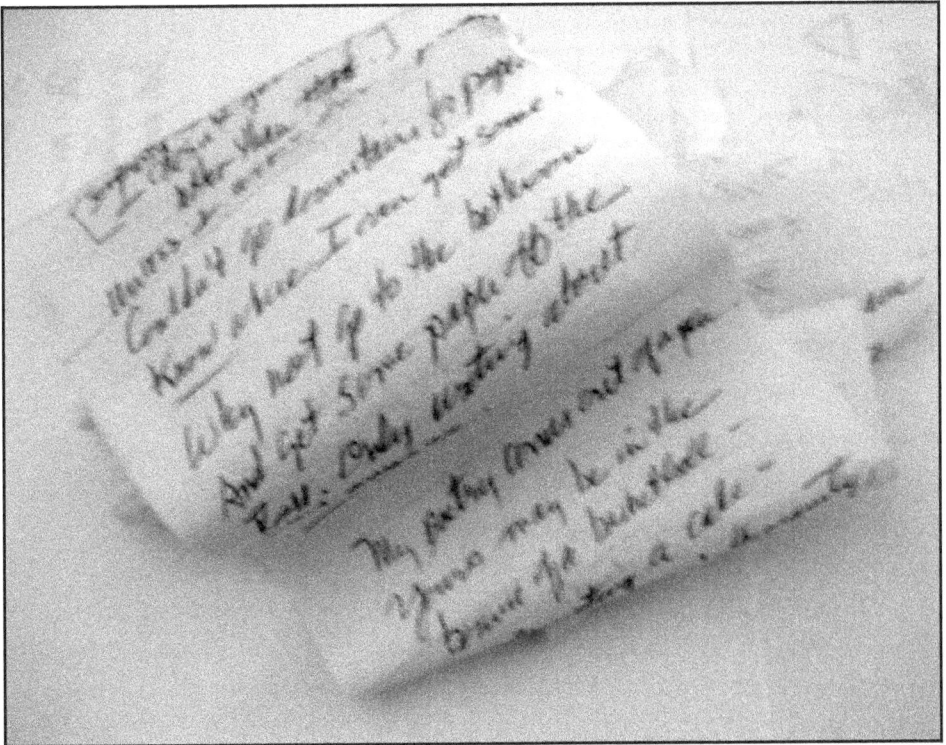

Fried Sounds

Fried sounds ringing
On; Why now?
Really want to sleep.
Grinding noise
Especially loud
Tonight. Have to write.

What about?
Ah, let's see. Why do I have to
Remember what
Started the noise?

Finding That As …

Finding that as years ramble
On I still
Reflect and carry things with me.
Guess they'll always be there
Except when asleep – during those
Times I don't ask

Why is it that young people
Are the ones
Recruited to die?
Seems like such a waste.

Filosophically Speaking

Filosophically speaking
Or, it it philosoficlee speeking?
Really, unless we find other
Good conventions to use,
Exceptionally good,
Then knot ever going to win.

Will always be
An off-beat word
Restling its way in.
Something's not write.

Troublemaker. We look at people who may have this label, but sometimes we don't know the whole story. While stationed at Illesheim, Germany, there was a man in the unit who was getting drunk on a regular basis. His roommate shared the following information after the "beacon light arrest."

/T/R/O/U/B/L/E/M/A/K/E/R/

HE GOT A LITTLE *w**i**l**d*
SUMTIMZ ¢¢ Take/forexample/the
night he rode the beacon light

AROUND and around & AROUND
  as it flashed across – flashed across – flashed across

  the air strip at Illesheim (Germany) ....
  His roommate said he was drunk ><><>< as usual -&-

    Then there was THE INCIDENT when
he was #I#m#p#r#i#s#o#n#e#d# for
st irrin g   up up up   trouble on base,

wielding a Baseball bat, chain &
      bro><ken beer bottle.
  his roommate said he was drunk <><><><> as usual -&-

when the contents of his locker were
inventoried there was a stack of
BABY WORD BOOKS .a=.l=.o=.n=.g=.s=.i=.d=.e==
a   STACK OF   PHILOSOPHY   BOOKS .
  his roommate said he would read from
  either set with complete seriousness.

his records said he had served
HONORABLY in Vietnam,,, his roommate
said his younger brother had b   t   d   b   t   d   b   t   d
                              l   o   e   l   o   e   l   o   e
                              e   a   e   a   e   a
                              d   t   d   t   d   t
                                       h   h   h
there in his arms*#%*.
Hi$ $quad leader said he would be
out of the (S(T)O(C(K)A(D)E) in a week now
and hoped the hell he had learned his lesson.

You Can Take the Boys Out of the War, But ... P/H

You can take the boys out of the war,
But that war won't come out of the boys.
When will we ever learn the fact
Our young men are more than toys.

God, country, Mom, apple pie.
Girl next door with whom we used to play.
Added them all up and decided they still fell short
Of the price we had to pay.

Soldiers at an early age, games of younger years.
Back then lots of laughs we had.
Later it was more than games,
Memories etched with things we did (so bad.)

And God didn't smile on kills we made,
And country just didn't seem to care,
And Mom's apple pies were rotting,
And somehow girls next door weren't there.

Bloody friends are in our lives now, along with
Tangled memories burned so deep.
Hooches aflame, dwellings destroyed,
Accepting Vietnamese lives as cheap.

Useless P/H

Until the day the bullets
Sort of caught him by surprise,
Emptying out some blood,
Littering the Vietnam soil,
Even though he didn't know why
Someone had drafted him to
Serve until his untimely death.

And so we may leave the location where the war, abuse, or loss, or … occurred; yet, we can never leave. We can, however, learn, grow, and reach out to others who may be entering, crossing, or departing similar treacherous waters. There are many who trod the pathways trying to "shake themselves dry" of the waters as they continue moving forward.

5

The Tip of the Spear (SFC Jacob Goble)

"'The tip of the spear', that's what they called us," said retired SFC Jacob Goble. He was referring to his job while on duty in Afghanistan. He had been in Bosnia in 2000, Kosovo in 2002 (peacekeeping missions); in 2006 he helped establish the ROTC program at the University of Pikeville, and then in 2008 went to Afghanistan. His unit traveled all over the country, from Kabul to Kandahar, as they engaged in route clearing operations.

"My wife is a teacher," he said, "and she used to have her computer homepage set to MSNBC News, but she changed it. The reason; one day she opened it to a headline which read, 'The most dangerous job in the most dangerous place in the world'. She did not know exactly where I was at the time, but she knew that I was with the unit the article was about."

The reason SFC Goble's unit had the above description, and why it was called the tip of the spear, was because they were the ones leading the way in troop movements. Their vehicles were like armored tractors with panels in the front that were mine rollers searching for IEDs (improvised explosive devices.) The danger level was high as, sometimes, there were almost daily "blow-ups." When the Army first tested the new Ground Penetrating Radar System (GPRS), his unit was the first to use them.

"One thing I'll say," he said, "my unit was given the best equipment available for the job. Our job was to save lives, and they equipped us to try and do that. Our platoon saw a lot of men wounded, but due to advances in medicine, most of them received treatment, and came back to us."

They also led the way to firebases under siege. A day in particular that stands out to SFC Goble is August 10, 2008. His unit was engaged in an intense firefight for over an hour and a half, completely surrounded. When he became aware that some of his men were pinned down, SFC Goble went out and brought them back into safety. For his heroic actions he was awarded the Bronze Star with "V" device (for valor under fire.)

SFC Goble retired from the military in February 2012, with Traumatic Brain Injury (TBI.) He also deals with tinnitus, the continual ringing in the ears. Both the TBI and tinnitus came about over time due to his repeated exposure to combat which included around 100 IEDs and 40 – 50 firefights. During one 33-day period, they had almost 30 IEDs blow up, and, the longest firefight he was in was against some 300 – 400 Taliban; a time when, even beforehand, he thought he might die. SFC Goble said he was able to visit with his wife by phone shortly before his unit went out on the mission. Although he did not tell her, he thought it might be the last time he talked with her.

When I asked him how he felt heading out on the mission, he answered, "There was a peace; I was okay."

However, after the firefight, figuring that he couldn't encounter anything worse than what he had just been through, he "stopped caring." When I asked if they used the same term we did in Vietnam, "don't mean nothing," he laughed. "Yeah," he answered, "'don't mean nothing', and we also used 'embrace the suck.'"

SFC Goble got real serious again. "I mean, when you pull one of your guys out of a vehicle after an IED, and he's lost both legs, it's hard. These guys were like your family over there. If you lost any, or saw them hurt, you want to get the guys that got them. And, I've had to deal with guilt in this area. On the one hand, our mission was to sweep a path through the area so that those coming behind us would be safe. If we left IEDs undiscovered, it would kill those men. On the other hand, I had to order my men into situations that put their lives in jeopardy in order to accomplish the mission. But I also began to want to come upon Taliban in order to destroy them; I wanted them dead. When I left Afghanistan I planned on going back, but my being diagnosed with TBI prevented it."

I asked SFC Goble about the TBI. "Well," he started, "I knew something was wrong. I had trouble coping, I kept losing things, forgetting things. I can only speak for myself, but I wondered, how could I let this happen? I'm losing a part of who I am. Of course, now, part of who I am is who I was in Afghanistan, too. And I feel guilt over the larger role my wife has had to take on. When I was gone she had to keep the family running and together, and now, again she's had to take on more, even though I'm back. She has completely taken over finances; I can't keep my memory organized enough to do that."

SFC Goble and I talked some about the role that military spouses take on when the other is on deployment. They are left to handle everything, functioning as a single parent, working to keep their children focused on doing well in school, and not worrying about the absent parent. "For the person be-ing deployed, you're assigned to new territory, jobs that call for a lot of focus; in order to stay alive; you have to concentrate on the mission. You really don't have too much time to think about other things, at least at the beginning."

I asked what the hardest part was for him when deployed, a total of three times, about a year each time. "My family; my kids now are seventeen, fifteen, and eleven. But being away from my wife, and them, was hard. You miss a lot of their growing up; you miss them. He said that his kids wouldn't watch the news so as not to worry."

"It's different than past wars in some respects," he added. "During WW II the whole nation was involved; some of that with Korea. There was a lot of national attention during Vietnam, but much of it was negative. In Iraq and Afghanistan, it seems that much of the nation goes its own way. Except for family or friends, when you're deployed, you're pretty much out of mind. And these wars have had repeat deployments; the average being 2 to 3, but some have gone as many as 4- 6 times."

SFC Goble said he had some questions that still remain. "We were in-volved in a major firefight one time because we were trying to retrieve a five-ton truck that didn't even run. Maybe they didn't want the Taliban to try and duplicate it, I don't know. But I do know I have the question, why? Guys al-most died, some were injured, some scarred for life; the question still remains, was that mission worth it?"

"And there was a situation where we had some EOD technicians from the Air Force pinned down, and we had to get them. We killed some Taliban, but I really remember this particular battle because there were some people we were getting ready to shoot up, and then we realized they were just kids. We came so close to killing them; I still have to deal with those memories."

"I feel like I functioned well in what I call 'controlled chaos'; I was able to stay calm in the middle of everything going on, and, to a certain extent, en-joyed it. Some may condemn me for that, but I realize that trait is also part of who I am. I could go for 14, 15 days in chaos without things making me sick. But after we were all safe, I got sick."

We talked about General Ulysses S. Grant who was criticized because, in his words, he "had a stomach for violence." General Grant realized that that was part of what made him a good soldier, being able to function in the midst of turmoil and circumstances of war. The simple fact is there are those who can, and those who can't. SFC Goble and I talked a little about how we tell ourselves sometimes; I hope I never have to be in combat with the person who can't. (Those who have been there will relate to this.)

SFC Goble said that in reference to those who served in the war theater, but spent their whole deployment in the more secure areas, he had no trouble with that. "Some guys seeing frequent action called them 'Fobbits' and kind of looked down on them. I didn't. I figured they had their job to do, and they did it. Someone has to make sure that those out in the field get their mail, their money, their food. That was the role they were in. I can't hold that against them."

SFC Goble said that the places where he finds the most inner peace is when he is exercising, or running. I asked him what advice he would give to others trying to cope with traumatic situations, military, or otherwise.

"Find what you enjoy doing, and do it. Talking may, or may not, help. It's probably different with each person. For me, I like to run."

Typing this, I am aware that his advice sounds similar to what I have been hearing in other interviews; get occupied with something you enjoy doing. And so the recurring theme goes along with the title, war wounded: let the healing begin.

SFC Jacob Goble

Sometimes you can
Find the heroics of
Controlled chaos involve
Just doing what needs doing;
A rescue of someone pinned down,
Carrying someone wounded to safety,
Or, as the First Sargent, just
Being there if someone wonders what is
Going on. Perhaps, "Sarge, why are we
Over here?" or, "Do you think we'll all make it
Back okay?" People ask these questions, and
Lots more, when daily dealing with Improvised
Explosive Devices, especially along the "tip of the spear."

6

Wake Up, Sam; Dad's Deaf (Sam Waddell)

"I was sound asleep in my bedroom with the door closed, and I never heard a thing. Then my younger sister awakened me saying, 'Wake up, Sam; Dad's deaf!' When I asked her what she was saying, she repeated herself, 'Dad's deaf!'"

"I got out of bed and followed her into my parent's bedroom, and my mother was sitting on the bed, cradling my father. At the angle she was holding him, I didn't see anything gruesome on him, but I could see blood spatters and hair on the wall. Then I understood; that my father was dead. I was in 6th or 7th grade; thirteen years old; I'm forty-four now, and that is really the main image that has stayed with me from that time."

"I was named after him; he was Sam Waddell I. He had been a good dad; we used to go camping and he'd take me out on a boat, fishing together; we did that quite a bit. I don't know if you remember the old yellow Pinto he had, but he took me over to the University of Kentucky Commonwealth Stadium parking lot and taught me how to drive there."

"And as a good typical parent, he had certain boundaries, or restrictions, for us. But shortly before his death, it was like he lifted them. If my sister or I said we wanted to do something, my father would say, 'Okay, let's go do it.'"

"I have never been angry at him over killing himself; he had been acting a bit strange and I realized that he didn't really know what he was doing. The next few days afterwards seemed dark, and I was numb, but I didn't blame him."

"He was in Vietnam, but he didn't talk much about it. He had a picture album, but most of them were of when he met up with my mother for R&R in, I think, Hawaii. He said he inspected cafeterias, and that you couldn't trust people. He said you couldn't even trust the little children in the area. With his other pictures, he did have a picture of a helicopter riddled with bullet holes. There was blood on it, and he said the pilot was the only one who survived. But he didn't say anything more than that."

"After my father's death, my grandfather came to Lexington and picked us up and took us back to eastern Kentucky where we lived, and the next couple days the family was getting ready for the funeral. I had an uncle, Danny VanHoose, who was fun to be around, and he was there, and it was good to be with him; it helped me cope, I guess."

"My grandfather, his name was Estill, immediately stepped into the role of father figure for me. He knew my dad and I fished together, so he took me fishing at some pay lakes. At first he took me with some friends and dropped us off, but then he started joining us; he loved fishing too."

"My grandfather was in WWII, and he said in France that he was with a unit that would go through towns to make sure they were clear after an advance unit had fought and secured them. He didn't talk a whole lot about the war, but the thing I remember the most was he would talk about the waste; how things in the houses were just destroyed, pictures, furniture; he said he was struck by the waste."

"My freshman year of high school, my grandfather passed, and that was really hard for me; harder even than when my father died. I remember it was the most pain I have ever felt in my life. When my dad died, my uncle and grandfather helped me cope, but by the time my grandfather died, I did have a faith in God, and that helped me cope with his death. Besides, he had a massive heart attack while fishing; he was actually reeling in a big fish when he died; he died doing what he loved. I was twenty-three when my grandmother passed, but I saw her death as merciful; she didn't have to suffer anymore."

"Still, after my grandfather died, I think my personality changed; I started keeping my distance from everybody; I became guarded, didn't really trust anyone. Maybe if people had been more like my grandfather I would have let them in. But I also guess I was afraid if I got too close, they would leave me too."

"And I guess I have continued to keep my distance, except when I got married. I have let down my guard with my wife, Tonya, and now our two daughters; they're ages six and ten."

"When I say my personality changed, that included my, I guess you would call it, my emotional level. I'm moderate; I don't get real excited, but I also don't get too sad. I really only remember getting real excited a couple times. The first time was when I received notification I had passed the Pharmacy board. I was opening the large envelope sure that I was getting word I had failed the exam, and my license feel out of the envelope onto the floor.

And, when my first daughter was born, she was six weeks premature, and the doctor wasn't sure if her lungs were developed enough. We were told, 'If you hear her cry, it's a good thing'. When she cried, I was excited."

"I started college at Prestonsburg Community College because my mom wanted me to. That's the only reason I went, and I didn't do well my first year. I was more interested in hanging out with friends and having a couple beers than I was in studying. Of course, at the end of the first year my grades reflected my lack of interest; I think I had a 1.9 GPA or something like that. Then I saw one of these posters on the wall of the college 'asking if you wanted to be a Pharmacist'. I thought that's what I would do, and my grades substantially improved. I was doing it for myself; for something I wanted."

"During my rotations there was a time when I was observing an operation on a man in his 40's at the Appalachian Regional Hospital in Hazard, and I remember thinking that I was really learning a lot from the experience, and I was feeling pretty good about that. Then I walked out into the hallway and there were several of the man's family members standing around waiting, and it really hit me hard emotionally, I guess similar to a flashback."

"I remember a lighter time too. There was a man who had asthma so bad he could barely breathe and they were working to clear out his lungs. He was unconscious, and then they finally got him cleared enough that he started breathing. He opened his eyes, looked at the doctor and said, 'Oh, thank you; you just saved my life'. The way he looked, and sounded as he said it just struck me as funny."

"I do think that my experiences have helped me relate to others suffering. I have comforted some friends going through a loss, and encouraged them to turn to God for strength. I feel a strong sense of spirituality; I know I have a personal relationship with God, but, I guess I'm not a real religious person; I don't much go to church. My advice to anyone experiencing a trauma like I did is to be aware that the clock keeps ticking; time doesn't stop just because we're going through a difficult time; we have to go on; we have to find a coping mechanism and go on. Fishing and spending time with my grandfather, and then later pursuing what I wanted to do in school, and finding God; these all brought me to where I am today. Things started out rough, but I really feel blessed now."

"I was having minor surgery on an ingrown toenail once, and was watching the doctor, and I felt real detached, like I was watching him work on someone else's toe. I think about that feeling sometimes. I think that now as an adult, if I were to observe me as a child, I would feel sorry for that boy. But at the time, as that boy, I didn't feel sorry for myself."

Sam Waddell
Suddenly awakened in the middle of the night
And told by his younger sister "Dad's deaf," is a
Memory that will always remain.

What troubled his dad enough to end it
All will always remain a
Deep mystery; he was becoming increasingly troubled.
Did the picture of the bullet-ridden helicopter
Enter into the equation? There are some things in
Life we have to submit to God,
Let go, and then, go on.

My comments: My family and I lived next to Sam and his family while I was taking graduate courses at the University of Kentucky. My sons Ralph and Rocky played with Sam and his younger sister. I had an early morning paper route, and the morning of the day Sam died, when I went past their apartment, he was standing at the window, arms stretched upward, praying. The image sticks with me because it was unusual. I had waved at him, but he stood transfixed with his eyes upward. At his funeral his pastor read a letter Sam's father had written a couple days before he shot himself. It was a somewhat rambling note filled with imagery and talk of the loss of innocence in the world.

One of the hardest things I think I have ever had to do, while a grad student at the University of Kentucky was pick up Ralph and Rocky from Glendover Elementary one day, walk home with them, and on the way tell them that the father of their two friends had died the night before. It was more difficult because I also had to try and explain how he had died, of self-inflicted gunshot wounds, and then try and answer the questions that naturally followed.

Where is he now?

Questions my sons asked after our neighbor committed suicide were, "Where is he now; Can people that kill themselves go to heaven? Do you think he's happy now, or sad?" My answer then is the same as I would answer now.

I told them, "We are here in your bedroom, all together, and we'll let that door represent death. Now let's say I died, and, it was because it was just my time to go. (I then went and stood just outside the doorway.) So let's say I can still see you, and I can see that you are sad, but there are some smiles at times because you're recalling some of the good times we had together, and you know that through those memories, I'll always be with you in a good way. I didn't want to leave you, but I'm here in this doorway, and it is okay, because I can see I left you with some good memories. However, let's say I chose to come through this doorway before I had to. I'm still watching you, and I can see that you are real sad, and don't understand why I did what I did, and maybe even feeling guilty that perhaps it was something about you. Now how do you think I'd feel?"

They said that they thought I'd be feeling bad and wishing I hadn't left early. I told them I thought they might be right, and, that seemed to take care of the questions for them.

Sam
Sam took a real deep breath as he decided about death.
Mem'ries made life not much fun.
A Vietnam tour spoiled his beliefs in innocence.
Those memories helped pull the trigger on the gun.

Sam II
Sam was a good dad; one I admired. He didn't seem easily perturbed,
And I used to wonder if I could ever see my way to be as gentle as he was.
He seemed troubled by the loss of innocence in the world.
His kids loved him, as did his wife. I perceived Sam as very kind,
Though, admittedly, sometimes blue.

Way in the background of Sam was a yearlong stay in Vietnam
Where it seemed something had affected him. *
Whatever it was apparently caused some deep inner pains that
He felt he couldn't share much about. Bothered him enough that
One night Sam took a gun and pulled the trigger.

*In a conversation with Sam's wife a few months after he committed suicide, she said she had been re-reading letters he had sent from his time in Vietnam and was realizing there were some things bothering him, much more than she had been aware of.

Sam III

Sam felt beaten by the past
And saw no other option.
Memories pulled the trigger.

Contacting Sam: I was conducting an interview with SFC Goble (Chapter Five: The Tip of the Spear), and he was looking at a large, 2' X 3' watercolor I had painted, which is on the wall behind my desk in my office; the one shown under "In Memory" at the beginning of this book. He saw the name "Sam Waddell," and asked me about him.

After I told him about Sam, Jacob said that Sam Waddell's son was married to his sister, was his brother-in-law. Jacob put me in touch with Sam; we exchanged a couple E-mails, and set up a time to catch up with each other, and, also do this interview. It is good to see him in his own place of business and doing well.

This is an interview where I have an image I can't totally break away from. I find that as I am editing and re-editing the book that I choke up every time I read the words of Sam's sister, "Wake up, Sam; Dad's deaf." I guess in large part because, before that night, my perception of her was, my sons playing with one of the neighbor's children; innocence personified.

Death P/H

Does it seem so horrible
Even though it finalizes
A life here on this earth
That daily wonders
How to go on.

7

Cold Turkey Quit (Greg Hicks)

It takes different things to get the attention of different people; for Greg it was seeing a friend in a coma for over three weeks, induced by an alcohol overdose. And then the funeral. Greg quit drinking cold turkey, but then had to face an even bigger demon; reality.

"I guess I tried to cope with the war and its aftermath by trivializing things. I realized that I enjoyed what I was doing while I was in Afghanistan, and when I got back to the States I had to sort that out. Some things started to fall apart at a personal level, and I totally blamed myself for all of that; I was angry at myself; but it wasn't just me, there were other issues involved and I had to accept that later; I didn't right away. I started drinking heavily, about a fifth a day for about the next five or six months. I still did all the stuff I was supposed to do, work, school, but I hid in alcohol."

Greg chose his next words carefully; he seemed fully aware of the sad paradox. "What 'saved' me was when my friend overdosed." He continued, "I realized I was going down the same path and I didn't want to do that. Of course, then I had to cope with myself, and face reality, without alcohol." The reality included nightmares of mortars crashing all around.

He served in the unit nicknamed "The tip of the spear," led by SFC Jacob Goble. Greg operated a mine-sweeper on route clearance operations, and was diagnosed with TBI (traumatic brain injury) over time after his "truck was on the receiving end" of three IEDs (improvised explosive devices); he suffered a head concussion each time. These injuries are also the most-likely contributors to the sporadic "phantom noises" in the ears, a form of tinnitus.

He said he functioned well and remained calm and clear-headed during these times; "It was only afterwards that I would 'get the shakes.'" We talked of how this compared to having a "near-accident" in a motor vehicle, and how, shortly afterwards, then the body system reacts to what has just occurred. I asked Greg about any firefights he had been in, and he said that to him, they were more an annoyance than anything else.

Once, Greg injured his hand in an accident, but he didn't go to the medics as he didn't want to miss out on any missions. He was able to go out on the next three, before an officer found out he was hurt, and made him seek medical assistance, whereupon Greg found out his hand was broken.

He told of a five week period when they were unable to get regular supplies. He said probably the hardest part was not being able get fresh changes of clothing. They weren't able to get hot meals airlifted in, and ate MRE's (meals ready to eat) for four weeks; with one notable exception.

"We were in an area where goat herders sometimes came by. They made the equivalent of $1.50 a day. After days of only MRE's, we paid one herder $20 for a goat. It made a really good stew; it was real good eating, and still sticks out in my mind as one of my more memorable meals."

Greg is currently enrolled at the University of Pikeville with a double major of Criminal Justice and Sociology. He wants to eventually work with a Metro Police department, although he has not ruled out trying to get accepted into the State Police Academy.

When asked what has been a restorative or healing device for him, Greg said, "The gym; I replaced alcohol with exercise, and a turning point in my coping came when I was able to talk with a friend about how I was feeling."

His advice for people dealing with traumatic situations in their lives; "Realize that you 'don't need to be tough'; don't be stubborn in seeking help." He added, "Be ready to listen to other people because you never know what they are going through, or have gone through."

Greg hit upon some of the same themes as with others I have talked with recently; the importance of family and/or friends, being responsible, and finding something you enjoy doing, and immersing yourself in it.

Greg Hicks

Getting blown up by IEDs is not
Really the best way to add
Excitement to your life. The blasts aren't
Good for your head either (as in TBI.)

How each one facing this, deals with it,
Is varied, and usually quite
Complex. One thing that Greg
Knows, when you realize that your
Strategies are destructive; you change them.

8

The Long Road Home (Ronnie Hylton)

I first met him in October 2010. I had a booth set up at "Winterfest" in the Expo Center in Pikeville, Kentucky, advertising my character monologues, and selling copies of my book, *Poetic Healing: A Vietnam Veteran's Journey from a Communication Perspective*. A young woman, Kim, stopped to look at the books, and then bought one, saying that her boyfriend was an Iraq veteran and was having trouble dealing with some things from the war. Later, she came back by with Ronnie, and we chatted a few minutes. Along with connecting on the "veteran level," he was also a student at Pikeville College (later the University of Pikeville) where I taught (I subsequently had Ronnie as a student in several classes.)

Backpedal to March, 2007. Ronnie Hylton had been looking forward to the fishing trip for some time. He had been stationed in Iraq for almost half a year and was flying back to the States for the long-anticipated R&R (rest and recuperation) leave. Two weeks of fishing; he and his dad could pick back up with something they loved to do together, and talk, maybe even a chance to sort out some of the feelings that went along with being in war.

As he stepped off the plane, his father wasn't there to meet him, but others were, and immediately Ronnie found out that his father had just died; Ronnie said his memories are vague of that period because something "snapped." In the midst of a "hazy fog" he helped with the funeral arrangements. The initial R&R period was two weeks, but he was given a one week extension for bereavement leave. Then, three weeks after arriving back in Iraq, his unit received notification they were facing a three month extension of duty. Although that was later changed, at the time, it just added to the confusion Ronnie was already experiencing. In the midst of his regular work-related routines, bombs and mortars fell almost daily on the airstrip where he was stationed in northern Iraq.

"My father was my best friend." Ronnie said, "I grew up 'riding shot gun' in his coal truck; his death overshadowed everything, and my attitude changed to one of don't give a damn."

Ronnie was a wheeled-vehicle mechanic and served in Iraq from September 2006 until September 2007, his tour overlapping "the Surge." His shop was part of an artillery battery with the 1st of the 14th Field Artillery. As mentioned, the airstrip was bombed and mortared regularly, and the ones that "fell short" landed on or near the maintenance shop. He laughed as he said, "I twisted my ankle once running from the shop to a nearby bunker."

They also had to deal with improvised explosive devices (IEDs.) After discharge from the military, Ronnie received a disability rating for post-traumatic stress disorder (PTSD), and continues to receive annual scans that test for traumatic brain injury (TBI.)

Three weeks after Ronnie finished his tour in Iraq, in October 2007, his grandfather died, so, obviously, as he got out of the service, he was going through a rough time. Ronnie said, "I am aware that what I went through was not as bad as what some did, but, still, everything that happened did bother me a lot, and dragged me down. I did some fishing, but also drank, to try and kill the pain. I started down a destructive path, but some things happened over time that helped me realize I need to turn around. My girlfriend came into my life in 2010 and she has been a very positive influence for me. I've never known anyone as gentle and kind as her. But, one thing that really concerned me was, when drinking with friends, sometimes I would have outbursts of anger, and the next morning I would feel horrible about it; just horrible."

Ronnie and I talked a couple minutes about Abraham Lincoln describing his "religious statement of faith"; "when I do good, I feel good; when I do bad, I feel bad; and that is my religion." It appeared that Abraham Lincoln's religion was also starting to convert Ronnie; he was getting tired of the "feeling bad."

Ronnie said he decided to start spending more time alone, especially fishing and hunting, where he could reflect, and try to get some thoughts in order. He cut back on drinking, and started to go to bed earlier, and get up earlier (fishing's good earlier.) He didn't want to be "all medicated up" and his early morning fishing and his walks in the woods were putting him smack into the middle of the process of "the long walk home," so he declined some of the medicines doctors suggested for PTSD.

Ronnie and I also discussed those times when anger wells up and one might not really understand why. I told him of a time a few years after Vietnam when at a ball game, during the national anthem I was suddenly engulfed with anger when the lyrics were sung, "and the rocket's red glare; the bombs bursting in air." I just didn't want to listen to it. Ronnie said that he had once experienced a similar reaction. We also found commonality in talking about reactions to fireworks; they make you "jumpy." He told how in September of 2012, his vehicle was "T-boned" by a car in a parking lot. The driver, high on pills swerved off the road into the lot, and hit the passenger's side where Kim was sitting. Ronnie said feelings and memories of the war immediately surfaced as he angrily jumped out of the vehicle and headed toward the other driver, but then he realized where he was.

We then talked for a few moments about all those things that can bother you which may sometimes be triggered quite easily, and, it seems, always unexpectedly.

Ronnie started classes a while after his return from Iraq at Big Sandy Community and Technical College, and a year later transferred to the University of Pikeville. He said that writing became another factor in his healing process, especially after his enrollment in Dr. James Riley's creative writing course. He wrote about fishing, and PTSD, and some poetry about war, and engaged in other journaling.

Some of his advice to others is, "In your darkest hours, don't quit, realize that it's a long walk. Get involved in something; school, work, whatever, and keep going. During my roughest times, when I was drinking more, and at my angriest, I still went to my classes, and did my assignments. Show up and be responsible toward your duties; I guess the Army ingrained that into me. I was in a 'dark stretch,' early on the long road home, when I started college, but I still graduated with a 4.0."

He continued, "Spend time with, and appreciate your loved ones. Find the things you love to do, and do them, as often as possible. Realize that money can't buy happiness. It's nice to have, but it can't bring contentment. I see people chasing after money and the things it can buy, and I have decided I don't want to work 70 to 80 hours a week for 'stuff'. Once you lose everything, you find out what's important; you can get jaded if you think it's all about money. I'm happy with a small house and an old truck, as long as I can find a good spot to fish and a place to go walking with my dog in the woods. You can't put a price on those things."

Ronnie added, "Something else that bothered me while in Iraq; I just don't trust politics much. There was a time when we needed Humvees, and the funding was delayed by Congress because of other non-war related projects that politicians wanted to tack onto the bill. I just hate the way wars are fought. We used to say that if we could sit down with the farmers over there, we could probably agree to put away our guns and each head on back to our homes."

I laughed at this point and told Ronnie that in Vietnam we said similar things; "Just let us sit down with 'Charlie', and I think we will decide we can both go back to our families and call this whole thing off."

Ronnie talked about a Sargent he worked with who had served four year-long war tours of duty in Afghanistan and Iraq. "He taught me a lot of lessons about life; especially respect. He had high expectations. I learned from him that some people demand respect, but then there are others who deserve respect. I want to try and live in such a way that I can be someone who deserves it."

Ronnie wrapped up our interview with a couple more thoughts on how the war in Iraq was handled. "Particularly in the job areas of security and drivers," he said, "there were civilian contractors. They received much larger salaries and were able to ride big buses, and their living areas had Taco Bells, Pizza Huts, and the like. But the people who cleaned the latrines and performed laundry services were from 3rd world countries, and were paid less than minimum wage, and just treated differently. If they were on a supply convoy, they didn't get the same level of protection as contractors; as far as I'm concerned, these people were some of our unsung heroes of the war. One time something really bothered me. They were not allowed access to the Post Exchange (PX), and, of course, this was where you could buy phone cards, so it affected what they would have to pay if they wanted to call their loved ones back in their home country; they'd have to pay higher reverse charge rates."

He continued, "One time I was going into the PX and one of these guys held out a $20 bill and asked me if I would buy a phone card for him so he could call his wife. I took the money and said I would, and when I got inside I decided to buy the best card there was; I think it was for 60 or 70 dollars. When I got back outside I gave him his card, plus his twenty back, and told him to enjoy his calls to his wife. He started crying, and hugged me. I'm not bragging, just telling you what happened. I don't know; but I think if we could all do a little more of this, and treat others better, the world would be improved, a better place to live; it might even help us all on the long roads we sometimes travel."

Ronnie Hylton

Really, he said, when I think of what
Others went through, I have to say, I'm
Not so bad off. But some things will, nonetheless,
Never fully let you go. For example, the sound of an
IED going off, mortars, other types of
Explosions. I think what we

Have here is the fact that
You can never fully
Leave the war behind, or all the other
Things that happen to us on
Our long journey home from the
Numerous side trails we find ourselves on.

9

What God Has Joined Together (Kelly and Shawne Wells)

You may have heard the expression, "joined at the hip." Although this is not literally the case for them, Kelly and Shawne Wells have a rather unique understanding of its implications.

Kelly Wells was playing college basketball his junior year at Morehead State University (Kentucky) when a routine physical for the whole team showed that he was having some sort of problem with his kidneys. A biopsy confirmed he had a rare kidney disease, IGA Nephropathy (Bergers), and he was told that in a matter of a few years he would need to have a kidney transplant. Because he was so young, Kelly was in disbelief and sought a 2nd opinion, which turned out to be the same as the first. He was also told he could not play basketball his senior year unless he had a medical override. He sought and received one, but in his 2nd week of the season, his knee went out and he had to sit out the rest of the year anyway. In retrospect, Kelly feels like maybe God was sending him a message.

Kelly's goal had been to play basketball all four years of college, hopefully go pro, and then go as far as he could in the coaching realm. Those dreams seemed to shatter with the kidney failure diagnosis, but due to the way he had been raised by his parents, Mickey and Doris Wells, he still feels like he was blessed by God; it was just that he was not yet ready to start a career that did not include playing basketball. However, Kelly said that, for him personally, one of the biggest obstacles he had to face dealt with concerns like living wills, etc. It really bothered him as he had just never thought of those kinds of issues before, and all of a sudden he was being forced to.

After his diagnosis, Kelly met and started dating Shawne Marcum who was playing women's basketball at Morehead. He said their common interest in basketball was what got them to noticing the other, but then they got to know each other better, started dating, and in 1997, got married. Eventually he taught full time and coached high school basketball for the Mason County High School Royals. He was starting to feel effects of the Bergers disease, but still experienced success in 2003, guiding his team to the Kentucky State

Sweet Sixteen Basketball Championship. One of the members of that team was the future University of Tennessee All-American, Chris Lofton. In a USA Today article on February 25, 2004, Chis Lofton was quoted saying, "his (Coach Well's) show of strength characterizes the attitude of his whole team."

In the same article, his Principal at Mason County High said that Kelly was "not only a coach, but carried a full-time teaching load, and, although he had missed some time from being sick because his immunization system was weakening, he fulfilled all his duties." Kelly had managed his medications according to doctor's instructions, but, nonetheless, in 2004, after seven years of coaching, his kidneys were functioning less and less, and doctors told him it was time for a transplant. Of course, the most important step in the process was finding a donor that matched.

From family and friends that had volunteered to be tested, there were four people that were matches. Shawne, his wife was one of them. Shawne had told her husband that she prayed about it, and, if it turned out she was a match, then she wanted to be the donor.

For Kelly, having Shawne as the donor was mentally excruciating. He realized the truth about it "being easier to go through something yourself than to watch a loved one go through it." Even though she was not the one with the kidney failure, still, putting herself at some risk for him was difficult to deal with. But Shawne was sure in her prayers, and firm in her desire to give him a kidney. Kelly said that Shawne showed him the purest form of love.

So at the age of thirty-three, 8 ½ years after the initial diagnosis, Kelly underwent the transplant procedure, receiving a kidney from his best friend and partner, Shawne. The procedure went well for both and they were able to soon resume their "normal" lives, bonded in a way they had not been before.

Back in 2003, along the pathway to the State Championship with his high school team, Kelly learned many valuable lessons about coaching that would pay off further down the road, at the University of Pikeville, where he was hired in 2006 as head coach of the men's basketball team. But as rewarding as the 2003 State Championship was, and the lessons learned along the way, Kelly feels like his kidney failure has taught him even bigger lessons.

"It keeps me grounded," he said. "It gives me a strong sense of what is most important in my life. And, with both coaching and in my life, I have learned I must stay focused on the positive. I can't focus on the negative."

Things that have served as restoring/coping devices for him are his family – being a husband and father to daughter Kaylee and son Mason; his church – being involved in service to others; and, athletics – being involved with basketball and other sports. Kelly said his "disability" has opened doors of opportunity for him to reach others he might not have been able to otherwise, sharing with them the good news that they can bear heavy loads with the help of God, and, God working through others.

He is involved in organizations like KODA (Kentucky Organ Donor Affiliates) that make others more aware of the importance of organ donations.

He referred to Mike McCarthy, who talked about the "paychecks" we receive along life's pathway which have nothing to do with money. Kelly said he receives some of those via calls from players who want him to know how they are doing, about the birth of a child, or, sometimes, former players telling him about incorporating some of the things they learned from Coach Kelly into their own coaching practices.

In 2011, the University of Pikeville men's basketball team had a pretty good regular season, enough to get them an at-large, non-seeded bid to the NAIA national tournament. Under Kelly Well's leadership, they became the first team in NAIA history to knock off only seeded teams (five of the top nine – including the top seed, the defending national champions and runner-up, and third seed (in the title game)) on their way to what initially seemed an unlikely NAIA Division I National Championship season. He was also named the NAIA Division I Men's Basketball Coach of the Year. Kelly will tell you that he senses the presence of God with him daily. He is also aware of another friend as an on-going part of everything taking place, not only watching from the stands, but in the court-side huddles, locker-room, wherever; after all, "what God has joined together …"

Kelly and Shawne

Kidneys. Kelly found out they needed to function well
Every day of his
Life. His didn't, and he
Learned quickly about possibly limited
Years; what is important;

And, sidetracked dreams.
Now there were new medications, but, still,
Dating, and after a while, marriage.

So when it came time for a kidney transplant,
His wife, Shawne, was a match,
And prayed about it.
Wisdom came to her in the form of a
New way of sharing, truly being a part of Kelly's life
Every day (enjoy the game; I'm right there with you.)

10

The Losses We Bear (Jeff and Lynn Waldroup)

I was sitting with Jeff and Lynn at the kitchen table discussing the most difficult time they have ever gone through in their life.

"It was very hard," Jeff said. "You're not supposed to bury your children; it's not right. They're supposed to bury you."

"People have said," Lynn had a pained look on her face as she spoke, "Time heals; it will get better with time. They don't know," she added, "It doesn't get better with time."

In 2000, Jeff and Lynn lost their eleven-year-old daughter, Lindsey, to Cystic Fibrosis. Lindsey's older brother, Lamar, was also stricken with the same disease. Jeff said they buried Lindsey on a Wednesday, and had to take Lamar to the hospital that Friday as he had a downturn. Jeff said that, looking back, they didn't have time to focus on Lindsey's death right then because they had to shift attention immediately to the worsening of Lamar. It was another five years of emotional peaks and valleys, and then they had to lay their oldest son to rest. Lamar was twenty.

Their youngest son, Lance, was fourteen, so again, after a second heart-wrenching loss of a child, they immediately re-focused on being parents to the remaining child. Jeff said, "Although you never get over the ones you've lost, you need to appreciate and enjoy the moments with those you have. We hold Lance close."

"But," Lynn added, "you always live with thoughts of the others; they're always there." Jeff also said that as far as any favorite memories; they have all become favorites.

When I asked Jeff if there was anything in particular that helped him get through the times right after losing each of the children, his reply was quick and certain. "Knowing that I'll see them again someday, and fishing."

Soon after Lamar was born the doctors made the diagnosis of CF, and he was in and out of hospitals from there on out, more so than Lindsey. Because of that, everyone thought Lamar would be the first to go, but not so. Three years after his sister's death, and two years before his, Lamar was able to have a lung transplant, and Jeff said that Lamar enjoyed living every day to its fullest. "He loved to fish; we fished together a lot."

"If I can live my life as full as he did in those two years," Jeff said, "I'd be living a lot. He had received a gift of life with that transplant; most people don't know what it is to get the gift of life. I know I look at life differently now."

As parents, Jeff and Lynn were concerned with the dignity of their children, and so they learned how to give the necessary treatments at home. "They had no privacy in the hospital," Lynn said.

"That's no way to live," Jeff added.

There's something else they have had to live with. Jeff talked about survivor's guilt. "Sometimes you just can't help feeling it," he said. "They're gone, and you're still here." We talked a little about how common that is. I mentioned that I could relate to that as an Infantryman in Vietnam, knowing that some had died, and here I was, still "bumbling my way" through life.

"And people don't know," Lynn said again, "it just doesn't get easier with time."

"But we do know we'll see them again, someday," Jeff added.

Jeff and Lynn

Just can't tell you how much it turned
Everything upside down. It was hard.
First, Lindsey, and then Lamar; both from Cystic
Fibrosis; just five years apart.

And, until you've lost a child, there is
No way you can understand the
Daily pain you still

Live with. Their illness is tough, and then
You have to give them up, lay them to rest.
Now there's some comfort in knowing they have
New bodies, and you'll see them again, but, it's still hard.

Organizing, then writing, about Jeff and Lynn has been the most difficult thing I have done so far in relation to this book. First, I do not want to bring fresh pain to anyone, but rather reach out in a way that helps all of us in our "woundedness." Secondly, I run everything I write past my main proofer (my wife, Cora.) I was reading to her what I had written in this chapter so far, and had to stop a few times to regain my composure in the midst of weeping. My feelings were so mixed. So far, my loss experiences (including during Infantry time in Vietnam, other friends, and with the loss of my mother) only touch the surface of what Jeff and Lynn, and so many others, have been through.

Yet, I am becoming increasingly aware, that at one time or another; we have all been left hurting, some at much deeper levels than others. My prayer for all of us is that we can see others "through the eyes of God," and try to reach out "with the heart of God."

Losses

Little,
Or
Sometimes, nothing, can be
Said to bring comfort;
Especially to those in
Sorrow over the loss of a child

Losses II

Losses unbearable beyond belief,
How can they …?
Yet they do, somehow, go on in hope.

Life to the Fullest and Its Shadow World

Jeff mentioned how Lamar lived life to its fullest in the two short years he was given after his lung transplant. Many people have talked (and will continue to) about this concept. The paradox of this is the awakening occurs so often with those who are keenly aware of their limited time in this life, and then, soon, those left behind have to suffer to the fullest.

Jeff and Lynn are examples of dignity in the face of extreme difficulty, and of holding close to their hearts the precious moments and memories they still have. They seem very aware that, as brought out in the play *Shadowlands,* and the writings of C.S. Lewis, especially *A Grief Observed,* we live in a world where there is pain, but these are only passing shadows in the world to come.

Losses III - My Prayer (02/02/2013, Saturday,12:45 a.m.)

Lord, help me to write,
Or pray, and live, every
Single day with a
Sense of your
Eternal vision, and with a
Sense of your love for others

All I Want is …

All I want is fulfillment of a
Little request. Pain of the losses to
Lessen, even leave! Be gone! Scat!

Is that asking too much?

Why can't you give me a break
And move along? Why can't you be
Nice enough to
Take my advice?

I know life doesn't work this way,
So, Lord, help me one day at a time.

11

The Losses We Bear (The Glue is Gone)

Elisha Taylor

"I think that initially, the most traumatic part for me was realizing that the glue that held our family together was gone. For a couple years afterward, a disbelieving part of me hoped, every time I heard a car in the drive, or the front door opening, that he was coming back to 'fix things.'"

"I was fifteen when it happened; a sophomore in high school. School was over for the day and I was waiting for my dad to pick me up as usual, so I was real surprised when my brother came for me instead. When I got in the car he just said we were going to Mamaw's house."

"Most of the family on my dad's side, and a lot of his friends, were at Mamaw's (my dad's mother) house; dad had been in an accident. My best friend had heard and she came over, and, soon after, the police arrived with more information. There had been a head-on collision, and both my dad and the driver of the other car were killed. As details came out, it turned out the driver of the other vehicle was someone that I knew and had gone to school with. That didn't matter anymore, now he was the teenage driver on drugs, running from the police, who had killed my dad."

"As I mentioned, I really was in disbelief for some time; shock, then that hopeful disbelief. Although I never dwelt on anger, I touched it for a while. I'm not a person who normally holds grudges, but, reflecting back, I was angry at the driver of the car that hit my dad, and the circumstances, a high-speed chase. Like I said, I knew the boy driving, and I always felt that his involvement with drugs came from peer pressure from some of the friends he chose to hang with, so I was angry at them too. I guess for a while I was just angry at everyone over what had happened to us; the question of 'why us?' My Mamaw was real distressed, and my mom was real troubled by it, and there was no one there to fix it."

"When I was eighteen, my best friend and I became roommates, living in the family house (without my mom.) Others had moved out, but I guess I was consumed with 'the weight of the house'; I felt that by living there I was somehow still 'keeping my dad alive'. I kept that role until I was twenty-one."

"About a year ago, a turning point for me, I guess you could say a significant point in the healing process, was when circumstances dictated that it made sense to move. At first I was against it, but then my roommate and I did move. That was when I started to let some things go; especially realizing that it was not 'on me' to keep my dad alive. I mean, I'll never fully be over it; you don't ever fully get over things like this, but you don't have to be consumed by it; you can move on."

"Of course, things are different; better or worse, I don't know; just different. I've achieved some things I might not have otherwise because I had to struggle, and grow up rather early. If my dad was still alive I would probably be a twenty-two-year-old still living at home, but I was forced to become independent."

"And, another thing, back to thinking about any anger that I felt; I guess I used it as a motivator, to keep the fire going, so to speak, to help me focus on where I wanted to go, and to survive."

"Something else that has been a major factor in my healing is my dogs. I have four; one from when my dad was alive, one I got the Christmas after he died, and then two more since. They have helped me a lot, just being there. The support a pet can offer is irreplaceable."

"Another thing, one month after my eighteenth birthday, I got a tattoo of a cross with my dad's initials. He probably wouldn't have liked it, just because he wasn't the biggest advocate of putting permanent things on your body. However, whenever I get too overwhelmed, or miss him, or catch myself wishing I could change everything, I touch that tattoo, and know he's with me wherever I go. He's infinite now; never changing, never moving forward, or going back."

"I'm closer to my family now; more appreciative of who is still here, and of what I have."

"If I have any advice for others it has to be; grieve on your own schedule; don't let others try and determine 'where you should be' in the process. It's different for each person. It is okay to hold on to the grief for as long as you need to; don't let it cripple you, but realize the world won't stop its day to day demands."

"If after some time you feel you are not where you think you 'should be', then you might want to reassess where you wanted to be in the first place."

"You can reach out to others who are grieving, but if you can't be comforting, then just don't say anything. At the funeral someone told my brother that 'it would always be there'. He felt like they were throwing a hot iron at him at that moment. Sometimes it is better to just be quiet; give a hug."

"I've found that talking about it when I can, helps. It makes me stronger. It is also a way I can try to reach out to others. You need to realize, that although it may feel like it, you aren't alone; you're not the only one who has gone, or is going, through this. Yes, the circumstances may be different, but the pain and loss are universal."

"Social work terminology includes the word resiliency. When studying it, I found it most interesting that some people have it; some don't. So sometimes I wonder what someone else might have done in my situation, or, even, what I might have done, had I not determinedly pushed through day to day."

"None the less, wondering aside, I am where I am. I'll never know if I am better off, or worse off. I do know that from that day forward, things were, and always will be, different."

I have known Elisha for some time. She is a survivor, caring, reliable, and someone who affects others in a positive way. I repeat what I said about Jeff and Lynn (Chapter 10); Elisha is an example of dignity in the face of extreme difficulty, and of holding close to her heart the precious moments and memories she still has.

Different (February 2013)

Does it really matter if
I can tell whether or not I am
For sure, better off, or,
For sure, worse off?
Everything changed; I
Really know that for sure.
Eventually I may have
New thoughts regarding the situation, but until
Then, let it suffice to say, it is different.

Elisha

Everything before that day was pretty much
Like what most would call normal
I thought my glue, my dad, would
Surely remain in my life for a long time.
How I was surprised and shocked
As different realities appeared.

12

Finding a Way; Turning Fear into Faith (Dr. David A. Smith)

"I was five, and one of my sisters was four, and when we went to school we realized that the other kids had more than one pair of shoes. So we decided to start changing shoes, actually brown boots, with each other every day so it would look like we had more than just one pair."

The thing that was reinforced to me as I listened to Dr. Smith tell this was just how young we can be when we start to notice something is different about ourselves, and how creative we can become in trying to hide those differences from those around us, especially our peers. Of course, what we frequently find out, sometimes later on down the road, is that some of the things we did were seen through; we really weren't fooling anyone.

Dr. David A. Smith is Associate Professor of Business and MBA Program Director at the University of Pikeville. He is an internationally recognized speaker on corporate behavior and the impact upon capitalism. The road he traveled to get to where he is started out with doubt, unbelief, and fear, but he learned in life to turn these attributes into confidence, belief, and faith. This is an insight into his journey.

"I was born in Harrodsburg, Kentucky, one of ten children. My mother passed thirteen years ago. She was married to my father for fifty-five years and was an amazing little woman. She accepted standards based on her Biblical beliefs, so when my father wanted to leave, she accepted that, but would not grant a divorce because she believed marriage was for life. So he left to go into business in Cincinnati, and she stayed to raise ten children on her own. We were poor."

"When you're four or five years old, you don't think things are irregular, when your family doesn't have a car, therefore you never travel; your neighborhood is your globe, your world. Everyone around me was African-American, and all were poor, so I believed that was the way it was with the whole world. I thought all drinking glasses started out as jelly jars, and as I got a little older and visited some white friends I was surprised because their glasses didn't have the little rings around the top. I also wondered why their whole houses were carpeted instead of having tile, or cement, or, as in the case of our bathroom, just ground. I noticed another area where things were different; my mother was always working."

"Like I said, my father lived in Cincinnati. He only came around about once a year and I vividly recall the first time I saw him; tall, 6'3", a giant in my eyes, and very black; to this day, he is one of the blackest African-Americans I have ever seen. He never really talked to me, was there for a short while, and then left. I asked my mother why he didn't live with us, and she replied, 'He does what he wants to do.'"

"I found out he was worth about a million dollars, and back in the 1970's, that was quite wealthy. He lived in a nice, new house and drove a new Lincoln, always had women around him, and was in business with white people. My skin was black. I began to compare. All the poor people I know have the same color skin as me, and the people who aren't poor have white skin ... I began to conclude that black was bad and white was good. I got to thinking, my mother reads the Bible faithfully. Even though she works a lot, she goes to church regularly, and she talks to the 'Lowud'. I knew the 'Lowud' wasn't Santa Claus, but from the pictures I had seen, I knew he was white, and he did nothing for black people."

"I heard all the time that just like cleanliness, being poor was next to godliness because Jesus was poor. Some things didn't make sense to me. God owned everything, so he was rich, but he sent his son down to this earth and his son was poor. If this was the case, then, I decided, this 'Lowud' I've been hearing about must be a 'no-good daddy', just like mine."

"On my first day of first grade I also noticed that all the white children were there with two adults, and I was just there with my mother. I also observed that this was true of a lot of the other black children. I told myself that either their daddies were at work, or they were 'no-good' like mine. This reinforced to me the idea that black must be bad."

"I compared clothes too. I cried to my mother because other kids were teasing me about what I was wearing, and she said, 'Don't worry, Honey, the Lowud will provide'. I got angry, and I kept it to myself, but I was saying, Stop talking about this Lowud! When he does provide he doesn't get his clothes from very good stores! Someday I am going to have all the things I need, and when I get there, I will share my situation with others like me so that I can help them get out of their circumstances."

"I hated giving speeches in high school. I would rather take a zero than give a speech or book report. I had headaches, sweating, and my hands would shake. Some of my friends would skip another class just to come and watch me, and my teacher would allow them in. But they were there just to laugh at and ridicule me. The teacher even let other teachers know when I was presenting, and some of them would come to watch, too. It was terrible. I figured no one wanted to hear what I had to say. After all, I was black. I had no confidence, didn't think what I had to say was important, although I did know I was just as smart as my peers."

"So, after high school I enrolled at the University of Kentucky, which at that time was known as the 'white university'. Most of my African-American friends had gone to 'black' universities. I had to take public speaking my freshman year, and the instructor would make us get up in front of the class every day. I don't know if it was because he was more mature, or a man, but I started to view him as a male role model. With his encouragement I started to realize, the other people in the class didn't know me, so I had nothing to lose. Some of the students had parents who were paying their way, and some, like me, were on grants. But none of us had a lot of money left over, and I realized that as students we were all equal. I started to feel at home."

David paused and gave a little smile. "Of course," he continued, "I have since come to realize that God's name wasn't 'Lowud', it is Lord, and his son is rich. My mother interpreted her Bible wrong in this area; a lot of poor people do this and overlook scriptures that say things like, 'Above all, I want you to prosper and be in good health'. Faith comes by hearing the word of God, and acting on it. I came to realize the Bible is a living document. My situation was not something God did to me because I was black. Actually, Jesus was more like me in color than those pictures I saw when I was a kid. He was darker skinned; he was sent for everyone, and he loved me. When I arrived at that knowledge it fundamentally changed my life."

"Back to public speaking. With practice, I started to gain more confidence, and I realized that, for me, it was 'sink-or-swim' time. I had these little voices of doubt that were talking in one ear, telling me I was black, no one wanted to listen to me, and so forth. These doubts were the ones I had had for years, which only led to unbelief and fear. But there was another voice in the other ear telling me, 'The demon on your other shoulder is not as tough as he claims to be; if God owns the cattle on a thousand hills, why listen to your demon?' And so I started to turn my doubts into confidence, which led to belief and faith."

"Being black, I cannot place blame on whites. That's an excuse; people need to take advantage of opportunities. The enemy isn't white; it is ignorance and bigotry, and that is found in all colors and races. This knowledge freed me when I realized that in the Lord's eyes I was on an equal basis with everyone. They were, are, all my brothers and sisters. If someone didn't love me, it didn't matter; I could love them back. I decided to integrate more, see what else was out there. As a teen I did a lot of reasoning, and discovered there were a lot of things and people God put into my life for a reason, even those I might, at the time, have considered an 'enemy'. That person was there for a reason."

"As I read the Word more, my confidence grew. I came to realize that God loves me as much as he loves his son, Jesus. I have found he meets all my needs and has filled my life with many blessings. I'm not perfect, but I do believe I am here in this life, and in this particular place right now, to be a blessing to others, and help them through some of their hard times."

Dr. Smith laughed. "I just had that image flash in front of me again of my younger sister and I trading brown boots. They had white fur inside. Can you imagine what we looked like in gym class with brown boots?"

David A. Smith

Don't you know, he said, it must have looked
Awfully funny to others, maybe even
Very ridiculous, to see my younger sister and
I think we were pulling the wool over their eyes.
Dr. Smith has turned out to be a man who was

Able to transform those early years of doubts, unbelief, and fears, into

Some different times; times composed of
Much altered voices speaking
Into the ears. Resisting the demons trying to
Tear down and destroy, he was able to give
Heed to the voices of confidence, belief, and faith.

13

Why Me, Lord? Why Not Me?
(Mary Beth Webb)

In 1974, Mary Beth Ulrich was fresh out of undergraduate school, and a first year teacher of math and science at a middle school in a Chicago suburb. Things were going well; as a college student, she had to study, of course, but, overall, concepts "came easily." Now, she was finally getting to strike out independently; first apartment, first car, more social life, the usual dreams.

Starting her senior year of college she had dealt with headaches some, but didn't think too much of it. As a teacher she didn't focus on the headaches, but rather "the joy of teaching." But the children in the class noticed that she was bothered some by headaches, because one of the Christmas gifts from students in the class where she was teaching was a pretty silver jewelry box, with aspirin inside.

She still visited regularly with her parents, and her mother noted that she seemed to be sleeping quite a bit. In retrospect, Mary Beth says she believes it was a defense mechanism; when she was sleeping, the headaches didn't bother.

On Friday, February 1st, 1974, Mary Beth was working with two little girls in her class who did not know the answer to what is 9 plus 4. She said, as she tried to explain it to them, she realized, she didn't know the answer either.

She spent that weekend, like she often did, with her parents. That turned out to be providential. One of her aunts had had a stroke, and, on Sunday, February 3rd, her parents went to the hospital to visit. Mary Beth declined going with them, as she had a headache, and wanted to sleep. When her parents returned around 5 p.m., they found her lying on the bathroom floor. As best the doctors could determine later, she had suffered a stroke around noon.

She was seen initially by her family doctor who knew that the University of Iowa Hospital had the facilities equipped to deal with her situation. Mary Beth's father told her later that a very difficult thing for him had been signing a release for an angiogram. The doctors made clear that it could either provide information that would help save her life, or, it could kill her. Within the team of doctors working on her, some were saying that an operation could be very dangerous, but one of them said, that given the alternative of what her life without the surgery would be, they ought to "go for it."

The initial ordeal was successfully dealt with. Mary Beth was kept alive, and was in the hospital in Iowa for exactly a month. But the next phase was waiting in the wings; recovery. This involved going back home to Illinois, and starting the rehabilitation process.

Several things became huge factors in the process for Mary Beth; her family, her friends, and her dreams.

The family factor was first and foremost. After a few days, her father had to return to work, but her mother quit her job to stay with her. As she started to recover, many people sent flowers and cards. Mary Beth was not aware of them at first, but, of course, her mother was, and felt comforted by the outreach of others. As she did improve, Mary Beth not only started to be more aware of gestures of love and support, but also became aware that the ordeal was, by its very nature, putting added stress on her parents and her brother. She now believes that her recovery was in part strengthened and hastened because she wanted to be the best patient she could be so as not to add to their stress.

Her father later related to her that, after the stroke itself, the hardest thing for him to do was pack up her apartment. He told her it was extremely traumatic for him as he felt like he was violating her personal space, papers, etc. In addition, her mother felt guilt as she wondered if the stroke had its origins in genetics. However comfort came for both her parents as they celebrated the joys along the recovery path; the first time tying her shoes, walking without a cane, getting in and out of a bathtub. And later, they joined with Mary Beth as she decided to start celebrating February 3rd as her "second birthday."

Friends were also an important part of the recovery process for her. She was overwhelmed when she realized that the cards she had received filled up ¾ of a large, black leaf bag. It was life-affirming to her to realize how many people cared for her. It also was significant, Mary Beth realized, that through visits, and later, walks and other activities, she was receiving the message that, even though she had lost some aspects of her life, the core of who she was, was being recognized and affirmed by her friends. Also, as some friends encountered some difficult questions in their own lives, they sought her out for advice. Those people made her feel important, and feel good about the fact that she was able to help someone else rather than always being on the "taking end" of things.

Another dynamic element in the recovery process for Mary Beth was her dreams. She didn't dwell on whether she could teach again, but rather, how she could get back that part of her prior life. It wasn't a question of what she couldn't do, but rather what was still possible. At some point in her rehabilitation process she was asked to be a guest speaker at a Rotary Club meeting. There was a priest who spoke before her, and afterward, she realized that their two messages couldn't have been meshed together any better. The priest's message also reinforced her belief that God had something for her to do because of what she was going through.

A prayer she had was, "God, I can handle the physical limitations that come with this, but, please let me have my mind." At one point, when a thought reared its ugly head that maybe she was "done for" as far as teaching, Mary Beth asked her doctor if there was any hope in that area. His response was quick and to the point. He told her he wanted her to get back into the classroom as soon as possible; that that would become a restoring device for her. So within a year, she started substitute teaching.

One thing different that she felt made her a better teacher when she started back, than from before the stroke was, right after college she taught as a person to whom things "had come easily." After the stroke she saw and approached learning from the "struggling side."

After subbing for a while, Mary Beth was offered a position as a Graduate Assistant at Illinois State University. After earning her Doctorate Degree, in 1989, she applied for, and was offered a position at Pikeville College (now the University of Pikeville) in Pikeville, Kentucky, where she still serves as an associate professor of math education.

Mary Beth has become more aware of the fact that helping people understand concepts helps them gain more control over their futures. She recalls the frustration she felt when she had no control. This emotion overwhelmed her once when her mother and an aunt were getting her ready to take her to a rehab session early in her recovery process. Her aunt asked her mother, "What are you going to put on Mary Beth?" Mary Beth realized she wasn't a factor in the procedure of getting dressed at all, and she hated that absence of independence.

A while after she started teaching at Pikeville College, Mary Beth received an e-mail from a girl that she worked with while substitute teaching. The girl had been a senior in high school, and had to pass math in order to graduate. But she just was unable to grasp some of the concepts. The girl wrote to Mary Beth words to the effect of, "You may not remember me, but you were a substitute teacher when I was a senior in high school. There were some math concepts that were difficult for me to comprehend, and, as a result of the time you spent working individually with me, I was able to understand them. I graduated from high school, am happily married with three children. I want to thank you for your help to me. It means a lot."

In one of her classes not too long ago, Mary Beth had a soldier who had returned from Iraq and was facing some obstacles in his life. He told her, "I look at you and tell myself, if she can do it, I can too."

Once when she was in a medical supply store for prosthetics, she was talking to a young boy who had to just been fitted with a prosthetic and was trying to get used to it. She was able to encourage him by telling him to celebrate the little victories, and related to him how she had been able to do that with being able to open her hand for the first time, tie her shoes by herself, and other things. She could tell he was reassured that he could learn to function in life quite well.

After listening to a couple of people with spina bifada talk about overcoming obstacles, Mary Beth realized even more just how blessed she was. That even extended to the "repair work" necessary several weeks after her original surgery. During the first procedure, doctors had to cut a section of bone out of her skull, and then, after they did what they had to do to save her life, they put back a temporary skin cover. Later there was a second surgery to put the cut-out-bone section back into place. Pieces like this were marked and kept frozen during the interim period.

Somehow, Mary Beth's piece got misplaced. One of her doctors said in disbelief to the "keeper of the bones" (possibly a trembling intern who just knew he was going to lose his position), "Lost? What do you mean lost?" A thorough search of the freezer storage area turned up an unmarked piece of frozen bone. Tests showed a match for her, and so they were able to proceed. And, she said, the incident not only still brings her a smile, it adds new meaning to the expression, "I once was lost, but now am found."

Mary Beth said she has also been blessed with an attitude of "Why not me? God has decided that I can handle this 'adversity-blessing' as well as anyone, and has allowed it into my life for a reason."

Mary Beth

Mary Beth said she went
Along her way with no
Realization of what upcoming
Years held for her.

But she discovered that in
Every circumstance she faced
That God was there to
Help her each step of the way.

14
Illnesses that Hinder (and Have Their Effect)

I want to live each day to the fullest (Lanny Sparrow)

Lanny Sparrow had cystic fibrosis (CF.) He attended Oakdale Christian High School, now Oakdale Christian Academy, in Jackson, Kentucky in the late 1970's. I was attending college and working at Oakdale as a part-time cook. I remember sitting at the dinner table with Lanny one evening, and we became engaged in a rather serious conversation which carried on after the meal was over and even after others had left the room.

Lanny told me that both he and an older brother had CF, and that his brother had died from it a few years earlier. Lanny said that when his brother died, he overheard his mother and aunt talking about the illness; it turns out his brother was dying right about the age the doctors had predicted he would. Lanny added that he heard his mother say, "And the doctor says Lanny will probably go when he's around fifteen."

He got real serious and said, "That was almost two years ago. I'm going to be a senior next year, and I'm not sure what to do. I love Biology and I'd like to teach. But there's a part of me that says, 'Why bother going to college, and doing all that work? You're not going to live much longer, anyway. But another part says ignore everything and live as though you were going to be here until you're in your eighties.'"

We talked a while about the "unknown factor" for all of us; some just are more aware of it than others. Then Lanny expressed concerns about falling in love, marriage, and children. He said, "Although there's no one right now, I dream about the possibility of a normal life with a wife and children. But then I always ask myself if that would be fair to someone. Is it fair to ask someone to marry you, knowing that you probably won't be there for them very long at all, and, what about children? Would it be right to have children knowing that they would most likely lose their father early on?"

Lanny decided to go on to college, and later came back to Oakdale to teach Biology. He was accompanied by his wife. When he was twenty-six I invited him to be a guest speaker at convocation at Lees College where I was teaching at the time. He talked to the group about living each day to the fullest. "I love life," Lanny said. "I want to get the most out of each day that I can. The doctors said I would die at fifteen. I'm twenty-six now, and I'm shooting for forty."

Lanny died a few years after that, but not before he had the chance to have a huge influence on my oldest son, Ralph. As a matter of fact, I think that other than me, Lanny has been the most significant male role model in Ralph's life. I am forever grateful to Lanny for that.

A poignant side; shortly before Lanny's death, his wife gave birth to healthy triplets.

Lanny Sparrow

For someone who was quite a bit younger than me,
You taught me a lot about living.
I marveled at your fascination with the
Intricate, and the mundane.

Because of your love of Biology
The world opened her arms to you every day;
Invited you to step outside, and live.
You did too, to the fullest.

I am forever grateful for the positive effect
You had on Ralph's life. He was on a good track already;
You just helped keep him there. By the way, after you taught him,
He wound up playing the cowbells just as good as you.

I sometimes feel like you lived more – in less than thirty years –
Than I have in sixty-three (and counting.) Lanny,
I pray I find even more, your love for life;
Find a way to absorb as much from each day as you did.

Your favorite pet, of course, was a boa.
Why not? One of God's beautiful creatures,
And, I imagine that somewhere (in the place I hope to join you)
You are trying to find where it slipped away to (between the walls, maybe?)

Allergies and Extra Weight; Targets for Bullies

An article from *Reuters, Edition: U.S.*, on December 24, 2012, exposed an additional way that illnesses can have an effect on young people. It said that according to a study from Mount Sinai Medical Hospital, of 251 children surveyed who had allergies, a little over 45 percent of them stated that, because of their particular allergy, they had been bullied.

The *Reuters* article further went on to say that Yale University researchers also found, of 361 teens surveyed who were enrolled in weight-loss camps, around two-thirds of them were targets of teasing and/or bullying. The type of harassment varied, from physical to verbal to "cyber-bullying."

A point made near the end of the article was, that in the study of kids with allergies, only about half of the parents were aware harassment was taking place, and that parents, particularly those with children with allergies or weight problems, should work harder to be more aware of what is going on in their kids' lives. The researchers encouraged parents to be allies of their children.

The Target 2013

Yeah, I know I'm different; every day at school they let me know.
My clothes look like hand-me-downs (they are, actually),
My sinus trouble has me sniffling a lot,
I have to avoid certain foods that most people eat,
And you don't have to tell me, I know I'm overweight.
I'll bet I'll just love it when the acne starts.

All in all these things add up to the wide variety of excuses
Some people use to shove and push, and, verbally harass me.
I try to make like it doesn't bother me, but it does.
I hate waking up and realizing that it's not the weekend,
That I am going to have to get ready and go to school.
And, sometimes, even on the weekends, I get those e-mails.

Sticks and Stones

I remember when Ralph was about five he came to me one time and told me that his younger brother, Rocky, and a neighbor friend, Jon, were calling him names. I was preoccupied with something else and rather glibly said, "Well, Ralph, you know the saying, 'Sticks and stones may break my bones, but words will never hurt me'." Ralph sadly answered in a voice that got my attention, "Dad, words may not hurt you, but they sure make you feel bad."

COPD (Chronic Obstructive Pulmonary Disorder)
Cora's Story

"The first question I always get asked is, 'Are you still smoking?' or, 'When did you quit smoking?' Sorry (not really); I never started. I did grow up in rural Graham County, NC. All our heat came from a wood stove, and I was around second-hand smoke all my life. According to some doctors, those factors, and maybe a touch of genetics, are probable contributors."

"Those commercials for COPD that start out with the elephant sitting on the chest are right on target. And another way they portray the reality of COPD is when the woman walks down the street and the elephant, although no longer on her chest, is right there with her. I love the little 'brush away' move she makes with her hand against his trunk, but the truth is, that is all one can do, push it to the side for a while. He's still right there with you."

"For example, about three years ago, in the Red River Gorge in eastern Kentucky, Basil and I walked the trail from a parking lot to Chimney Rock. Not a difficult trail at all, but the elephant kept his place, close by, but 'behaving himself'. However, after we were down at the overlook, 'Mr. Pachyderm' decided to 'make himself a little more known', and it was a terrible walk for me back to the car. It took me some time to get over the subsequent pneumonia."

"Fortunately, medicine has come a long way since I was a kid. I know others may have felt I shirked on my chores when I was younger, especially outside ones, maybe even faking, but I didn't; sometimes I just felt like I was smothering. I guess it affected other areas of my body, too. One of my ears drained a lot, and it seemed like I had a constant infection until I was twelve years old. Those infections led to severe hearing loss. I was never allowed to go swimming as a child either because of my constant 'cold'."

"I moved to Maryland when I was eighteen. I knew I had these breathing problems, and was regularly under a doctor's care, but it was never mentioned that asthma might be a part of the picture. When I was in my mid-20s, I took my son to his pediatrician for a normal follow-up visit, and the doctor, because of my wheezing, asked how long I had had asthma. I said I didn't know I had it, and he told me I needed to get it taken care of. I wonder sometimes how much better my system might be now if I had been diagnosed and treated for asthma at an earlier age."

"Even with all the treatments available, I still feel like I am smothering sometimes, and I'm constantly wheezing or coughing. The coughing embarrasses me, although it shouldn't; that's how I get the 'junk' out of my lungs. I guess you could say, I'm just not allowed to 'suffer in silence'. Changes in temperature, and dampness, bother me a lot, shut down my system. In March of 2009 Basil and I went to the University of Minnesota, Crookston, where they were performing his play about a troubled Vietnam Veteran, *Starkle, Starkle Little Twink*. We arrived in a major snowstorm and freezing temperatures. There was a good turnout for the play, but in retrospect, it probably wouldn't have hurt to have had one less in the audience. That trip nearly did me in. When we got back home I had a lung infection for a long time."

"Something that bothers me is that the bacteria in my lungs build up resistance to the antibiotics; once I'm given one, the doctor has to wait ninety days before she can re-prescribe that particular one again. And I'm being told that each time I use them they are becoming less and less effective."

"When you have that smothering feeling, you're willing to try anything. The older I get, of course, the worse it gets. I know it has got to be an aggravation to others when I have to change plans because of what's going on with me at the time. But I still want to do as much as I can; I can't just give up; I just have to respect my limitations. Some of my limitations I put on myself based on how my lungs are behaving; some come from listening to my doctor; things like avoiding large crowds and making sure I always take my prescriptions and get my flu shots."

"Concerning advice to others, all I can say is, if times are tough, keep going; you can't quit. You may have some limitations, but you can still enjoy life.

And follow your doctor's advice. Realize that there may be things going on with someone that you can't see that may be contributing to why that person seems detached, or maybe even a bit anti-social."

"Along with faithfully taking my prescribed medicines, the best thing for me to do sometimes is to relax, read. But the panic can about overwhelm when it feels like the elephant is starting to sit on my chest again. Perhaps the most accurate statement in the world is, when you can't breathe, nothing else matters."

Cora

COPD is really something like the commercial of the elephant sitting
On your chest. I would like to go outside on hot days and enjoy a
Really long walk in the woods, or a swim, or even perhaps
A picnic in the woods, but I really shouldn't; I'd better stick to books.

COPD

It is tiring figuring out a way
To avoid explaining
Why I don't want to take a long walk,
Or go outside on a hot day,
Or go to a concert.

But even with my medicine, sometimes it feels
Like I can't breathe, and those COPD Commercials
(with the elephant sitting on the chest)
Are accurate, and my doctor recommends
That I avoid large crowds.

I guess I could just come out
And tell you I have COPD,
But I have always been a rather
Private person and I just don't want to
Share that information with you.

(She really is a private person, but I convinced her that the "COPD story" would help others understand what this "inner wounding" is like.)

15

Horse and Buggy; Speeding Van; Wheelchair (Paul & Linda Shirk)

"It was on C Highway here in Morgan County; April 4th, 2010, Easter Sunday," he said, "right about 4:30 in the afternoon. My fiancé, Linda, and I had eaten earlier with my parents and were on the way over to visit with and have the evening meal with hers."

April 30, 2013. I was visiting Paul at his farm in central Missouri, in an area where most all of his neighbors were, like him, "horse and buggy Mennonites." We had come out onto a concrete porch that ran along the front of the tomato-sorting shed where he had been working while sitting in his motorized wheelchair. He and three other young men were sorting and packing some of the biggest and best looking tomatoes I had seen in a long time, maybe ever. And later I discovered they were also very delicious.

He continued, "Actually, a car was passing us the other way, and I noticed the driver looking at me, or at least I thought he was, and I specifically remember wondering, 'Why is he looking at me like that?' Later I found out he was looking our way because he saw that the van behind us was about to plow into our rear."

Paul paused, and went on to explain about how a buggy was constructed. "I don't know if you know how the buggy is put together," he said, "but the part you ride in, the box, sits atop the basic frame. It's attached, but it is a separate unit. The van that hit us had a small hood over the engine, and the box part of the buggy, with my fiancé and me inside, went up on the hood against the van windshield while the van went over the rest of the frame and pushed it and the horse about a hundred yards down the road."

"People told me this later. I don't remember being hit at all; just waking up lying in the ditch. It was like part of my leg had disappeared; it was the way it was twisted under me, and I saw people running toward me and someone hollering, 'Call 9-1-1! Call 9-1-1!' I blacked out again; I never heard the sirens, or the helicopter."

"I woke up again as I was being carried to the helicopter, and talked with some neighbors. I asked about Linda and was told, 'She's over here crying.'

When I was in the air, I remember seeing clouds and how windy it was. The helicopter was lurching some. I blacked out again. I remember when they were carrying me down toward the emergency room it was cold, and they were almost running. 'Slow down!' I hollered, 'or I'm going to be sick!'"

"Linda doesn't remember much from the accident either. She gets around okay now although sometimes she has a lot of pain, but initially she was black and blue all over her face and collarbone, and several places on her legs and back, and she had one broken bone in her leg. I had only one visible bruise, and no broken bones, but the disc between my 6th and 7th vertebra was torn out, the doctors said probably because I was partly turned looking at those guys in the passing car. The guy that hit us was older, maybe 75 or 80. He had restrictions on his license, and he really shouldn't have been driving at all; his eyesight was so bad he was legally blind."

"I remember asking how the horse was and they told me it was still alive, but that it had been pushed along the road in front of the buggy frame. Later they had to put him down. Funny, but I recall thinking I was glad I had not hitched up my favorite horse that day."

"I didn't really feel a lot of pain at the time of the accident; I just knew something was going on, and I remember thinking, 'Okay; whatever.' In the emergency room they had to restrict my neck movement, and while they were putting the neck clamp on to hold my head straight, they told me it would only hurt a little bit. They were wrong about that; it hurt a lot! I realized I couldn't walk, but after a week and a half I started to have toe contractions. I was so happy. I told the doctor I was moving my toes and I would be able to walk, but he told me, 'No; it's just spasms in your muscles; you won't ever be able to walk again.'"

I asked Paul if he had any anger in his initial feelings about his situation, and he replied, "No, not really, although in the first week I was in a lot of despair. I felt like this really couldn't be happening. Then in the second week I just said to God, 'Thy will be done.' At that point, overall, I started to feel better about everything. Last winter, however, for the first time I cried about it."

I knew that Paul and Linda were married, so I asked him when they had wed. "November 23rd, 2010," he said. "We were already engaged. We figured that if we had already been married, we wouldn't get a divorce over this, so why shouldn't we continue with our plans to get married. We've been good for each other. She has a lot of back pain at times, and sometimes feels depressed. I get down sometimes, too. We encourage each other not to give up, to hang in, that everything will be all right. She says that helps her, even though sometimes you wonder if it really will be. Something that is difficult, too, is reading. I think that sometimes it takes longer for me to turn a page than it does to read it."

"When I am struggling sometimes, and feeling like, 'No way; this can't be happening', I start to feel like something bigger is going on. We wanted to have children. We're going to adopt. There is another couple in our church that has adopted, and we are planning on doing that too. In a bigger picture I have a peace that this is all working out for good. We are going to be going through our adoption process the same time as another couple, our best friends, so we're going to have that shared experience with them."

I asked Paul what were some other things he could say he had gained from the whole situation, and he thought a moment before answering.

"I have learned to appreciate even more my family and friends and the support they give. They have helped me during times I feel down, or in despair. I believe, even though I don't understand it all, that God knows best. I have a strengthened faith in God; in knowing him, and believing in him. If something good happened to me I would have no trouble in saying it was because God loved me, so why shouldn't I also say this is for some reason, and someday I will find out how this fits into his plan for my life. I've learned not to give up. I feel a stronger sense of hope that our adoption will work out."

"I was twenty when the accident happened; I'm twenty-three now, and, you know, I actually have a pretty good quality of life. If I need to go somewhere that I can't access in my wheelchair, my younger brother, he's twenty-one; he picks me up and carries me. We have a second floor in the house. I don't go up there very much, but if I want to, he carries me. He's my partner on the farm here. We grow tomatoes, blueberries, and pumpkins. I had a friend who owned this place and I was going to be a partner with him. I lived across the road in that house over there, and worked on this farm for years when I was younger. Then he sold the place, so now I own it and am partner with my brother. I pretty much put in a full day's work every day. Although," he grinned, "some afternoons I do take a short nap. We plant our tomatoes in the greenhouse in January, and that's how we have such big ones ready now; we started picking in March."

I asked Paul if, after the accident, he had ever seen the man who ran into him and Linda. "Oh, yes," he replied. "He came by one day when I was at my parents. I feel sorry for him because I don't think he has a real good life with his wife. As he telling me he was sorry for what happened, his wife came over to us in an agitated state and insisted, 'Let's go; let's forget this ever happened; you need to leave right now and put this whole incident behind you.' I saw him last winter in a store and I wanted to talk to him and tell him I forgive him, but he walked away and avoided me. I don't know. I do forgive him, but I just don't understand. I don't understand the way his wife reacted, and I don't understand how he was even out on the highway driving with the restrictions he has."

"And something else." Paul straightened up in his wheelchair some. "Sometimes people have told me that everything will be all right, and I want to tell them, 'unless you have been here in this wheelchair with me, you don't know.' They can say they understand, but they don't. You can't really understand something that you have never been through."

Understanding

Unless you have been through something, he said, there's no
Need to say you understand all about it, because you
Don't really empathize with someone until you have walked their pathway.
Easy enough to say, it will all turn out okay for you.
Really? Walk down, or maybe I should say, wheel down the
Same pathway I am on. And if I am feeling despair, please don't
Try to make me feel better by saying I'm going to be just fine. However,
And this is important; realize that I am at peace. Now, I'm
Not saying I don't question, and at times I really
Do wonder why that guy was even on the road.
I wish he had heeded all restrictions on his license, but wishing will
Not change reality. I don't even understand it all sometimes, and unless you
Go down this same road, you can't begin to either.

16

Good Kid; Mad City (Branden Teasley)

"I grew up in Compton, California. There was a time, due to gang violence; it was called one of the most dangerous cities in the United States. It's gotten better; there are still some problems, but there are some things that have been improving. My mother was pregnant with me when she was fifteen; my father was twenty. My father was murdered when I was three; he ran out of gas in the wrong neighborhood and a local gang member targeted him. He ran and tried to hop a fence and was shot eight times in the back. So my mom and I were left to find a place to stay with family and friends. My dad's family hardly knew us, but they reached out and took us in. My grandmother and my mom raised me, and looking back, I can see the odds were against me. I was being raised by a black single mother in a ghetto, not a real bad one, but, still, it had a reputation for gang violence. I was fortunate; I didn't get into the gang lifestyle too much, for a couple reasons."

"First, my mom had to work and so she wasn't there a lot of the time, but I saw a lot of things, and learned from the gangbangers, the homeless, and people on drugs. I was almost paranoid when living there that something was going to happen to me. What I learned was that I wanted my life to be in the opposite direction; I guess you could say that the gangbangers taught me the difference between right and wrong."

"Now, my grandfather didn't live in the ghetto area where my mom and I did, but I visited him a lot. He had some guns, and one time, when I was thirteen, I was playing 'gang-wars' with a cousin, and we got ahold of a 9 mm Glock and were taking turns putting the gun to the other's head and clicking the trigger. I didn't know my cousin had a bullet in the chamber, and so I clicked the trigger, accidently shot him in the face, and he almost died from the wound."

"For the first time, life got real for me. I had almost killed my cousin, and I would have thrown my own life away in the process. I could have gone to jail; and my cousin dead. That really got my attention. My mom and the rest of the family were real upset with me; I moved to live with my grandfather. This was when the second main factor kicked in that got me away from the gang lifestyle, my grandfather, who was a veteran, became the main influence in my life; he raised me kind of old-school, less emphasis on rules, and more emphasis on values, morals, respect, and responsibility."

"I had a lot of respect for him, and, the things he said to me. This was a man who saw signs that said 'Whites Only' when he was growing up; he truly knew what it was to be held down, but had a lot of ambition, and was goal-driven."

"Once I came out of the ghetto, I took 100% advantage of the opportunity. I started getting better grades in high school, and then after I graduated I started junior college. When I was a sophomore I met a girl on Facebook, we got together, and before long, she got pregnant. When I realized I was going to be a father, I knew I needed to be responsible. My daughter, Lyric Teasley, was born when I was a freshman at the University of Pikeville where I had decided to go in order to play football."

"About a year ago I was at a club in Williamson, West Virginia, and I was dancing with a girl, and I'm not sure why what happened next, happened. One thing I was told was the girl's brother, he's the one who stabbed me, didn't like me dancing with her. The other thing I was told was that since the guy had gotten into an argument with some guys on our football team, he thought he might get beat up and so he 'struck first'. Anyway, I was out on the floor dancing with this girl and her brother came up behind me and sliced me with a knife across the back. I've got about a nine inch scar running from my vertebra over to my right side."

"I didn't know what happened, but I was losing my balance and my vision was getting blurry. I stumbled over to some friends and told them to call 9-1-1; that I had been stabbed, and they thought I was joking. I knew to keep my composure and tried to get away from the crowd, but then I collapsed. Luckily, there was a nurse there who took my shirt and slowed the flow of blood. I got my cell and called a friend from junior college who called my daughter's mom, and she called my mom and put us on three-way. I was sure I was dying and I told them to tell my daughter that I loved her. Things kept shrinking and getting littler and littler, and I started going into some kind of hole. The nurse said later I stopped breathing and she was able to revive me. When I came back out of the hole, my mom was on the phone crying, there was a brawl going on in the back of the club, and police were there with Tasers."

"Someone had called 9-1-1 and they transported me to a hospital. I was told if the wound had been 1 cm either direction I would have bled to death, or been paralyzed. They told me I stopped breathing again at the hospital but they, also, were able to bring me back. I got eighty-six stitches inside the slice and fifteen staples on the outside. They told me at the hospital they didn't know how I had survived because I was in such bad shape when I got there; that really frightened me, and got me thinking even more seriously about my life."

"My mom begged me to come back to live with her as she said it was too dangerous here for me. I told her, 'No; I'm not going to let these people scare me out of my future'.* The doctor said it would be a couple months before I would be able to walk, but I did it in two weeks. When I got back to the University, a good friend, Jocelyn McCown, helped me a lot. She nursed me, cleaned and changed my bandages; if I remember right, she e-mailed you and then you called me while I was still in the hospital. She was there for me which is a nice feeling when you are so far from home. Also, for a while I got depressed some; actually got paranoid every day for some time, but I kept pushing on through the darkness. My good friend, B J Iverson, he helped me a lot with my attitude and gave me a lot of encouragement."

"I figured if I went back home I would just become part of the crowd; with no education to help me. My GPA had been a 2.3, but I bounced back the next semester and got a 3.5, and this last semester I got a 4.0. I'm getting a degree in social work, and I started to get more involved on and off-campus. I got involved with Black History Month, and I also went to some middle schools in the area to talk to kids about not bullying, and take their education seriously. I did a practicum with the WestCare Homeless Shelter. I want to do anything to show people you can overcome when odds seem against you."

"For a while I was angry a lot because I didn't really know why I was stabbed. I was sad because people were telling me Williamson was a dangerous place to go, and I thought that it was crazy, because I had come from a real ghetto, to be stabbed here. I was also angry because the guy couldn't come up to me man to man and face me if he had a problem; I mean, I was 5'9" and weighed 200 pounds, and he was 6'4" and weighed about 250 pounds. I mean, why did he have to stab me in the back? But like I said, B J and Jocelyn encouraged me and helped me through these times."

"When I was growing up, as far as religion goes, I guess I only had my mom's faith, but now I've found my own; it's more of a spiritual thing. I want to tell people to take advantage of every day; you never know, you could be gone in an instant. Be responsible and get an education. Don't let procrastination keep you from achieving your goals; learn to make smart choices. I'd rather have my mind full of 'what ifs', like what if I had stayed in the hood and gotten into a gang, than regrets over actions I didn't take."

"I have something I want to say to the black population. Quit limiting yourself. Don't feel like if you are goal-oriented, or getting an education that you are 'becoming white', or betraying your race. People fought and died for us to be able to take advantage of opportunities. There are a lot of things you can do now that you couldn't sixty or seventy years ago. Do them. Use your God-given abilities for good."

"That's why I went into social work; to help others and be a role model. It is so easy in today's society to be influenced by the negative. I'm going into the Air Force this summer, and I want to get my Masters Degree and use my time promoting change for the better."

* I met Branden's mother when he graduated from the University of Pikeville in May 2013. She exuded pride over her son's accomplishments.

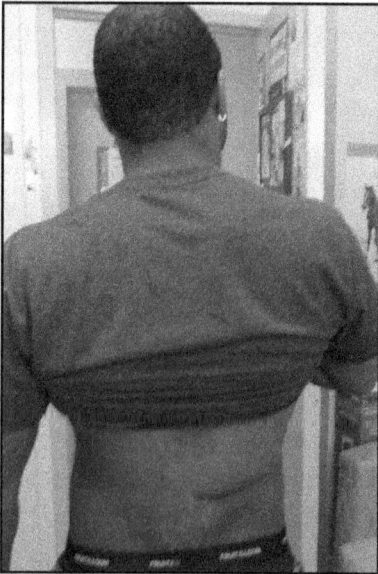

Teasley

There were a few things along the way,
Especially a foolish game with
A gun at age thirteen, that weren't the
Smartest choices. But at
    twenty-three, when
Lying on the floor, bleeding to death
    from someone
Else's choice to stab me, I realized that
You have to get goal-oriented,
    and push on.

17

Every Day is a Bonus; Don't Waste the Bonus (Doug Lange)

"As you know," he said, "the biggest event in Pikeville is 'Hillbilly Days'. Crowded streets; everybody loves to go downtown. I get tensed up; check windows. You had to do that in Khabul and Khandalhar, and you just don't leave that behind. One thing that people who have gone through some form of inner wounding come to realize is, there are a lot of triggers around."

Doug and I were talking together a couple days after he had started reading some of my earlier writings. He commented on *Starkle, Starkle, Little Twink*, the play in Appendix B of this book which he had just finished reading the night before.

"You might not have said it exactly this way," Doug said, "but you nailed it with, 'no man is an island; at least not for long'. When PAM picked up that something was different about DAN when he returned from the war; and he couldn't tell her about everything that was bothering him. When people go through certain experiences, sometimes they can't describe them to someone else who has not been there; they have difficulty communicating about them. And yet, there's a connection that people make with others who have gone through like experiences."

Doug referred back the play again. "After the war, DAN and PAM still connected and communicated at an emotional and intellectual level, but there were some levels they could not relate to each other on because they were in separate lives for a year, and with DAN, the veteran, there were some things at a deeper level he just kept inside. I think I've done that with others at times; kept my distance."

We talked a couple minutes about the idealistic visions people can build up about others when separated by war; the almost fantasy-like vision of 'he or she is over there fighting for his country, or, the other is back home, holding everything together'. "We can get very idealistic," Doug said, "but we reconnect at the new reality of 'different experiences for a year', not idealism."

"However," Doug went on, "let me give you an example of when you can communicate with someone at the 'experience reality level', and you know

you should. From my experience in Afghanistan, I know how it feels to sense-
lessly lose friends, co-workers. So when the shootings took place at Ft. Hood,
Texas November 5, 2009, which were senseless killings, I had a nephew I
knew I had to call. He had served two tours in Iraq, and returned to an assignment at Ft. Hood, a place where he, and his Army buddies thought they
were safe. When I got him on the phone, he just started to 'spill over' with
his feelings. I just knew he would need to do that; I was aware because, in a
sense, I had been there."

Doug was a Civil Affairs Officer, Deputy Commander, Brigade level,
with approximately 230 personnel in his command. His jurisdiction included eight cities and some storm troopers from the 101st and 82nd Airborne
Units, also known as 'helmets'. He spent twenty-seven ½ years with the military, ten ½ of those on active duty. He was with the Reserves when called up,
both to Kosovo, and Afghanistan.

"I was fortunate to be part of the early units both in Kosovo in 1999 and
in Afghanistan in 2002. At that time, a lot of the locals were happy we were
there. That changed. But, still, maybe one of the lessons of Vietnam was there
are times and places where we can be more effective talking with the locals,
than fighting with them. My real job was to coordinate aid and work with a
'Khabulcentric 'government as liaison. But I really enjoyed it more working
directly with the people. I have been told that that 80% of the people are honest and industrious and the other 20% are politicians and crooks. That's the
way it was; maybe I should say, was then."

"I felt a strong sense of responsibility for those people under my command. The most difficult days for me were those 'groundhog days'; the same
thing coming back around again. I hated looking at those metal boxes being
loaded onto planes. They were bearing real people who gave their all, heading back to loved ones in mourning. Those are images you don't want in your
mind, but they're there. It gives you a different outlook. You find yourself
saying, 'I didn't expect my life to turn out this way.' You face your own
mortality."

"Those images create a certain pain. My dad was in World War II, and
he never talked about his experiences. I was talking with him when he was
eighty years old, and asked him a question about the war. His answer caught
me off guard; he said, 'I can't talk about it; it hurts too much.' He lived a very
full productive life, and I never knew how he was feeling inside. Now I know.

There are images many of us veterans have, whether they originated in Iraq, Afghanistan, Kuwait, Vietnam, Korea, any war; we don't want to see them, but they are there."

Doug paused for a little while, thinking, and then he went on. "I tried to help my people in any way I could, to try and help them stay grounded which also meant using tough love at times. Sometimes it takes that to help people grow and develop into what they can be, and also, to survive. You want to keep them from being in those metal boxes loaded onto planes."

"I had something interesting happen one time that hit me at a couple levels. We were in an area where there were a lot of nomadic Afghans; they herded sheep, and basically their way of life had remained unchanged for centuries. They would migrate to the north, and back south with seasonal changes. When we were checking out villages, there were usually a lot of kids standing by the road, and we would give them any leftover MRE's (meals-ready-to-eat) we had. We would take their pictures, and of course then they could see themselves on the camera. They were always in awe. I was talking one time with this boy who was maybe ten to twelve years old, and he asked me what it had been like for me growing up. I told him I had spent a lot of time with relatives on their farm, with the animals, and growing and picking fruit. He said to me, 'Oh, you know agriculture; so you're a shepherd'. I had never thought of myself as a shepherd."

"Then it hit me; in actuality, I was a shepherd, of 230 people. Sometimes I had to go out looking for the lost sheep and bring them back to the fold, and I was always trying to keep them safe. I realized that was, and is, my calling; this is when I feel completed. Often you seek 'lost sheep' one at a time. The journey of life is all about helping others. As people we all want something, and to feel like we have lived a worthwhile life. Things happen that change your outlook, but, still, we all want to feel like there has been a reason for us being put here on this earth."

I asked Doug what he considered was his best day in Afghanistan. He smiled. "There were a lot what I could call best days. I enjoyed working with people. Throughout my life I have volunteered for things, because I don't want to look back and say, 'what if?' But now, one of my best days I was able to have, due to my position, was spending an evening with the king in his palace. We had a nice conversation about life, Christmas, and God, dreams and goals, families."

I asked Doug what he has found to be a source of healing in his life after Afghanistan. He was silent for a while, reflecting. "I pray and meditate more; I study my Bible differently and try to internalize goals on how to live my life. Meditation for me is time away from the noise of life, certain memories. Of course, I have mild tinnitus, milder than you do, so there is a certain sense of never getting away from the noise; but we work at it. I read a lot more. I like to walk with my wife. I think more about the difference between what I do and who I am. They are not the same. I crunch numbers; that's what I do. And I'm a little oxymoronic. There are times when I am a little OCD; and other times when I feel a strong sense of compassion and realize I have a heart to help. I'm here at the University of Pikeville for a reason. What I do is function as Vice President for Finance and Business Affairs. Who I am called to be is a helper, a shepherd. I believe that what we do for others flows out like the ripples from a rock being thrown into a pond."

He continued. "I have no right to have survived when others didn't. Every day is a bonus; you don't want to waste the bonus. I want to know at the end of the day that I made a positive difference in someone's life. If I did, it wasn't a wasted day. There are images out of Afghanistan I don't want to see, or live again. But I wouldn't trade the experience. It has helped form who I am. From both the good and the bad, I have learned so much. I don't want to waste my bonus days."

Doug Lange

Does it really matter what I do
Over the course of a day? By my way of
Understanding, yes, it does. I believe we must
Give our best to helping others; seeking the lost.

Little did I know how that young
Afghan boy would speak to me. He probably
Never knew the implications of his words, but he
Gave me new insight into my calling. I can't erase
Everything that's happened, but I can be a shepherd.

18

A Country Boy Can Survive (Mark Rogers)

"I may have had it tough in the early years, but that's how I learned to survive. We had it rough; there wasn't any such thing as money. There were times we nearly starved. If we killed something, then we ate meat, and we had a garden. I'm fifty now. When I was growing up in the 60's there weren't a lot of government programs; didn't want help anyhow."

"Like I said, it was rough. If we got sick we just had to deal with it. There wasn't money for doctors. But at school, it seemed like anybody I looked at had it better. I didn't understand the differences until I was older. That's just the way it was. When I look back on it, I realize my mother was like a lot of other people in the area; she did the best she could."

Mark sat back on the couch in his camouflage jacket and relaxed a bit. I was visiting a sister-in-law in Graham County, North Carolina, and Mark had come by the house to visit for a while. He and I left the others in the kitchen and went into the living room for this interview.

"My dad wasn't around when we were kids. My mother remarried; some of my uncles pretty much raised me. When I was around seventeen my stepdad got killed in an accident while working on the Cherohala Skyway. A packer rolled over on him. But one of my brothers and me, I guess we were maybe eleven and fourteen, we had already left home, and raised ourselves. We learned responsibility. More kids these days need to learn that. We lived together in an old house for some time. I stayed a lot in the mountains and just did what it took to survive. I married when I was thirty-one; that didn't work out so well. I did better this time. I've been married for fifteen years now."

"I never did like school. I would just sit and think about hunting and fishing. I quit going when I was fourteen." Mark grinned. "They never did come looking for me, so I just stayed out."

"I learned to hunt when I was eight. A couple of uncles helped, but I pretty much taught myself. So I knew how to trap, fish, hunt, and stay in the mountains. I'd work construction in the summer, and in the winters I'd go to one of the camps I had in the Santeetlah Mountains for about eleven weeks. That's where I've always been the happiest, in the mountains."

I asked Mark what was the hardest part of his life in the mountains. "Even though I was happy there, sometimes it was hard when I was all alone. You can get lonely out there with no one."

When I asked if he was able to make any pets of the animals in the mountains, he laughed. "Had to eat; didn't think of making pets of any of them. I shot my first big deer when I was thirteen. That was before I even left home. Before then I ate a lot of squirrels and other small game. I love squirrel meat. Since then I've shot a lot of bears and hogs. I have an old wood stove, and I can most of what I shoot. Can the old fashioned way; outside sometimes. I can just about any kind of meat, and taters, any kind of vegetables, trout, and other fish."

I told Mark I had never heard of canning trout before. He laughed and said he liked canned trout even better than salmon.

Mark got quiet and thoughtful. "You know," he said, "in the mountains is the only place where I really feel normal. In a way, the world ain't changed there. It's the same as when I was a boy. I'm at peace there. I like the old ways."

I asked Mark if he had any days fishing or hunting that stuck out to him as the best. He was quick to reply. "I've had a lot of them; there've been a lot of them good." He thought a moment. "I guess with fishing, maybe the day I caught a 28" brown trout. That was really good. And hunting, the biggest animal I ever killed was near Wilkesboro. I got me a 530 pound wild hog." He smiled. "The biggest bear I ever got was 438 pounds. That old hog was even bigger. I've killed lots of bears and hogs; canned a lot of the meat. Of course," he added, "we got us freezers now, so we save some that way. I like to garden, too." He grinned. "And make a little shine. My uncle taught me. I've been around stills ever since I was a baby."

I asked Mark what advice he had for others who might find themselves in particularly tough circumstances.

"People need to appreciate what they have, their health, the people in their lives. All that can change quickly. Enjoy each day. I believe we're supposed to be happy, so you need to find what you like to do, and do it. My peace and happiness is in the woods and the mountains. I'm not a real religious person, but I'm spiritual. My communion is with nature. I learn about God in a garden and in the mountains and in survival. A country boy can do that."

Mark and I went back out to the kitchen to join the others. A family friend was there with her young son, Conner. Mark asked her if it was okay to give Connor some candy. He laughed and said, "The youngun's like candy."

Mark Rogers

Mostly I learned to survive, he said,
As he thoughtfully looked down, because of the
Rough times. I had to learn what to do,
Know how to become

Responsible for myself. I'm at peace
On a mountaintop, and when I
Go fishing. Caught a 28" brown trout once, and
Even killed a 530 pound wild hog.
Right up there as some of my better days. No; I have to
Say, he added, all days are good in the woods.

19

What Doesn't Kill Me Will Make Me Stronger (Name withheld)

After she was seated, we talked about a direction for the interview, with the goal of finding what the turning points had been for her in her situation, and the paths to healing she had discovered.

"Which situation do we want to talk about first," she asked, "my mother being on drugs and my dad drinking, or the abusive boyfriend who almost killed me?" We started with her parents.

"I grew up around alcoholics and potheads. My dad drank a lot, and my mom was always smoking. There was pot being grown in my room when I was little. I've also seen my mom have seizures when she couldn't get a fix, and there were always people coming in and out of the house. I still get along with my mom okay, though. She was high a lot, but she was there, well, except I couldn't count on either of my parents to be at my games. I felt like I was in a normal home. I thought all parents had their friends over and did drugs with them. Then one night I slept over at a friend's house, and it seemed so different. Later I learned about drugs being bad for you, and I think I was eleven when I decided I didn't want drugs to be a part of my life."

"We ate, but there was other stuff lacking. I didn't have any dolls; we had one TV, but I never got to watch anything I wanted to. When it was time for shopping for clothes for school, if I was lucky that year, I got one pair of shoes, a pair of pants, and a shirt."

"We lived way out in the country, down an old road, and there was a creek nearby. I used to love to sit by the creek with a friend. I found peace there. There was just something calming about the water."

"I started in a relationship with a guy when I was eighteen. In the beginning he seemed like the perfect boyfriend, but then he started to become controlling, and mean and hateful at times. I foolishly excused this because I knew he had a rough time at home. His parents did drugs, too. But by this time I guess you could say I had already allowed him to get 'his hooks in me.' I didn't leave."

"The first time he hit me, we were arguing about something. I don't even remember what, and he smacked me across the face and hollered, 'Shut your mouth, you stupid whore!' I tried to leave and he told me I couldn't. He apologized and said he was sorry and talked me into staying. Like I said, I had already allowed him to 'get his hooks into me.' Later we had another argument and he pushed me down a flight of stairs. I had some marks on me when I graduated from high school, but I covered them as much as I could with make-up. My parents asked what had happened, and I told them, 'Oh, you know me. I'm such a klutz; I tripped and fell down some stairs.'"

"We broke up during the summertime, but he had my number and was texting daily, and said he had changed, so, I went back. I started as a freshman in college, but after 2-3 months, he was telling me that if I really loved him I would 'quit that stupid school' and live with him."

She raised her eyebrows with a sort of "I know, I know" look, and then continued.

"So, with only three weeks left in my first semester of college, I quit school. I quit on a Wednesday, and early Thursday morning we were arguing, and he kicked me. I said I was leaving, and he told me the only way I would leave was in a body bag. Friday he asked where his ball shorts were. When I told him they were in the dryer he asked if I had folded them and I told him 'no'. He went and got them and hollered at me, 'They're wrinkled!' and threw me down the steps. I tried to fight back but he kicked me and knocked me out. I woke up in the hospital. A next door neighbor had heard the fighting and then saw my boyfriend leaving with some blood on him, so he came into the house and found me and called 911. As I lay in the hospital I thought a lot of him saying that the only way I would leave him was in a body bag, and now I knew he meant it, and I was afraid of what would happen if I stayed with him."

"Naturally, I left him, for good this time. I saw him once, accidently, at a gas station. I quickly got in my car and locked the doors. He came over and started beating on the door saying he wanted to talk to me. I told him to 'get away' and drove off. I wanted nothing more to do with him. I know he was raised like that. His dad was abusive to his mom and he learned from that, but you don't have to be that way."

"My Mamaw told me that if someone loved you, they wouldn't hurt you. When I left him my self-esteem was dirt low. He told me I was a whore and that no one would want to be with me. I felt just as low as anyone could. When I had been with him, if we were out somewhere, I didn't even look around for fear of being hollered at or hit. I lived with him for almost nine months, and for at least five of them I was in constant fear."

"After I got out of the hospital I worked as a CNA at a nursing home for six months. I had gotten certified while I was still in high school. But, after a while doing that, I knew I didn't want to stay at that level the rest of my life."

"I knew I couldn't live with my parents or my Mamaw, and I kept thinking about how good I had had it when I was in college. I knew that the only way I was going to make something of myself was to go back to college. I want to make something of myself. My people back home are all in the same pattern. I feel that's no excuse. I'm going to survive and get beyond this. I started thinking about why I started college in the first place."

"When I was a junior in high school we had a visit from an admissions counselor. I thought my ACT score was too low and thought I couldn't make it. Well, he came back again when I was a senior, and talking with me, he called me by name and asked if I was interested in an overnight stay at the college. I thought to myself, *If he remembers my name from a year ago, I need to check this out.* Of course, like I said, I quit, but, when I decided to come back, I was readmitted, and I'm almost at the end of my first full year. They have a retention counselor, and a developmental program, and all the teachers in that program are awesome. I have shared my story with some of them, and they have always been there for me. They've listened to me, and cried with me. They're the main reason I've stayed. I consider this place my home right now."

I asked about things that helped her cope and she answered, "I've sought a deeper spiritual life. I pray a lot more, about everything. I write in my journal, and," she smiled, "I write a lot of poetry. I've already mentioned I've received counseling from teachers and staff here. I'm always looking ahead; I tell myself there will always be a tomorrow, and it will bring an even better day."

I questioned her as to whether she had ever wondered, "Why me?"

"Oh, yeah. I can see now that some things I thought were true, maybe I learned in error. I'd always heard that good things happen to good people, and I used to think, *I'm doing well in high school, good grades, in the band, I don't get into trouble, and I'm good-hearted, not mean.* So, yeah, I wondered for a while. And my Mamaw told me that God will never give me anything that I can't handle. That has helped me, made me stronger. I recently got a tattoo that says, 'What doesn't kill me will make me stronger.' I figure if I can go through this and still smile, then it has made me stronger, and if I can face this, I can face anything. It has all made me want to try even harder."

I asked if she felt any sense of her experiences working into a bigger purpose for her life.

"I'm still not fully settled on what I want to do yet. I really like math, but I'm still leaning toward pediatric nursing. I want to help other kids, let them see that if I can come from poor circumstances, and abuse, and survive and do well, they can to. I'd like to be able to inspire them. Also, I lost some friends at a very young age, and I'd like to be able to help other children cope with these kinds of losses."

When I asked her if she had any advice for others who might be in similar circumstances, she was quick to reply. "If anyone is in an abusive relationship, get out. Even if they say they will change, they don't, so just get away from it. If I had stayed with him, I believe I'd either be dead now, or, if not, he'd still be trying to do it. Find friends that are positive, that don't hurt you, and seek counseling."

20

Addictions That Held; Moving On (WestCare Program)

The local jail facility in Pike County has a rehabilitation program that inmates can volunteer to go through. Bill Baird III, a long-time University of Pikeville board member, works with a ministry through the program and makes weekly visits to the jail. He invited me as a guest speaker a few months back, and so I asked Bill if he would see if there were any inmates who might be willing to talk to me about the role addictions played in their situations. Four men talked with me, and here are their stories.

I Never Thought It Would End like This (Tom – Not his real name)

When he walked into the room for the interview I was a bit surprised. He wasn't my age, but he's getting there. After we shook hands and introduced ourselves, we sat down and he began to talk.

"It wasn't my upbringing that was a factor in my being here. I was raised in a strong, traditional family; my parents are still married. They sent me to a private school, a good Catholic one. They made sure I got a good education, stronger than most. It was in 1986, after college that I enlisted in the Air Force. My test scores were high enough that I could have been an officer, but I've always been more of a hands-on type of person, so I chose to go into the enlisted ranks. I did my job well, and overall had what I guess you would call an "uneventful career" until I was deployed to Saudi Arabia in 1990 and 1991 for operations in Desert Storm."

"I volunteered to be with a crash recovery team. We would go to where a plane or helicopter had been downed, and, after certain items were retrieved that could be used, made sure the rest of the aircraft was destroyed so it couldn't be used, or studied for information, by the enemy. One time, when we came under fire, it was the first time ..."

He stopped, clamped his lips tight together, and fought back tears. He was quiet for a moment before continuing.

"It was the first time that I killed someone."

I was right there with him in that moment as I recalled my own experience of being aware that I was responsible for taking the life of another. I told him that in the book I was leaving with him (*Poetic Healing: A Vietnam Veterans Journey from a Communication Perspective*) that there was a poem I had written about the same feelings and questions. We looked at each other, college professor and jail inmate, with the bond of brotherhood that combat veterans understand as he paused again, regrouped, and then continued.

"And there was a warehouse that was hit by a scud missile in Saudi Arabia with over 150 Third World Nationalists caught in it. The sight, and smell, of those bodies was awful. I guess now they'd say I had PTSD (post-traumatic stress disorder) but it wasn't really talked about during that war, not like after Vietnam, or Iraq, or Afghanistan. I started to have nightmares, and I started to use alcohol to self-medicate."

"Meanwhile, my military service progressed along until budget cuts enacted by Congress in 1994 brought it to an end. I planned on making it a career, but in 1995, after 9 ½ years, my time on active duty was over, due to downsizing, but eventually I was able to serve in the Reserves."

"However, things started to fall apart at home. My drinking was causing problems, and my wife left and moved away with our only son, and I thought I had hit bottom. My boy and I didn't have contact with each other for a long time, although we are close now."

I asked him about other turning points, either positive, or negative, and he paused and smiled before continuing.

"I've had several. For a while after I thought I had bottomed out, I guess you could refer to it now as my first recovery, I remarried, started going to church, and thought things were getting better. I became active in the VFW, and, in 2004 I bought a motorcycle. I was drawn to the allure of it. But, I started to hang out with the wrong group of people, some unsavory characters. I started drinking again, which created a lot of friction with my third wife."

"Our house burned in 2006, and, later, I was raking through the charred remains trying to see if there was anything salvageable, any kind of mementos or keepsakes. I was by the refrigerator, and there were some steaks that had burned, and while I was raking up those charred pieces I had a flashback to that warehouse in Saudi Arabia. Then the dreams started back, and I got back into the cycle of drinking. I tried to justify it by saying that I had to in order to get to sleep. Then in August 2008 I broke down and was committed to the psych ward at the VA. I spent some time there, got out, and went back to the same cycle."

"Things got worse with me and my wife and there was a divorce. I was at the bottom again. I had a good job, and was getting ready to start another tour at Fort Knox with a salary upwards of $125,000. I had all the toys, but they didn't mean anything, and I was ready to end it all. I went through several days of debating whether or not to take my life. I wanted to talk to my ex, but she didn't want me there. The police came, and I resisted arrest. I grabbed a 12 gauge shotgun and pointed it at the officer, so, of course I was charged with a violent crime. I understand all that, and I was in the wrong. My world was just collapsing around me."

He thoughtfully paused again, and then went on. "I never thought my life would be like this, the way it has been. But it's okay. I'm at peace now. Ironically, one of the areas I received training in while in the military was counseling, and I have had jobs as a counselor. Now I'm a player instead of being the coach. But this has been good for me, a turn-around. Actually, after I get out of here, and go through the follow-up programs, there is a good chance that with my background I can get into the program as a counselor. I've worked before as a counselor following the basics of the Twelve-Step Program. This program is faith-based, and it has helped me get back to a place of spiritual peace with who was once my first love, my Lord."

I asked him if he had any words of advice to pass on to others. Again, the thoughtfulness, and then he said, "It's okay to cry; that's the beginning of healing. Too many people try to maintain a tough attitude. Crying about things that have hurt deeply help purge, give you a clearer perspective, help you move on to the next step. When I say I'm at peace with my Lord, I'm not talking about being 'churchy.' I'm talking about a one-on-one relationship. That's where the real peace comes from."

When we talked about a bigger picture in life, he said, "Although it's hard to see sometimes, if we can learn from everything that happens, even though it may be a result of some poor choices we have made, there's hope. Like I said, even though I never thought my life would be where it is right now, it is okay, because I have found peace and a hope for the future."

My Advice; Don't Go down This Road
(Jack – Not his real name)

He sat at the table with me after our self-introductions and started telling me his story. "I'm forty-two now. It's been over twenty-five years since I heavily started using alcohol. I was sixteen when I let a buddy of mine take my car. A little later I was with another friend in his car, and we were going down the road when we saw the wreck. It was my car, and when we got out and went over, the ambulance crew had already covered the body with a tarp. It was my friend who had borrowed my car."

"I wish now I had never done it, but I lifted the tarp. One arm and his head were nearly cut off. I wish I had never seen that. I wish I hadn't let him use my car. I've always felt guilty about that. He might still be alive."

"When I was about six, I remember my mom and dad bought some property and cleared all the trees and brush off it, and we built us a home. It took about four years, but we moved in when we got enough of it done that we could. I remember those years as a good life. Still, and I don't know why, I was just always in trouble most of my childhood. When I was younger, me and my brother got a BB gun for Christmas one year, and we sure got in trouble because we were shooting BB guns at a telephone repairman who was up working on a line. We were just mean. We shot at him five or six times each before he got down from the pole. We took off running for the house, and he followed us there and told my mom. We got a bad whippin' for that."

"We had to walk about a quarter mile to the bus stop, and there was this big bee's nest of hornets. I could not walk by them without throwing a rock, and every evening I would try to throw to tear their nest down. Every morning they had it built right back up. I got stung three to four times a week, and my mom kept telling me to leave them alone and they wouldn't bother me. But I would not give up. I had to get even with them until one day I got stung about thirty times and had to go to the hospital with big red welts all over me and get a shot. I guess that learned me the lesson to leave them alone like my mother said."

"Later when we were older, I was about eight, me and my brother got in trouble in school because we hung two guys; we didn't kill them, but it scared them. They were going to tell on us for something we did, and we didn't like snitches, so we hung them. I felt sorry for them and let them down, but we still got in big trouble over that. We had to go to court and the judge asked me what part I had to do with it, and I told him, 'All I did was hold the rope.' He said I was just the one he wanted to talk to, and suspended me and my brother from school, and my mom had to take us to an alternative school for a year."

"I would see a lot of people come and go as I grew up. I remember everyone would come to my dad's to party. I made a good friend, and me and him would get into his dad's beer and take some, find a place to hide, and drink them. We did this every weekend for a long time. When I turned sixteen I thought it was party time, so I got me a car and a driver's license."

"It was after my friend was killed in the car wreck that I was shot with a .357 Magnum. That was after I got in trouble in school for smoking pot, so I had quit and moved away from home. I had a pretty good job at a factory, and there was plenty of money, women, and pot; I grew a lot of pot. I had a fight with a neighbor one night and I whipped him. The next day I was coming home from work, and when I started down my driveway I heard what I thought was firecrackers, and then I heard my back window bust out. I realized someone was shooting at me and I felt one hit me in the back. So I floored the car, got to my house and got my gun. I loaded up and started firing. He was running back to his car, but I hit him a couple of times. Then I got in my car and drove to the hospital. The cops were all over me there. They didn't arrest me while I was in the hospital. I was there for a month, but as soon as they released me, a cop was waiting to give me a court date. I served time for attempted murder and wanton endangerment. That's the first time I got in trouble with the law for drinking. The bullet was still inside me, and I drank a lot then because it helped kill the pain. I still have the bullet inside me."

"I've had a lot of wrecks from drinking, and a lot of DUI's. On some of those arrests, I would try to fight and got arrested once for assault on a police officer."

"In 1998 I was hurt at work. We were working on a dozer taking up the slack in a chain with a binder. It broke and hit me; broke a disc in my lower back. I began drinking even more; again saying it was for the pain. I quit drinking once for quite a while but then was hurting, and got prescribed some 30's and Xanax. But then I got to feeling like I could handle a six-pack, so I started drinking all over again. I got into these loops. I'd quit drinking for a week or two, then I'd have a bad day. I've spent ten to twelve years of the last twenty-five in jail. I wrote the parole board I needed the S.A.P. (Substance Abuse Program.) I've got five kids. My first two were with my first wife; she died of an overdose. I realize now I've robbed all my kids of so much. They've had a dad who's been living 'lifestyles of the not so rich; and dumb'. I'm surprised that I'm not on America's Dumbest Criminals."

He paused a moment, started taking about his children again, and brightened a little.

"My kids are doing well. One's graduated from college; another's started college; and a daughter, after her grandmother died, she wrote a poem about her, and it was published in a poetry book. I'm real proud of her. I got my GED while here in the program, and I want to try and make some things up to my wife and my kids. I've been married twenty-two years, and my wife is waiting for me. She's hoping, like I am, that this program is my big turning point. I've got to make good choices and make it work."

"I'm a good worker. I always worked hard when I wasn't in jail. I like to read a lot, and fish. I like to work with wood. I make some real nice bird-houses. I'm thinking that now I have my GED I will go to school for auto mechanics or auto body work. I like to do both of them."

"WestCare has been a major turning point for me. It's helped me step back and look at all the things that brought me here, and see the things I need to avoid so I don't get here again. It's changed my way of thinking. They say insanity is doing the same thing expecting a different outcome. That was me. I'm open now to all suggestions. I'm forty-two and there's got to be more to life than what I've been doing. I've got three grand-babies now and I think that's going to help too."

When I asked him if he had any advice for others, he thought a moment. "My advice to others," he started, "is, don't go down this road. Deal with life as it happens, on its terms. Don't be afraid to talk about what's bothering you. I might have been a lot better off earlier if I had talked to someone about what was bothering me. I never really could get away from the sight of my friend when I lifted that tarp, or the guilt I felt over letting him use my car."

"But, you know, I come from a small town where a lot of people have died of overdoses; a lot of drugs. I thank God I'm alive. I want to try and help others now because of what I've been through. I want to try and make up some things to my kids, but I do have to say, because of where I am now, in this program, I'm at peace; I'm the happiest I've ever been."

It's all in the Choices You Make   (Stan – Not his real name)

We shook hands, exchanged names, and I explained to him what I was writing about, and the general questions I would be asking him. Then he started talking.

"I was twelve when it happened. My sister and I came in from school and saw a note on the table. My older brother John, he was sixteen, was upset because he was being grounded. We hear a pop from his bedroom and ran in there; he had killed himself. I saw him; it was a mess. It took its toll on the family. I started sneaking and drinking my dad's beer, and smoking weed when I was thirteen."

"When I was sixteen, I started drinking even more. One day my dad was home in Edmonton working on his car, and I was supposed to help him. However, I chose to go with a couple friends to Bowling Green and get drunk instead. When I got back I was told I had to go to the hospital. My dad had had a massive heart attack while he was working on the car that I was supposed to be helping him with."

"I was a freshman in high school, and I quit. That was when I started taking acid and crank; I'd cook crank. I was in jail from when I was eighteen to twenty-two. When I got out I stayed straight for a while; I had two kids. Then I started substituting illegal drugs with legal, so I thought it was better. I didn't see it at the time as hurting anyone, but it was. I was taking from my kids to support a $200 a day hydrocodone habit."

"My mom's on probation. She gets off pretty soon. She's clean now, too. We worked together at the same time on meth, but never in front of each other though."

"I'm a repeat offender. I've got over fifty felonies against me: violent crimes, stealing, fleeing and evading the police. I've made some real bad choices. I was caught for possession, and was put on probation for five years. I was two months away from getting off probation when I was arrested for shoplifting. That put me where I am now."

"I enrolled in the WestCare Program because I want to change. I think being here will help me do that. I've got three kids: two biological, an eight-year-old son and a twelve-year-old daughter, and a fourteen-year-old step-daughter that's the same as mine. My goals are to stay off drugs and support my family. I love logging; that's what I want to do when I get out. My grandparents and my mom between them have several hundred acres I can log enough off of to support my family."

When I asked him if he had any advice to pass on, he was quick to reply.

"It's all in the choices you make. For me, things started to snowball, and then I lived almost fifteen years in a blur. I was trying to get away from pain, mental pain, but you've got to deal with it. My sister, who saw all the same stuff I did, made different choices with her life and she's doing okay. She moved to Florida right after our father's death, made good choices, and today she is a dispatcher in a County Sheriff's office."

"Me, I've lost my wife due to all this trouble and drugs. I plan on supporting my kids still. It's just that now it looks like it is going to have to be from afar. It's going to be hard to make it all right with the people I hurt, but I can, with different choices than the ones I've been making. But I can do it better without drugs. I know that."

I Don't Want a Lot of Material Things; I Want a Family (Hank – Not his real name)

After we introduced ourselves, and I explained what the interview was about, he started talking with pained look.

"The hardest thing I've ever done was hold my mom in my arms when she died of cancer. It took me a long time to come to terms with that. I was real angry at God. I had a lot of anger toward my two brothers, too, because they weren't there for Mom when she died. They've spent a lot of time in jail. I don't talk about them much. But one thing about this program is it has helped me realize I can't stay angry at people."

"When my uncle died, he was my best friend, I was real angry at God and other people. I worked in the coal mines, but I had also started selling pills. I was all the time running around. I never thought that my family would rather have me than the money I was bringing home. I didn't really see the pain I was causing others. I had fifteen or more years go by in the blink of an eye. That's what it seems like. My ex-wife told me that she dreaded every time there was a phone call, because she thought it would be about me in trouble again; another problem. If I'd kept going the way I was, I'd a probably been in the graveyard in two or three years."

I asked him about the WestCare program he was in, and how it was helping him. He took a deep breath and started.

"When you've been living like I have, you've got to change your way of thinking, got to start doing things differently. I think God's letting me be here for a reason. I've lost a lot in life, lost a lot of relationships. I'm not mad at my ex. I don't blame her for leaving. I used to think I knew it all; now I know that I don't."

"I have some regrets over things I did, choices I made, but I can't dwell on them. I've got to start thinking ahead. I've got to learn from my bad choices and go on. I was always searching for something, and I didn't know I had it, a family. They were right there in front of me, and I lost a lot due to dope. If I hadn't been on dope I could have spent more time with others, with my ex. I wish I was here in this program eight or nine years ago; things might have turned out different. But I can't change that. She got someone new, and he's good to the kids. I'm glad for that, but it still hurts that it's not me there."

"I am proud of what I'm doing here. It's helping me look at life in a bigger way. I can see a reason for everything that's happened. It's helping me learn a lot. I'm trying to change for the better. It's gradual, but I do see I'm changing. I like this new way that I'm thinking. They've taught me here that I've got to take care of myself before I can take care of others. Trying to get a lot of material things isn't important; I want a family. I need to repair relationships with my kids. I was married thirteen years and I have three kids: fourteen, eight, and four. When I look back, I realize my best times were with my children. I'd like to be a good role model for them now. I want to prove to others I can do it."

"I've taken classes here on anger management, and parenting. I need to re-establish relationships, and I think what I have learned here can help. I want to show love toward my brothers; stay sober. A real man needs to see his children, provide for them, and set an example."

We talked about how much time he had left in the program and he said he had almost completed it, and was getting out soon.

"I love my children, and I want to see them again, but I'm nervous and anxious about it too. I've got some goals. I want to get a job in the mines again. I loved working in the mines; I love to work. They told me where I used to work that they liked me as a worker, and that if I would get help with my drug problem they would give me a job again. Having a job offer helps. A lot of people don't know what they'll do when they get released. It helps to have a job to look forward to."

"I've always had a good bond with my daughter, and I want to spend time with her. I miss seeing her and the things she does. She's a cheerleader. I have an aunt that's always been close to me, and she keeps me in touch with my kids. That's my mom's sister. She's always stuck by me. She tells me she's so proud of me in this program, and that means a lot to me. I look around at other guys in here, and a lot of them don't have family. I need to do some work to fix some things, but I do have family. If you do the right things, family can help keep you on track. Like I said, my best times were with my children."

"I thought I was having fun with my friends, but they weren't really friends. None of them have contacted me in here; said they hope I do better. Real friends don't throw you out as soon as they're done with you."

I asked him if he had any advice to offer others who might be in a similar situation as he, or headed down a path in that direction.

He paused a moment and then said, "If something is bothering you, find someone you can talk to. Seek professional counseling if you need to, even go into rehab. If you go to church, find a friend who can help you. Don't try to be alone. If I had put as much time into trying to get help as I did into getting high, I'd have been a lot better off. Pick your friends better. Enjoy each day; it might be your last. Think about your choices. I never thought I'd be here."

He wrapped up the interview saying, "I really do want to be a blessing to my kids, not an aggravation. I hope that when I'm out I can help someone who is headed down the wrong path. I'm in the stage of the program here now where I'm helping teach responsibility to some of the guys just starting in it. I really like the way I feel when I'm trying to help someone else. I hope some will listen. Everything we do, we can say 'yes' or 'no'; it's our choice. Like I said earlier, I like this new way I'm thinking. I'm starting to feel a lot better about myself."

You may find, like I have found, your heart weeping for people who want to do the right thing, but will find, especially upon release, that they are going to have to fight like never before in their lives. Choices carry their consequences, and gullies worn over time will take even more time to get filled in with positive choices, actions, and directions. My heart and prayers are with these men as they fight back against their earlier life activities.

Fight Back

Figure that if
I only have one life to live,
Grating, negative aspects of it
Have to get
Turned around.

Besides, there is still
A certain satisfaction that
Comes from
Knowing you can fight back.

21

I Once Could See, but Now Am Blind (or is that ...?)

I discovered a few years back that, although our determination and courage are a large part of overcoming obstacles, our humanness also seems to come equipped with additional tools. I learned this from observing and listening to Bill Irwin, at that time, the first blind person (there have been a couple more since then) to hike the entire Appalachian Trail from Springer Mountain, Georgia to Mt. Katahdin, Maine.

Look out AT, Bill's on the way

The Special Events Committee at the University of Pikeville, then Pikeville College, had invited Bill, author of Blind Courage, to speak. I was coordinator for the event, so I made arrangements for him at the Landmark Inn, and, upon his arrival met him there to bring him to the college dining hall for the evening meal before his speaking engagement. My oldest son, Ralph, was there to hear Bill, so I introduced them. After Ralph said hello to him, Bill's response was, "Ralph, so you are a little taller than your father." (Okay, six inches taller, what's your point?) But Bill was focused on what height the sound was coming from.

Before his presentation Bill was chatting with several different people that he was meeting for the first time, and during the question and answer session after his motivational speech, I noticed that he called a few of them by their names when they asked a question. When I asked him about that, also during Q&A, he replied (calling me by name) that after he lost his sight his sense of hearing became much sharper, and he focused in on vocal differences, much like we might pay attention to how people look, or what they are wearing.

Also, during the presentation, Bill said that after he lost his vision, his senses developed to the point where he could walk down the middle of a hallway that had several doors and tell you which ones were open, and which were closed. It is amazing to me how our system automatically compensates for other deficiencies. Bill also described some occasions on the trail where he stepped out in faith, and later was told he had made the right decision. He added that losing his sight was the biggest blessing that God had ever given him.

All in all, I became much more aware that evening of the tools we are equipped with, not just in our body, but also in our mind and spirit. Bill was, and is, a powerful example of how we are "fearfully, and wonderfully, made."

In addition, he talked about falling down, and getting back up. Someone estimated that in Bill's nine-month trek, he fell down about seven thousand times. That sounds "reasonable," as I was picking myself up from losing my balance or footing some three or four times a day on my Long Trail hike. Had I been nine months at that rate, it would have been over five hundred falls, and that's with eyesight. But the point Bill was making was, when you fall, the only thing you can do is get back up and keep going.

Bill Irwin says, "Get rid of some of the baggage."

In his presentation, Bill told of how he started out with everything he was sure he needed, plus extras, just in case. He was packing over one hundred pounds. After a few days on the trail, at a stop to replenish food supplies, someone went through Bill's pack with him and helped strip away unnecessary baggage. He then talked about taking the time in our personal lives to evaluate the loads we carry around in our hearts and spirits, and see if there is baggage we need to shed. He told the audience that, about things in our lives, to ask ourselves the question, "Is this item worth the weight?"

Baggage – too much?

I know first-hand from my (short?) 150 mile backpack trip in Vermont what a relief it can be to get rid of extra weight. If you are still out on the trail, then you leave what you are shedding at a shelter as there may be someone coming along who will need it, or at least think he or she needs it. At one shelter, Kid Gore I believe, someone had left a rather heavy duty sleeping bag. I

Little things add up (Basil on The Long Trail – in Vermont. Photo by Raj Singh.)

was experiencing a little chill at night with only the blanket I had opted to bring, as it was still getting into the low 40's. So I decided to pack it. About a half hour into the new day, headed north, I dropped my pack, and while Raj, my traveling companion for 45 miles, took a break, I hustled back to the shelter we had just left to leave my newly acquired, but short-lived, "bag-mate" for someone else to consider carrying. It weighed more than I wanted to add on.

I've discovered this with personal baggage too, be it fears, cautions, habits, memories, materials things, or other. Sometimes I can let little things start to add up and before long I'm starting to feel down in my spirit. I have discovered that if I allow adequate quiet time first thing in the morning, I can sort out the day, and it's easier throughout the day to stay on track. Personally, I can't just jump out of bed, shower, and rush out the door, without feeling weighed down in my core.

So, back to the title ...

I once could see, but now am blind; was blind, but now, I see. This is a common theme in literature, and with good cause. Sometimes there are things we can't see until we can't see. We are so bombarded with messages, visual and aural, that sometimes we don't take time to reflect on what the next step is, or should be. And so the baggage begins to pile up.

Many of us are familiar with the saying to the effect of, "we spend a lot of money buying things we don't need to impress people we don't even like." For me, this is another example of where we can see all the things around us, but are blind to what we are doing. If we can spend more time in reflection, blind to the things of the material world, then we can start to find out what and who the really important things and people in life are.

Baggage

But if I don't
Always carry this
Garbage around, I might
Get to the point where I
Am aware of all the
Good things I could
Engage in. Oh, no!

22

Minor to You, Maybe; Major to Me

I wrote the following when my sons were younger and I was reflecting on things that would be important, say, some forty years on down the road. Reaction to some things may seem minor at the time to the parent, but have a major impact on the feelings and attitudes of the children involved. I decided there were some things that might not be as significant later on as they seemed at the time. But, of course, as a human, I know I have had my share of failures in these areas. Thank goodness, I was able to compensate in the overall relationships enough that my sons, seem to at least, enjoy my visits to them, and their visits to me.

Damned Kids [PH]

I try to concentrate on my paperwork
And think...
Damned kids...
Why can't they hold down their noise?

I pick up scattered crayons and torn papers
Off the living room floor and mutter...
Damned kids...
Why can't they pick up after themselves?

I look at the speeding tickets my teenage sons just got
For racing and holler...
Damned kids...
Why can't you stay out of trouble?

I gaze out the window as I slowly move back and forth in my rocking chair
And sniffle...
Damned kids...
Why don't they ever come and visit me?

Time with our children, and how we spend that time, is important. Our lives, especially with our children, are filled with words, looks, and events that may be minor to us, and yet, so often, major, to them. There is the old adage of being careful of how you treat your children when they are younger because they may well be the ones in charge of how you are treated in the later stages of life. Food for thought; that's all I'm saying.

I made all …

I have a plaque in my office that says, "Half of being smart – is knowing what you're dumb at." I believe this is, yes, so very true. For a year at Lees College in Jackson, Kentucky, I was the Dean of Students. You could quadruple my salary and offer me a Dean of Student job again, and I believe I would have to turn it down. On top of "being dumb at it," I didn't like it; maybe there's a correlation here; maybe?

Anyway, 1988, near the end of the spring semester, a student managed to steal someone else's telephone calling card number, and soon it got passed around to several students, and then the president and I were contacted by two parents wondering how they had received a ninety page phone bill for around five thousand dollars. The chairman of the board and the president handed me the phone bill with the instructions to "find out who was involved and take care of it."

Long story short. As students were confronted with evidence of their home phone numbers being some of the ones calls were made from, or to, using the stolen card number, I was frequently faced with belligerence and anger, like I had done something wrong in catching them. I recovered about 2/3rds of the money, but with a "price to pay"; I certainly would not have won a popularity contest.

At the end of the year we had our annual faculty-staff meetings with reports from all the administrators (on what a wonderful year I had, I did this, I did that, ad nauseam.) I kept my report short and sweet. It was:

"As you know, there have been some problems this year, but, I did make all of my sons' basketball games."

And then I sat down. The fact is, years later, making their games is the only thing that has mattered.

The Best Day In-Country (With a Bomb-Sniffing Dog) (LTC McLean)

"I had it pretty good; I wasn't injured and I had a good job. Sure, we were mortared almost daily, but I didn't return with the traumatic moments and memories that so many have to deal with."

Lieutenant Colonel (Retired) Todd McLean went to Iraq in 2005 and was assigned to the 18th Airborne Corp at Camp Victory where he oversaw rotary wing aviation; meaning, he coordinated the helicopter support for missions, and dignitaries visiting in-country. However, having a good job didn't necessarily translate into it being an easy one; it involved prioritizing missions for the likes of the Vice President of the United States, the Secretaries of Defense and the State Department, and Presidents of other countries.

Lieutenant Colonel McLean said the Joint Operation Command where he operated out of looked like something from a Star Trek movie with its wrap-around giant screens and seating. He was daily involved with two big pictures; the one he and fellow officers played out on the screen, and the one the screen helped play out with what was going on in Iraq; coordinating ballots for elections, bringing together representatives from different tribal areas, congressional delegations, and the like.

Todd said that although they did receive regular hostile incoming mortars, the most difficult part of being over there was what affected almost everyone regardless of their circumstances; being away from family, and the accompanying feelings of isolation and loneliness that come with that. In his case, he was absent from the daily lives and routines of his wife and two young children. He said that after his mid-tour R&R back home, it was most depressing to return to Iraq, especially the first month back.

"My son was old enough that he did everything with me. I had friends in Iraq, my 'family' over there, but, I really missed my wife and kids."

"I had a friend who was a kennel-master for bomb-sniffing dogs that were used in detection of IED's. He had a large German Shepherd that he brought to me in my office while he attended a meeting. And, years later, that still stands out as my best day in Iraq. Sometimes someone does something for another that doesn't seem like a big deal to them, but it turns out to be very significant to the person on the receiving end. That was one of those times."

When asked about advice for others, Todd said that he was more aware of the impact in life of the "little things" we do for others. "Sometimes we get a break, or give someone else one," he said, "and it changes the direction of a life. We can treat people right, or treat them poorly, either way they will remember."

He told of an incident several years ago where a young Lieutenant's home had burned, and he helped him with food and furniture. Years after the incident the man, a Captain by that time, contacted Lieutenant Colonel McLean and told him he had never forgotten the kindness shown to him.

On either the "giving end" of kindness, or the "receiving end," many times it still translates as "minor to you, maybe; major to me."

Deadness from abuse

When someone is being abused, physically or emotionally, there is a kind of "deadness," or maybe just a form of "accelerated indifference," that creeps in. For many of us, reconciliation may be reached with the person later on, but one may also recognize that there is an area of feeling about that person with a numbness still attached to it. This is especially an area where counseling may help. And sometimes maybe we shouldn't overanalyze, but rather, accept that's the way that it was, and just go on.

When my older brother died several years ago, I did not really feel like I had lost a brother, but a name. That feeling still basically exists to this day. We visited and had some good times off and on in our adult years, but there were some things involving fear and anger on my part that we never talked about. I didn't feel like it would serve any good purpose, and, of course, now, I'll never know. We did have a form of relationship, but the years of subconscious numbness really couldn't be restored. There were probably several things that factored into this, but two occurrences stick out.

When I was around six or seven (he was four years older), he had a couple of captured woodchucks in a cage behind the house, and one evening we were out feeding and watering them After the cage door was closed, one of the woodchucks put his face to the wire. I stuck a finger through the wire to try and pet him, and he bit me. My older brother, who, for what reason I can't remember, was holding a hammer, raised it over his head, and hollered at me, "You stupid son-of-a-bitch, I ought to kill you!" I still recall the intense fear, not only of the moment, but also, fear of telling my parents. I guess I was afraid of what my brother might do to me if he was punished.

Another incident occurred when I was around eleven years old. My brother had a donkey, and one day I wandered around behind Pinocchio, and he kicked me. Then, perhaps for added emphasis, my brother kicked me too as he hollered, "You stupid idiot!"

Again, these are small incidents, but I believe they were contributing factors to the overall relationship. As time went on, I did not hold these things against him, but the memories were still there, and we never had a close relationship. We made some visits, talked on the phone several times in later years, and, shortly before his death, both ended the call with "I love you." And I believe that we both were sincere.

Again, harmony may be achieved, but there still may be areas of the emotional realm that cannot be restored. I do know I arrived at a place of peace with him, and my mother said that when he died, he was very peaceful. My biggest hope is that none of my younger siblings have any of these types of incidents lingering in their minds about me. I don't think so (but maybe I need to double-check so forgiveness can be asked for, if necessary.)

There are also things we do that we usually don't think much about (minor) that might be a big deal (major) to someone who can't do them anymore.

After surgery in the 3rd Army Field Hospital in Saigon, I was shipped to a hospital in Japan for further recuperation. One day I decided to take a walk down the hallway while wheeling my IV alongside me. I was not feeling on top of the world, was in a little pain, and started feeling a bit sorry for myself. About that time a soldier smiled and nodded as he went wheeling past me in a wheelchair, both legs amputated. That got my attention quickly. Here I was feeling sorry for myself, while walking on my own two legs.

Later that afternoon the Chaplain came through the ward, and as he talked with me for a few minutes, I mentioned to him how I had been chastened in my spirit earlier in the day. The chaplain responded, "I know what you're talking about. A little while ago I was with someone who is on a dialysis machine eight hours a day. I had never thought before about what a blessing it is to 'be able to relieve myself quickly, without the aid of a machine.'"

This is definitely an area where an activity that may seem minor to most of us is a major deal to someone who loses the opportunity.

Nursing old wounds

Some time ago I was on vacation, and while on a trip into town, a couple relatives and I stopped at a yard sale. I was wearing my US Army Vietnam Veteran cap, and a man approached me and said, "You were in Vietnam, too? Welcome back." When I told him thanks, he went on to say, "Yeah, the only welcome we got when we came home forty years ago was a kick in the ass."

We talked a few minutes, and in the course of the conversation it came out that he had experienced a lot of difficulty with the VA in getting a certain disability compensation rating. Generally, he came across as bitter, and I'd be willing to bet that it spilled over into other areas of his life, too. I got his address and told him I would send him a copy of **Poetic Healing**, hoping there would be something in it that might be of some assistance to him.

I later received a letter from him thanking me for the book, and stating that the fact I had followed through with what I said I would do had renewed his faith in mankind again. In response to that, I say what I put in the "Comments Section" of my annual self-evaluation form we have to fill out at the University of Pikeville, "Just glad to be here and a part of it all." But the fact remains, what seemed small to me was big to him.

Actions toward others

My mother was someone who was very involved in giving to others, but she always felt like she wasn't doing very much, or, doing enough. An example; she was working in a nursing home in Missouri, and she and my dad were on a vacation visiting me in Kentucky for a couple weeks. There was a 104 year-old woman named Leticia that was one of the residents at the nursing home, and Mom called her a few times to check on her and see how she was doing.

After Leticia died, my mother received a letter that included the following:

"Dear Marvel,

As you know, some time back, my mother was in the nursing home, and the saddest day of her life was when her only daughter died. She was lost in sorrow and despair. Then, Marvel, you came to the res-

cue and provided her with loving care. Marvel, you made the last few years of her life worthwhile, and, in many ways, even enjoyable. For the unconditional love you showed her, I truly thank you."

(Signed by Leticia's son)

I believe Mom may have been met at the "Pearlies" by, say, Mother Teresa greeting her with, "Please, Marvel, come on in. Our Lord will join you here momentarily, and, as always, our theme for the day is, 'Insomuch as you have done it unto the least of these, you have done it unto me.' Oh, and actually, Marvel, you made a mistake in thinking that you didn't do very much for others. You failed to realize the significance of every good deed you were performing. We could substitute your name for Bethlehem in Micah 5:2, paraphrase, and say, 'But you, Marvel Clark, though you thought yourself little among the thousands, yet out of your works came forth things that are everlasting.'"

Part Two:
Inside Wrestling Matches

23

The Stories We Can't Tell
(or I Am Who I Am, But I'm Not)

First, the good news

I Samuel 16: 7 reads, "The Lord does not look at the things man looks at. Man looks at the outward appearance, but the Lord looks at the heart."

The flip side

I say this is good news, but we also have to realize it works both ways; we may be "looking good" to those around us, but the heart "ain't lookin' so good."

Unfortunately, another factor that comes into play is the people who think they are horrible inside due to erroneous images they have let others put on them. How many people, especially young girls are caught in the trap of the following poem.

What the Mirror Says 2013

If you could only hear what my mirror tells me, you'd be surprised.
Actually, you probably wouldn't, because I really
Believe you're thinking the same thing. Oh, you tell me I'm pretty,
But I know better; I heard the truth from my looking glass,
And mirrors don't lie.

My mirror tells me I'm ugly, I'm fat, and, you know what else?
It can even see inside my head, test my IQ; tells me I'm stupid.
It's psychic; it lets me know what other people would think
If they knew the real me. I hide all my secrets, but I still know,
Because, you see, mirrors don't lie.

Aaron   (not his real name)

"I feel that I always have to keep up my guard and not let people see me for me. I pretend every day that I'm strong, brave and a people person, but in reality I hope nobody ever figures out that I wear a mask, and frequently feel ashamed that I'm not who I pretend to be."

Don't Unmask Me (P/H – revised 2013)

When I am down and covered with shame.
I often wonder if there are others who feel the same.
I know I can't be the only one in this precarious game.

So I'll suit up and race time into eternity for now.
Please don't unmask me for this is only how I can look at myself as I plow
These furrows deeper in the sands of time, still moving, somehow.

Fear of Rejection

For all I know
Everyone I see
And interact with will
Reject who I really am.

Oh, they think they know me,
For they spend time with me.

Really, though, the truth
Eventually must stay
Just below the surface
Even if it wants to
Come out. Why hide? Because
The truth is, people may say,
I accept you for who you
Obviously are, but they'd really rather
Not.

Standing in the Corner

Cora and I were talking about how childhood feelings can stay with someone for a long time, and she made the statement that some kids spent a lot of time in the corner when they were younger, and that, even as adults, they were afraid to leave that place of punishment. She said, "It's like they were sent to the corner as a young child, and told not to speak until they were spoken to, or maybe, 'Don't you move until you are told to do so.' Their bodies moved on years ago, but emotionally, it's like they are still standing in that corner."

Standing in the Corner

There are a lot of cartoons about children in the corner.
Maybe like Dennis the Menace they are in a rocking chair.
I even saw one of a little girl saying that she was trying
To figure out how not to get caught next time.

Many images of a child in the corner for wrong-doing.
Some get out, and go right back to play;
All grow up, but, even then, as adults, some of them
Still spend half their lives standing in the corner.

Standing in the Corner II

Now I want you to go stand in the corner,
And don't come out until I tell you!
(Corners and timeouts can be effective
Forms of discipline.)

The burden is on each parent to
Find out which methods work for
Each given child, and
Each given infraction of the rules

(No sense using a "hammer"
When you can fix it
With a "screwdriver"
Or corner, whatever.)

But, for various reasons some children
Never leave the corner, and,
Even as adults,
Feel like that's where they belong.

You'd better watch out, you'd better not cry ...

Unfortunately, the above way of thinking, can be instilled at an early age, in a variety of ways. We are in the Santa Claus trap; and we know, he knows. December 1982, while a graduate student at the University of Kentucky, I was the weekend Santa at Turfland Mall. (It paid 4 dollars an hour, and I needed the money – those "pesky" sons and their desire to eat occasionally.)

Probably more valuable than the paycheck, though, were some of the insights into human behavior. One such time was when a mother stood in front of me with her young son, probably about three-years-old, and very sternly said, "He's been real bad, Santa; he won't mind me. You tell him that you're not going to come and see him if he doesn't start being good, and helping, and minding me." The little boy had tears in his eyes, and the look on his face was one of the saddest I have ever seen.

So I did what any Santa worth a candy cane would do. I got down on my knees so I was the same height as the boy, and hugged him as I told him, "Don't worry, I love you, and I'll be there. Now it makes me sad when you don't listen to your mother, so I hope you'll start helping her, and minding her, but I love you anyway, just because you're you."

His little face brightened, and he smiled and hugged me back and said, "I will, Santa, and I love you, too." I hope that in some small way I was able to make a positive impact on the boy's life, maybe even help reduce time for him of "standing in the corner" in his mind.

What the mother took away from the incident, I don't know; as far as I'm concerned, she was the one qualified for a piece of coal in her stocking.

The masks worn to keep things hidden from others may work, but the reasons they are put on in the first place linger close by; like the elephant in the COPD commercial referred to in chapter fourteen.

Difficulties, or maybe, Screw This

Sometimes functioning is difficult unless
Concentrating hard enough on something –
Really focused – but
Even then knowing that eventually
Whether I like it or not

The "situational facts"
Have to come back
Into their usual
Superior place.

The noise in the following poem can be two-fold. In my case, if I am feeling a bit down, for any reason, including just being tired, I am more aware of the tinnitus. But, for some, the psychological noise can be the culprit that enters in. If that is the case, it is just as aggravating.

Quagmire?
Depression falling, perhaps over a poor choice, or
Responding poorly to
Other life pressures.
And when that occurs then it seems the
Quagmire of internal noise
Starts to overwhelm.

Whenever the next step – or phase –
Of this universe happens,
Hopefully there will be some quiet,
And maybe even peace.

I'm asking too much, aren't I?
So just shrill on. Have at it.

And, The Stories We'd Rather Forget

For many, there are stories that can be told, may have been told, but in reality, are stories one wishes he or she could just forget. But the human mind does not work this way. Some find relief through counseling or in focus on other activities, but others remain tortured inside.

Still burning

I was told by someone how his father emotionally couldn't escape from an incident that had occurred years earlier. His father had been on a hunting trip as a teenager with a couple close friends, and there had been a fire in the cabin where they spent the night. His father escaped; his friends were not so fortunate. This person related, "My father does everything he is supposed to do; he goes to work, provides for us all, lives what most would see as a normal life. But I know from what he has told me that he is still chained in his mind to that night in the cabin. I don't know if he'll ever be free."

And it burns; this scream of fire

I don't think I'll ever get his screams out of my mind. Andy may have thought he was dying, but I think his screams were coming from the sheer pain emanating from his burned back. We were setting up for the night; digging foxholes, setting out observation posts, eating, etc. The only thing different in this location from most was there were still some tall trees burning from an earlier fire. Suddenly we heard a loud crack as the top of a tree broke off, and when it fell, Andy was underneath. The wood scraped across his back, leaving embers in the flesh. The medic injected morphine to try and ease the pain, but that made Andy delirious. His anguished yells became louder as we waited on arrival of a medevac helicopter. Fortunately for Andy the medevac arrived soon. But screams like that, for him, and those of us with him, you don't forget so soon.

Thanks, Mom

My mother used to work in a nursing home, and one time she told me of a situation she had to deal with that was so gross I have never repeated it to anyone, and never will, because I don't want to "put that image" on anyone. There are still occasional times when the story comes into my mind and it takes a while for it to leave.

This is a minor example, but I believe it exemplifies the way it can be with serious abuse, or other traumatic images and situations. They stay lurking in the background, ready to push their way to the forefront. Fortunately, we can reach the place where they don't have to stay front and center, but, the fact is, they will never totally leave.

Like the Lapping Waves

They come back again and again, never giving a moment's relief,
Like the waves on the seashore swimming toward me.
Isn't it funny how sitting and watching the real waves
Gives a sense of peace, whereas, knowing that the memories,
True to their pattern, are moving back in again, gives the
Sensation of tight knots in my stomach. When the waves
Head back out you start to watch for the return of them;
When the pain eases momentarily, you dread the return,
Yet know that as sure as the moon rises, and the tides ebb
And flow, they'll be back; you can count on it, they'll be back.

Could kill him without regret

I read where a POW was reflecting on the first guard he had after he was captured and thrown into a prison. He stated that, even years after the encounter, he believed he could kill the man with no guilt or regrets.

There may be times, with some inner woundings, where victims may have perpetrators they feel this way about. There may be some guilt attached for feeling "the urge to kill," but the fact remains, some wounds run deep, and people feel what they feel; thank goodness we can make choices not to act on every feeling.

Many veterans have gone, or are still going, through feelings like this, especially if they have been in situations where they saw friends shot up or otherwise maimed or killed under fire, or as a result of IEDs, mortars, and other explosive devices.

24
The Stories We Don't Want To Tell (or Places of Secret Insanities)

Tina (not her real name)

In the late 1980's, when I was teaching at Lees College in Jackson, Kentucky, a student talked to me about what she called "her place of secret insanity." Tina was a non-traditional student, probably in her late 30's, and happily married with a couple children. I guess she felt free to talk to me because she knew I was a Vietnam veteran.

She said that years earlier she was engaged to a soldier serving in Vietnam who was reported "missing, presumed dead" after a battle. Tina said she had mourned, and waited for a couple years before going out with anyone. After a while she became engaged to the man she eventually married. Fast forward almost twenty years. Her life moved on, and was good. However, she said a secret fear that she couldn't talk about which stayed in the shadows of her mind was that someday her former fiancé would show up at the door, having somehow survived and eventually finding his way home.

Even though by this time Tina knew this was extremely unlikely, it was still "her place of secret insanity." She moved on, she functioned well, was an excellent student, but the fear could not be totally erased.

Bedwetting (The author)

I guess it was expected when I was in diapers, maybe even a little beyond that. When I was six I went off to a summer camp, other than the annual church camp we went to every summer – this time there were counselors, and no parents. Every morning there was a cart that came around to collect the bed sheets from the boys who "had had accidents" during the night. Quite a few of us put our sheets out to be collected every day. As I grew older I was afraid that my friends from school would somehow find out that I was still wetting fairly regularly when I was twelve, less so when I was fourteen, and still occurring, though seldom, when I was sixteen. When I had any accidents as I was getting into this older category, the thing that frustrated me so much was it seemed that every time it occurred, I was dreaming that I had to go, would get out of bed to go, and then halfway through going, would feel the dampness on myself, from myself. I was so mad at yours truly, but in my dream I was doing everything I was supposed to; I somehow didn't seem to know how to wake up before the "action started."

The summer I turned sixteen I worked away from home on a small sheep and chicken farm. I lived with the family, "Mom and Pop," and their seventeen year old son. Pop teased me quite a bit about still being a "little pisser," and I really started to feel the embarrassment quite a bit. I don't recall too many incidents of bedwetting after that, though there were a few, stretched out by quite a bit of time in between.

The thing I do know is that things like this leave their mark inside, because, in time, you know it's not the norm, and it's not the type of thing you talk about with your friends, or anyone else, for that matter. But there is a certain shame that goes along with it that affects how one feels about himself during the formative years.

Name unknown (An experience observed when I was sixteen)

I was at the house of the pastor of the little church I attended and while we were sitting in the living room there was a knock on the door. A disheveled looking man was standing there and asked the pastor if he could spare a little money for something to eat. My pastor told the man he would do something even better; if the man would come in, he could have a meal. The man agreed and came in. While the pastor's wife warmed up some leftovers from the noon meal, I stayed with the pastor and the man in the living room. The pastor asked him where he lived, and I listened as the man launched into a story something to the effect of the following:

"I don't live nowhere, just wander around, do a little job now and then for something to, ah, eat. Alcohol's been the reason I ain't doing so good. I was married and had a couple boys, and I used to have a good job, but I couldn't stop drinking. My wife finally left me and got a divorce when I was 31, or maybe 32. She moved to another state, and I just went downhill from there. I couldn't find a job and I wasn't sending nothing to her to take care of my boys. I heard from a friend that she re-married, and I figured my boys was being taken care of. They probably don't like me too much no more. I'm over 50 now, and still drinking. I'm afraid I'm going to die before too long if I keep on the way I am, and I'm also afraid that if my boys did care enough to look me up they'd hate me after finding me still drinking."

"Sometimes I think of trying to kill myself in a car wreck when I am sober, just so if they did try to find me they'd know I died in an accident. But I guess they wouldn't know if I was sober, so they'd probably think I was drunk anyway." He stopped for a moment and then continued. "And I think God would be upset with me because you ain't supposed to kill yourself, but he's probably already mad at me because I can't stop drinking. That's another problem with my accident plan. I don't know if I can stop drinking long enough to get real sober."

Lunch was brought to the man, and while he was eating, my pastor talked more with him, telling him that God did love him. But the man kept going back to the fact that he couldn't stop drinking, and that he also had done other things that God couldn't love him for. After he was done eating, he said he was thankful for the food, and that he had to go. As I remember, he did let the preacher say a short prayer for him, then left and headed down the sidewalk.

I have no idea of what ever happened to him, but I do know the incident left an impression with me of just how chained we can get to our habits and be ingrained with the thought that God couldn't possibly love us until we make ourselves better. I have found myself in a similar struggle of the mind more than once over the years. But I have also come to realize that God comes to us where we are, and although it may be a long process, wants to help us get beyond the secret insanity that he may "walk in on our lives" at the wrong time.

Sign of weakness, or strength?

One of the outlooks some may have is that telling their story or seeking help for a particular problem is a sign of weakness. In an AP release in June 2012, the (then) Defense Secretary Leon Paneta said that Commanding Officers needed to get the message across to troops under their command that "seeking help for the stresses of war should be seen as a sign of strength rather than a sign of weakness." This was said in response to an increase of suicides by those serving in the military.

And even though we may accept the preceding as a true statement, the fact still remains that there are many who fear seeking help because they are afraid that it will become a part of their records, and perhaps be used against them at some point on down the road. It really does become a conundrum, not just for military personnel, but anyone. We know that sometimes when we are being evaluated on the job, whether or not we had sought counseling could be a factor. It is not supposed to be a factor, and others aren't even supposed to know, but, still …

Seeking help for addictions could also factor into the stories we don't want to tell, or places of secret insanities. But once a person admits an addiction, past, or present, there are those who will always see them as "the addict," kind of like the kid who has two car wrecks at age sixteen, and then never has another one, but at age sixty, some people will still label him as that reckless driver.

There are some "addiction poems" coming up in chapter 27 on "patterns," but I think the following one also applies in the realm of secret insanities, and stories untold.

Addiction

Always you are there, just
Devouring my strength and
Doing what you want with my life.
I may be the one who started; asked you to
Come in, and take charge of my
Time, but you're on notice.
I've had enough. No more looking back
Over my days with regrets. I am
Never giving in to you again (until next time.)

25

Living in the Fog
(I Can't See Clear Enough to Think)

While a student at Eastern Kentucky University I had a 65 mile one-way commute, and the schedule one semester required leaving the house around 5:45 AM. I probably shouldn't admit this, but I wrote the following while driving to classes one day in the fog. As daylight started to "come up," the following words came to me. I "played with the format" during a class later in the day. I'm hoping the statute of limitations has expired for both: (1) writing while driving under the influence of fog, and, (2) doodling under the influence of inattention during class.

Fog over the lake

FOG P/H

```
           SHE
      REACHED OUT
      ENVELOPED
         ME
         IN
        HER
FLIMSY, SHAPELESS
GOWN        AND                              NO
     C                  I                 COMFORT!
     L            SNUGGLED            GOD!     WHAT
     U          UP TO    HER         COMFORT     IN
     T          BUT      ONLY        THIS
     C          ENCOUN-  TERED       DISMAL
     H          GRAY-    WHITE       MIST
     E          DAMP-    NESS        THAT'S     HERE?
     D          AND      AN          I          CAN'T
     ME         ICY,   TASTE-        SEE        CLEAR
   CLOSE           LESS              ENOUGH  TO
   LY             BREATH             THINK
```

There are times when things from the past try to crowd their way into our minds, but they come in a hazy, faded way; we just can't bring the memories, or people in them, into a real clear focus.

Foggy Memories

Foggy, faded memories,
Or something, are walking;
Going delicately through my mind;
Guess they're trying to,
Yes, that's it; dedicate the

Moments to all those who
Eventually
Make the rounds.
Often all the cobwebs
Randomly squeezed
Into my brain are
Expecting a response, and,
Sadly, I can't answer (don't know what to say.)

What to Say, What to Do; Living in the Void

There can be experiences we have which are so painful or shocking that we have no response except a foggy emptiness. I mentioned one of these times when Rodney Evans was killed in Vietnam. Other deaths were numbing me, the tinnitus was in its early stages of letting me know it wanted a part of my mind, and Rodney was just too good a friend. He couldn't die.

And remember Ronnie Hylton (Chapter 8: The Long Road Home) who stepped off the plane ready for a fishing trip only to hear of his father's death. He said his memories were vague of that period because something "snapped," and he was in the midst of a "hazy fog."

These times, too, shall pass, but they are a numbing, foggy hell when you are in the middle of them.

When my allergies are bad (Name withheld)

"When my allergies are bad, I feel like I'm in a fog, like I'm on the outside looking in, but I can't quite get in. I can't answer questions, or think real well; I just sort of 'drop out of it'."

And there are so many different kinds of fog

The foggy emptiness applies to so many situations, and with that comes lack of focus.

Losses of people, pets, jobs
Allergies and other illnesses or injuries
Depression
The medicines prescribed to cope with the physical and mental ailments
Drugs and alcohol
Being overwhelmed by choices, or other events pressing in
And the list goes on

The Void

The emptiness is pressing all around,
Squeezing, yet providing nothing to hold on to.
I'd like to be able to grasp something to help me
Scale these high walls that are trapping me

Inside the nothingness that slams my mind
With so many thoughts that I can't quite
Sort them out enough to adequately express
The barrenness of soul and mind.

Wasteland

Words lost in
A wasteland.
Speechless. Confused.
Thoughts tumbling through my mind.
Energy drained. Unable to concentrate
Long enough to make
A "lick of sense."
No paper to write on.
Doesn't matter. Couldn't anyway.

Jangling

Just wondering if the jangling
Assortment of
Noises tumbling through the
Gray matter in my head can
Leave some sort of
Imprint of sensibility, then
Next up, of course, is a
Growing hope the fog will make more sense

Shades of Job (Job 6:11)

> Job felt overwhelmed
> In the depths of despair,
> Surrounded by the fog of advice,
> None of which applied
> As far as he was concerned.
> He wanted to find his way out,
>
> But wondered how he could go on, asking,
> What strength do I have?
> Is there room for hope?
> The fog keeps me from seeing.
> Are there any prospects that
> I should be patiently waiting for?

Several years ago I was sitting with a friend in a hallway outside a waiting room in a Nashville, TN, hospital when a man shuffled past. I have no idea what the circumstances were, but he was walking as if he were in a void, looking totally beaten down by life. My imagination kicked in, and the following poem came into fruition.

And Somehow Convey P/H

> The young man was moving down the hall
> In a dejected, shuffling walk.
> His body caught in disbelief.
> His face still showing shock.
>
> God, please help Sandy through this.
> Please, dear God, let her stay.
> Don't take her yet to heaven.
> Save that for another day.
>
> She'd only gone out shopping.
> Just like any other day.
> A driver flew through a stop sign
> Then an ambulance whisked her away.

The doctor came out and spoke to him
He bit his lip then cried through tears,
Oh God I don't quite understand this.
We've only been married two years.

And now I must go by her parents.
And pick up our little girl Kay.
And somehow convey to a one-year-old
What has occurred today.

This poem may have been a product of imagination, but we all know that regularly there are people who have to exactly do what is in the last stanza; explain unexplainable things to someone too young to understand.

Peering Through the Mist

I believe the Apostle Paul offers some words to hold on to during some of our "foggy times." In his second letter to the Corinthians, Chapter 4, verses 8 and 9 we read, "We are hard pressed on every side, but not crushed; perplexed but not in despair; persecuted, but not abandoned; struck down but not destroyed."

Or perhaps we can find hope in the end of Jeremiah 30 (out of context), "In days to come you will understand this."

26

Abuse; the Wounds Run Deep

While working as a teaching-parent in a group home, one of the boys who was admitted had been a victim of sexual abuse for a couple years when he was just five and six years old. Jonathan (not his real name), at the age of twelve, definitely had some serious social issues. The program was for a year, with up to six months extension time granted if necessary. Jonathan stayed the entire eighteen months. As he was released from the program, all of us working with him (teaching-parents, court counselor, mental health counselors, and social worker) felt like he should stay longer, but by law there was nothing else we could do. Six months after his release from the group home Jonathan was again appearing in court, and this time sentenced for a much longer period of time to a more restricted juvenile facility. His offense? He was the perpetrator of sexual abuse.

Abuse of a Child; Turning a World Upside Down

He was five when his parents let him start going
To stay at his uncle's house.
It was only later they found out that
Sexual abuse had occurred.

At age twelve, for major disruption at school, he was
Court-ordered to a year-long program in a Group Home.
Of course, if problems were severe a client could
Stay the maximum time. He did. Eighteen months.

At age fourteen, six months after release from the program,
He picked up on the early patterns, and became the abuser.
Abuse of children settles deep in their souls and systems and
Turns their worlds upside-down.

Abuse

And it creeps into the very
Bottom of your soul and
Unveils the core of your
Spirit and shatters
Every aspect of normalcy.

You Gotta Know

You gotta know there is a reason
Why I don't want to venture outstretched
Into the world beyond my walls.
It's dangerous out there!

Verbal arrows being flung at you,
Sometimes physical blows directed
Your way. I mean, Good grief, man,
Why would anyone want to put up with that?

There is evil …

Some who have struggled with a variety of issues over the years – some of our own making, others from circumstances we found ourselves in – may have found themselves doing what I recall doing a few years back. I was looking at a baby picture of myself, actually a really cute and innocent looking little guy, and, thinking of some of the things I had gone through, done, etc., and asking myself the question, "What the hell happened?"

I know some of the things I have done over the course of my life did not come from the goodness of my heart. And we could look at baby pictures of probably every wrongdoer, be he liar, murderer, thief, abuser, the list goes on, and ask, "What happened?" Circumstances, environment, genetics, the fight for survival, continuing abuse patterns, and a few other things we could throw out there just don't fully answer the question. There is a spiritual component to our lives that must be taken into consideration.

Interview with Ellen, about Doris (Not their real names)

"I'm a little over eighty, and, in talking with one of my sisters, Doris, shortly before she died, I found out about what happened with her when we were younger. I was the youngest of three girls; we all slept together in one larger bedroom. I remember when I was about five that, when it was dark, our Uncle Carl started coming into the room after we were all in bed, and he would always go to Doris's bed. Doris was eight years older than me, so she would have been about thirteen."

"I thought that he was just coming in to talk to her because she was older. I didn't know; I was too young to know what was going on, but when I think of what my sister suffered and had to live with all those years, it bothers me that I didn't know. I don't know if I could have done anything. Doris told me she never told our mother because Uncle Carl told her that our mother wouldn't believe her, and might even punish her for telling lies. So she just kept quiet, for years."

"Doris told me that she never even told her husband because of all the shame she felt over it, but that she was feeling like she had to share it with someone. Maybe she had to share, or maybe she just felt like she could ease her soul before she passed. Either way, it breaks my heart of what my dear, dear sister lived with all those years. It just breaks my heart."

It Still Burns

It still burns, burns, deeply inside my brain.
Sometimes I believe I'm going insane as the screams of memories
Linger, linger on and keep me living in a hell.

I didn't dare scream or cry to hold off the attacks,
And even since that time the tears cannot seem to erase
The memories of him coming back again, and again, and again.

Broken heartedness and banishment

What we read in Psalm 18, a writing of David, could also apply to Jonah. "The waves of death swirled about me; the torrents of destruction overwhelmed me. The cords of the grave coiled about me; the snares of death confronted me."

Good news for the above comes in Psalm 34, verse 18. "The Lord is close to the brokenhearted and saves those who are crushed in spirit." And more in I Samuel 14:14 "But God does not take away life; instead he devises ways so that a banished person may not remain estranged from him."

The summer of 2012, I met a middle-aged woman who had a troubled relationship with her mother. It carried over into their lives so much, that if the mother entered a party or other event, and saw that her daughter was there, the mother would "give a 'Hmpf!'" and walk out. It turned out that this was a situation where the mother really bore the brunt of responsibility for the poor relationship in the first place. But the daughter bore the brunt of the woundings. Years had passed, and the daughter learned that the best way for her to have peace was to not live near her mother.

A Smoldering Wick ^(Isaiah 42:3)

As the sun rises anew
And sends the message that
Another day lies ahead,
So hope within is a little spark.

Unfortunately, abuse can cover
And crush until it seems like
The spark is gone. But, Isaiah says in 42:3,
"A smoldering wick he will not snuff out."

So when darkness seems to prevail, and it feels
Like you are about to be washed away
In the streams of despair, give out a cry to God,
No matter how feeble, cry out, and hope.

In *The Long Walk*, the author speaks about traveling toward the Siberian prison camp in the train cattle cars, packed together so tight they could not even squat or lie down. They had to sleep standing up. He said that often he would be dreaming, and then awaken to the hard fact that his reality was back again. This may compare to the feelings of some who have been abused.

Awakening to Reality

When I came to the edge of the forest
I broke into a large smile at the sight of
A wide-open field of flowers.

Then I stirred, moaned, stretched,
And awakened to reality.
Anytime now, the abuse would start again.

As you might be able to tell, the book *The Long Walk* has left an indelible impression on me, especially in the area of amazement over just how much humans are capable of overcoming. I guess that part of my surprise comes from being able to relate in a very small way (negative 50 on scales from one to ten) with some of the experiences, and then hardly being able to comprehend how much these people endured.

For example, I still quite vividly recall spending a cold spring night camping with my two (then young adult) sons in a small meadow some 12,000 feet up on a Colorado mountain. We had been slogging along through up to two-foot-deep recently fallen snow, and when darkness fell, so did the temperature. It started to snow again, and the wind whistled around and made our small tent shudder and flap. My sleeping bag was not the best, and, at one point, I felt so cold and miserable that I really thought we might die. I guess all the sound effects contributed to my frame of mind.

After a long night, and short, troubled sleep, we finally awoke to sun and warming temperatures. But I knew in the deepest places of my heart and mind that I never wanted to spend another night like the one just undergone. So it is incomprehensible to me how these men endured an over-one-thousand-mile forced march from Irkutsk to Camp 303, wrists handcuffed to a long chain, in December and January during a Siberian winter. I just cannot wrap my head around it.

And I know there are those who have been survivors of many different kinds of wars, those listed in the introduction, and then some, and most of us just cannot imagine being strong enough to escape from, and survive what they survived.

And, again, reality

One of the strangest awakening experiences I can recall occurred when I was in the 3rd Field Hospital in Saigon, Vietnam. I had been medevaced after being struck in the face by a log when we were blowing up bunkers on a firebase. Later it was determined I had both sides of my lower jaw broken, an eardrum punctured, and some of my sinuses crushed. I had been swallowing some blood which weakened me a bit. I passed out in the emergency treatment area, and while passed out was taken to another room which had light green walls. Upon awakening, I saw these walls which were about the same color of the walls of the living room of the house we lived in when I was thirteen. For a few moments I thought I was waking up back in that house and that the past few years had been nothing but a long horrible nightmare. Slowly it started to sink in that indeed they had been reality. The moment was a hard one to wrap my mind around for a while.

I imagine this is a process similar to what some abuse victims go through on a regular basis as they awaken each day.

And, the Barriers are Huge

The next time you find yourself going past an enclosed prison facility, imagine how difficult it would be to break out of there going over those barbed wire fences. In *The Long Walk*, Slavomir Rawicz describes the barriers to escaping from Camp 303: coiled barbed wire, trenches, log barriers, police dogs, and more coiled barbed wire surrounding the whole camp. Getting out of there in a Siberian blizzard boggles my mind.

Although it is very subjective, this is what we may sometimes feel like we are looking at when faced with trying to escape from our patterns, thoughts, memories, abusive situations, or other things that hold us down.

I personally take hope in the fact that seven men did escape from the above camp during a blizzard, and then started on a 4000 mile journey to freedom. In other words, huge obstacles can be overcome.

Getting distance between us and the "place of captivity" is important, because if we stay nearby, we can get pulled right back into the place we just left.

Escape

Even though we
Say we won't become
Captive again, it is
Always best if we
Put a lot of distance,
Early on, in between.

After escaping from the Siberian camp, the men traveled up to thirty miles a day in the cold and the snow in order to get out of the immediate area. In fact, they had planned for the escape to be during a blizzard so their tracks would become windswept and covered up. But thirty miles a day? I have trouble comprehending this.

Over part of a spring break several years ago, my oldest son, Ralph, and I did a short (three-day) backpack trip, hiking the Great Smoky Mountain National Park segment of the Appalachian Trail. We had to get twenty-nine miles completed on the last day. Quite frankly, it kicked my butt! A few years later when doing a 150 mile backpack on the Vermont Long Trail, I averaged twelve to thirteen miles per day. Again, I have trouble wrapping my head around thirty miles a day, especially in the snow!

What the threat is this all about?

I was struck with disbelief at an article in the *Chattanooga Times Free Press* on Saturday, January 26th, 2013. In a criminal complaint, a man in St. Paul, Minnesota was charged with threatening his fifteen-year-old daughter with an AK-47 because she made two B's in her classes, instead of making all A's. This man is nuts; no other way of looking at it.

And, although the above seems way over the top, I commented to my wife that, unfortunately, there are far too many children who, while maybe not having a physical weapon pointed at them, still feel like they are "under the gun" as far as grades go. I have nothing against a parent wanting a child doing his or her best, and receiving good grades, but abuse, mental or otherwise, should not factor in. Crazy!

Our hearts all breathed a collective sigh of relief when the young boy from Midland City, Alabama was rescued from the bunker where he had been held hostage. As a witness to two killings in a week's period of time, we can only pray he finds the emotional and spiritual healing he needs. It will take time, and counseling, a touch from above, and something positive he can "throw himself into."

Never Resting

Those memories are sharp and cutting.
Their persistence is dragging me down.
They curse and harass me, like echoes
Bouncing back, back, back, and again.
They're damning, trying to kill my spirit,
Fighting me separately, or together,
With one goal in mind, to
Never let me, never let me, never let me rest.

Abuse of Broken Promises

There are many children across our land who can relate to the waiting on someone who doesn't show up, again. This takes on many forms and shows no gender boundaries, and the wounds can run deep.

Waiting

Why am I sitting here?
Always deceiving myself that
In this case, just this one, this one
Time, it won't be like the last time;
I know he has changed, turned to a
New page, and this time I won't
Grind my teeth in disappointment

??Find Your Quiet Time??

Okay, preacher, they hear you.
Finding quiet time each day to spend with God is good. The
Problem they encounter, religiously and otherwise;
It's hard to find the silence when encircled by noise of
Reminders, memories, replays; those damned replays.

The door opening quietly as he comes into the room; or,
His fist against the side of her head; or,
Damn; she emptied out the account again; how about,
She can tell by the way he's coming through the door,
He's drunk again; another fight, another mess to clean up.

So many people do try to find those times of meditation; or,
Maybe I should say times of dreaming, dreaming
Of a time and place where they are free, truly free;
With a mind that is not encircled by the noise of
Reminders, memories, replays; those damned replays.

Feelings of Worthlessness from Abuse --> Hope

It is a well-established fact that people who suffer from abuse, and/or other inner pains and anguishes may well experience times of worthlessness, and they may find it is difficult to believe that there is any relief on the horizon. And yet, at least in a symbolic way, I believe we can find hope in Isaiah 68:1 when the writers says, "As when juice is found in a cluster of grapes and men say, 'Don't destroy it, there is yet some good in it,' so will I do on behalf of my servants."

So if you are feeling like you are worthless, quite sure that you are not going to be able to be productive anymore, perhaps you could stand in front of the mirror, read the above verse, point at the reflection, and tell yourself, "and, yes, this means YOU!"

27

The Patterns May Run Deeper

Early Events that Can Lead to Long Patterns

The following occurred when I was five. I will not deeply debate the merits of whether I should have even been exposed to this preacher; the fact is I was.

At the small church my parents attended there was an evangelist who was brought in for a week of "revival services." At the conclusion of one of the services, as a five-year-old, very unaware, of course, of symbolic language and the meaning behind religious doctrines, I went down to the altar to "be saved," and then at the prodding of the evangelist, to follow-up with the subsequent "experience of sanctification," a doctrine interpreted by this group as a "removal of the sin nature," where one would no longer consciously sin (this must be real important because we don't want a five-year-old "spewing his sins" all over the place.)

So anyway, after everyone was up from the altar, and back to their seats, before the services ended for the evening, the evangelist further made a request for volunteers to raise their hands if they would pledge to fast and pray the next day for a real "outpouring of the Holy Spirit" on the next evening's service. Well, guess who raised his hand? After all, I had just been saved and sanctified.

I made it through breakfast and lunch, but around 1:30 p.m. this young boy was starting to get a bit hungry. Around two or so I said something to my mother, and she reassured me that God would understand how young I was and "not care" if I ate. So I did. But this five-year-old felt guilty. I felt like I must have "lost" both my salvation and my sanctification. I mean, God was depending on me, and I had let him down. I had failed on my very first "day on the job." Sounds a little strange to write it, but in a five-year-old mind, these things are very real. And so are the patterns that can follow.

Of course, we almost all can agree that I shouldn't have even been exposed to that preacher in the first place, but the fact is, at the time, my parents, along with many other parents, were doing the very best they knew how and were truly unaware of the consequences and/or unintended consequences.

But it took years to shake loose from the patterns of guilt that were set in motion in my five-year old head. In terms of understanding spiritual matters, I stayed on a roller coaster for years. It was like the little daisy-ditty kids used to sing as they pulled off petals, "he loves me; he loves me not." To reach the point of rest in the fact that God loves me, period, rather than major turning points, there have been a lot of "turning nudges."

It has been said that we tend to create God in our own image. I think there is a lot of truth to that, but we also create him from our own experiences. And sometimes it takes a lot of time, and different experiences, to "re-create."

And regarding the guilt, we slowly can work our way free, but like anything else in life, it's a process. I have wished sometimes that the processes I have been through hadn't resembled my exercise bike so much. For some time (actually, until I got a couple of undergraduate psychology classes under the belt, and then waded through the process of applying what I had learned), I felt like I was doing a lot of pedaling, only to get nowhere; I guess that's why guilt is called a useless emotion.

Repetition

We learn by repetition.
There is certainly truth to that;
So, what do we learn?
Water flowing down the same rut forms a gully;

Actors repeat lines until they come out without thinking,
Automatic, imbedded, ingrained.
So patterns from the early years can stay,
Done without thinking; automatic, imbedded, ingrained.

Following are some poems and comments dealing with the area of addictions. In the interviews in chapter twenty with four inmates in a substance abuse program we saw the grip that habits can get on a person, causing them to lose everything, including freedom. Thank goodness we also saw that when a person searches, and learns, there can be a path to regaining that freedom.

Addictions

This is an area where there are no quick fixes. Even if someone were to have an experience where they were a recipient of "shock therapy," or "delivered" through some other intervention, spiritual, or otherwise, there is an "activity-void" in the rut created by repetition of certain behaviors. The gullies must be filled in with other productive activities, or, the destructive patterns, returning and finding the "house still empty" will reclaim their old territory.

More on replacement

I recall reading several years back that if we were "totally healed" from anything in our life, physical, emotional, spiritual, money problems, whatever, and did not change the way we were currently living, in short order the problem would be back. I realize there may be exceptions to that idea, but in general, it makes sense. If we do not replace negative patterns with positive ones, the negatives will move right back in.

A few years back I was seeing a counselor about some issues I wanted to get a handle on. In the course of our meetings, the conversation of my eating patterns came up. We talked about strategies for change, and then she told me to track specifics about my eating until our next meeting. The following phrases were on the paper I gave to her the following week: "I replaced," "I took the time," "I chose." During our next session we talked about how keeping track keeps one on track, and how planning and replacement often are a part of being successful in pattern-breaking.

Rains and Addictions May Start Gently

Rains, and many other things, often fall gently into our lives
In such a way that they keep us flourishing, productive.
However, these very same elements can start to pour down,
And ditches appear and habits start to be ingrained.
There comes a point where the tides must be turned, or such
Deep ruts will form that they will become incredibly difficult to escape.

Addiction II

Around and around you come; every
Day enveloping me in your arms, enticing me to
Do what you want over and over again, plus once more.
Ingrained patterns grow deeper and
Come more easily into
The daily routine of my life.
I want to break away and switch
Over to a life of freedom, but find
No help in your sweet, ugly stare.

Addiction III

And I find that on a
Daily basis you knock on my
Door and want to know
If I am ready to
Come play again. As we slide down
The long slippery slope
I realize I have better things to do; the
Only problem is, I find
No way to break this hold you have on me.

Addiction IV

At the end of the
Day, I say I
Don't want to spend
It again with any
Controlling forces
That enter
Into my life,
Over and over.
Next? Oh, you again.

Addiction V

Although there are times where I say I won't
Do it again,
Don't you know (like the sun, as surely as
It rises in the east) you will
Come around, saying, "Just one more
Time, and then you are free to go."
If I could just simply believe you; but this hold
Over me lets me know that will
Never be the case.

Deeper Into the Abyss

And so I promise not to come your way again
Because you are not really in my best interests.
But much as I tell myself, no, I won't do this anymore,
I really have given up control, so when
The road into darkness tugs at my soul, once again
I blindly follow your lead, deeper into the abyss.

You are probably familiar with the fable of the monkeys who were captured by putting nuts into jars with small openings, and after grasping a handful of food, could not draw their paws back through the tops. In the story, they were easily captured because they refused to let go of the nuts. It seems like they would have the sense to release the very things bringing about their downfall, but, ingrained deep into them was something that would not allow them to let go.

We may identify with this tale as we substitute the nuts for ruts, which so often are comfortable, safe, and never-ending.

And there also may be the factor that life has "slapped us in the face so hard," and we feel so overwhelmed, that we dare not let go of the only things we have left to provide some measure of security.

The monkey on the back

We've all heard the above expression. I have a picture verifying its existence. (Now if I can only get Micah to forgive me for calling him a monkey.) I was struck with the parallel one day when Ralph, his dad, was trying to nap. Micah was bound and determined not to let him rest. How much like an addiction is that?

Like a monkey on your back (Sorry, Micah)

Another aspect that comes into play is the spiritual component of battles.

Spiritual Battles

Sometimes we
Pretend that
It is all in the
Realm of the flesh
Instead of the soul;
The realm of spirituality.
Unless we are willing to
Acknowledge this, the
Lessons to be learned will repeat;

Battering us
Again and again,
Telling us
To realize that
Life is more than physical;
Expect to also encounter
Spiritual battles.

Sometimes I "put my own spin" on a verse I am reading, and, as far as I know, that's okay. So, according to Basil, the following may also deal with negative patterns, addictions, etc. In II Kings 5:18, after Naaman is "cleansed of leprosy" in the River Jordan he is talking with the prophet Elisha before returning to Aram, his home country. He asks one thing from the prophet.

"When my master enters the temple of Rimmon to bow down and he is leaning on my arm and I bow there also – when I bow down in the temple of Rimmon, may the Lord forgive your servant for this."

I interpret that also that there may be those who, on the surface, look like they are going along with an "earlier master" in their lives. But the truth is, we cannot see into their hearts; we don't know what is really going on.

Always nearby

A few years ago I had a very small squamous cell cancer on my left hand. It is a very slow moving type of cancer, so the appointment to have it cut off was set for a couple weeks later. I was never in any danger from it, but it did cause food for thought. Sometimes I would look at the wart-like skin that was there, and think, if this is left unchecked for years it could kill me. Even now, if there is a new growth or age spot that appears, my first thought goes to squamous cell. I believe this is comparable to the way our minds work when it comes to dealing with the patterns, or perhaps we should say ruts, that we may have developed in our lives. We see or hear something, or go through a certain experience, and our first thoughts go right to the established pattern.

Fears lingering close by

Some people live in fear and find that it cripples functional behavior. We need to get rational about our fears. If this is your situation, heed the words in the *Apocrypha*, Wisdom of Solomon 17:12, "Fear is nothing more but the giving up of reinforcements that come from reason." Sometimes we may not want to accept this premise because we have already established patterns of fearfulness.

28

Abuse; Become a Pattern-Breaker

Breaking Patterns

In my opinion, one of the more difficult scriptures to understand, and/ or accept is found in Exodus 34: 7; "Yet He (God) does not leave the guilty unpunished; he punishes the children and their children for the sin of the fathers to the third and fourth generation."

This statement was satisfactorily explained to me when I was a student in an introductory psychology course. My professor had been a former pastor, who quit the ministry to teach psychology. He said he never could reconcile this statement with a loving God until he got into the field of psychology and started to understand better how family environments worked, and their impact on patterns, behavioral and psychological.

It's not a punishment to the next generation; it's more a natural consequence of the way we are wired. We have to seek out ways, spiritually, educationally, and from counselor assistance, to become a pattern-breaker, if for no other reason than the benefit of our children.

This idea, of "for the benefit of our children" seems to be reinforced in Deuteronomy 30, verses 15 and 19b. "See, I set before you today life and prosperity, death and destruction … Now choose life, so that you and your children may live."

Becoming a pattern breaker is moving into a cycle that may take a generation, or maybe even more, but a move that on the positive side can produce "better fruit" for years to come.

The first thing we must accept if we are going to be a pattern breaker is what Albert Einstein said, "I must be willing to give up what I am in order to become what I will be."

In Genesis 32, Jacob is described as wrestling with a man that later is identified as God. When daybreak came, the man told Jacob to let him go, and Jacob replied, "I will not let you go until you bless me."

Jacob was given a name change and told it was because "You have struggled with God and with men and have overcome."

Sometimes we have to wrestle with something and not let go, or stop struggling, until there is a breakthrough, I believe, symbolized here by daybreak. And it can be said that we are given a new name, or look at ourselves differently, because we have struggled, and, even if we never see the total transformation, we are still in the process of breaking patterns, and therefore, have overcome.

A few years back I was driving along the Mountain Parkway toward Lexington and noticed a hill where rain gullies were the prominent feature. The following came, so I jotted it down.

Gullies

I saw a hill with gullies etched all along her side,
And noticed some were quite deep; some quite wide.
The storms of life she'd weathered, that fact was plain to see,
But through it all, she stood her ground, and,
Actually, looked quite lovely.

I thought about a deeper truth affecting you and me,
The storms of life against us come and make us feel like we
Have gullies etched and scars from past that sometimes hold us down,
And keep us wondering day to day if we'll
Ever hold our ground.

So Lord, I turn my life toward you, and, in simple faith, just ask
For you to let the sun shine on, and let me in it, bask.
And let me find the ways where I can find your love, to fill
My life with beauty from my scars,
Like the gullies on that hill.

Richard (not his real name) working to be a pattern-breaker

In the Group Home there was a monthly "parents' night" when the boy's parents would come for some training sessions about techniques that would help them after their child was released from the program. One boy came from a home where his mother had left, and his father was frequently picked up for public drunkenness, and then sentenced to a few days in jail.

There was one time he was in jail when a "parents' night" rolled around. The judge in Juvenile Court arranged with the jailer for Richard, in civilian clothes, to be released to my custody for the evening, and after the parent meeting was over then I took him back to his cell. His son was happy that his father came to the session, and you could tell they were genuinely glad to see each other.

En route to and from the Group Home with Richard, knowing that he most likely felt some embarrassment over his situation, I told him how proud of him I was that he was coming to the session to learn some new ways to stay more positively involved with his son. He appeared to be pleased when told this. I honestly believe this father was on his way to becoming a pattern-breaker.

So many parents are involved in their own battles, and even though some of the things they are doing in the child-rearing area may be less than stellar, they may really be doing the best they know how. We have to be careful not to judge too harshly, and maybe even see if there is an area we can help them along the way.

How many of you were "Juvvies?"

I think the following passages from Isaiah 61 may well apply at least symbolically to a question teaching-parents were asked at a monthly training session at Morganton, NC.

The passages are, "to preach good news to the poor … bind up the brokenhearted … proclaim freedom for the captives … release from the darkness," and, "They will rebuild the ancient ruins and restore the places long devastated; they will renew the ruined cities …"

Several teaching-parents were at the session, and the group trainer asked the following question, "By a show of hands, how many of you were 'Juvvies', in trouble with the law at some point during your teen years?" More than half of us raised our hands, and we represented almost 90% of the couples there. He then went on to point out that many people who have had some difficulty in some area of their lives often go on to help others who are facing the same kinds of situations.

This applies whether it has to do with having been in trouble with the law, or facing some other form of traumatic situation. We can only empathize with someone else when we know exactly what they are going through. Then we are in better position to proclaim good news about freedom for captives in a variety of "darknesses," or rebuild, restore, and renew as we bind up broken hearts. Whether for a full time or volunteer profession, if you are looking for a place to help others, look at your past.

Escaping from the entrapment

In Psalm 124: 7, we read, "We have escaped like a bird out of the fowler's snare; the snare has been broken, and we have escaped."

I have a couple blueberry bushes off my side porch, and I try to keep the birds away by putting a net over them. Occasionally one will figure that it can find a way to the blueberries by getting onto the ground and flying up into the net. At that point, there is only one avenue of escape for the bird, and "my birds" have all figured it out. Go down low, and there is the "freedom trail."

There are negative patterns we can fall into that can hold us like a bird caught in a net over a blueberry bush. The Psalmist says that God is interested in helping us find that way of escape. In my blueberry bush net example given above, I don't know if it follows that we also have to get pretty low before we find the route to freedom, but, it sure seems that way sometimes.

Escape II
Entrapped with no visible way out
Seems to be a place I
Can relate to ...
A lot. A thought of hope; the
Psalmist says I can find a route of
Escape from the snare.

Escapes require planning

If we were preparing for escape from a facility where we were held captive, we would plan carefully, looking over every detail to make sure we were not thwarted in our plot, for primarily two reasons. First, we want our freedom. Without it we cannot truly live up to our fullest potential. And, secondly, we can be fairly sure that if we are caught and brought back into captivity, it is going to be worse than before. We do not want to go back to that.

So, why should an escape from habits, patterns, or abuse be any different? There must be assistance, be it from a friend, counselor, pastor or other spiritual leader, in order to make long-term and effective progress. The preceding may help us avoid some of the pitfalls that can set us back. To use a hiking comparison, if I am getting ready for a backpacking trip and I read an article on foot care, I may save myself a lot of anguish on the trail, and maybe even avoid having to abort my mission, which is to complete the trail (or escape from the inner wounding patterns that are dragging me down.)

I can relate to this example as I started a backpacking trip in the Smokies a few years back without checking my toenails first. Partway through the first day, the "dogs were talking to me." Fortunately my son had some clippers and that night I corrected the situation. Had I done it before I started, I might have saved the two nails that later came off. It was a result of poor planning on my part.

I guess maybe I could paraphrase Proverbs 21:5, "The plans of the diligent lead to profit, as surely as haste leads to poverty," to "The plans of the diligent lead to easier hiking, as surely as carelessness leads to distress."

Back to the backpacking trip, our last day of a 62 mile, three-day trip, Ralph and I went 29 miles because Ralph had an appointment the next day, and we arrived at our car in the dark. I "ran on adrenaline" the last few miles, was totally exhausted, and wasn't real full of energy the next day either. The same can occur when there is an escape from something that has been dragging us down, or wounding in some way. We need time to rest, and re-charge.

Weather patterns and predictions

We can see an example of how easily we humans fall into certain thought patterns just by observing "weather talk." Many, at least on the surface, judged by what we hear, evaluate the "goodness" or "badness" of a day by the weather. We ask, "How's it going?" and we often hear, "Well, okay I guess, but it's raining." How about, "I'm doing well, and my garden is happy."

According to whom?

One rainy day, while a student at Eastern Kentucky University, I entered the classroom a few minutes early and overheard the following exchange between a couple of students:

A: How are you doing?

B: Horrible.

A: Why? What's wrong?

B: Are you kidding me? Look outside! It's raining!

Now, granted, student "B" may have had something special planned for that day, and the weather forced a cancellation, but I did not hear any suggestion of that enter into the conversation. Based on what I heard, it seems that she might have been in a pattern of determining her well-being by the weather.

A Bad Day?

You may look at the rainy day outside
And decide that it's going to be a bad day,
But whether or not a day is "good" or "bad"
Depends on what we tell ourselves about it.
So, go ahead, have your bad day;
I choose to have a good one.

Self-fulfilling Prophecies/Strange Loops

There is something in the psychological and communication realm called a "self-fulfilling prophecy"; what you or others say about yourself comes to pass as you bring it about. For example, the "target" of "he's such a mean little boy," frequently grows up to be "a mean little" boy, then young person, then adult. Why? He lived up (or down) to the expectations and prophecies. The conversations might go as follows:

"Why are you mean?"

"Because I do mean things."

"Why do you do mean things?"

"Because I am mean."

The person involved in vandalism may answer the question, "Why did you do this?" with,

"Because I am 'bad'(as in tough.)"

"What makes you 'bad'?"

"Because I do 'bad' things."

This can carry over into adulthood. I know, because on the following, I "was there, and did this" for a long time, especially during my 20's and 30's. A phrase I used, and have heard other adult males use (women may too; I just haven't heard any say it) is:

"I guess I'm just a 'dumb-shit'."

"Why do you keep calling yourself a 'dumb-shit'?"

"You ought to know. I keep doing 'dumb-shit' things."

Parental reactions that don't help break patterns

Parental Fears

A moment ago I mentioned "parents' night" in the group home. One session we were involved in minor role-playing, and each parent had to respond to how they would probably react if they thought (or knew) their son was drinking and driving, or riding with a driver who had been drinking. Most responses were quite emotional, including ranges up to the effect of "I'll kill you if I ever catch you driving after drinking." (Care for a little irony, anyone?)

We discussed their reasons for what they had said, talked about fears, and then role-played the response. "Son, I love you so much that just the thought of police showing up at the door and telling me I need to come to the morgue to identify your body scares me so badly, I get irrational. Please, don't ever make me have to go through that. I just love you too much and it scares me."

Is that not why, as parents, we do get emotional and irrational in our dealings with our children sometimes? Think about it. After the role-playing and during discussion, we also talked about the idea of telling our children that if they were somewhere and had had something to drink, and shouldn't be driving, then let them know they could call for a ride home, and the issue wouldn't be discussed until the next day.

The following conversation with "Kevin" is a real-life example of how this played out for him.

Kevin (not his or his son's real names)

"I must admit, as a teenager I did drink and drive a few times. So, as an adult, I always told my kids that, although I hoped it wouldn't be necessary, if they ever were drinking and needed a ride home, call me. My kids all would adamantly respond something like, 'Not to worry, Dad. Not ever going to be drinking in the first place.'"

"Well, one evening, when Jason was twenty, I received a call. 'Dad, can you come pick me up? I'm over Tyler's house and I've been drinking; actually, I'm drunk. Will you come and get me?' I went to pick him up, and discovered he indeed was in nowhere near condition to drive. We stopped on the 20 mile trip home a couple times so he could open the door, and hang his head out, if you know what I mean. The next morning on the way to get his car, I told him that I was disappointed that he had gotten drunk, but I was so glad he had called, rather than get out on the road. He replied, 'Well, Dad, I sure didn't think I'd ever have to, but that's what you always told us to do.'"

"You just don't know how grateful I was he had called. If he had gotten on the road, I feel certain he would have either wrecked and hurt or killed himself or someone else, or would have been arrested, and had that as a blemish on what has since turned out to be, from there on out, a really good 'track record,' not only as a driver, but as a person and good all-around citizen."

Caution about what helps break patterns

Sometimes one may think that "escaping" into marriage and having a family, without dealing with certain core personal issues he has with himself, will take care of all problems, and put him on the road to becoming a pattern-breaker. Not so. If the problems are not dealt with, chances are, all that will happen is the cycle will continue.

Take Time

Having said that, I have experienced, and observed, there are some woundings we may have received as a child that we feel being healed as we spend time with our own children. Taking the time to do positive things with them is enjoyable, savoring the moments is satisfying, and healing can take place. We can make no

Troy with Nicholas – good stuff!

better investment than spending positive time with our children.

May I repeat; we can make no better investment than spending positive time with our children. Memories are being formed, lifetime attitudes are being shaped, and, I firmly believe, "juvenile delinquency rosters" are being shortened. Parents, a word from the children, "Take time."

Make it your ambition to lead a quiet life

I Thessalonians 4:11, 12 says, "Make it your ambition to lead a quiet life, to mind your own business and to work with your hands, just as we told you, so that your daily life may win the respect of outsiders and so that you will not be dependent on anybody."

Allow me to take another trip to the Group Home for an example. There was a client, Jerry (not his real name) who was admitted to the program when he was thirteen for breaking and entering. His father was an alcoholic, he had an older brother and sister in jail, and his mother had allowed him to start chewing tobacco at the age of five because, in her words, "He said he wanted to." Understatement of the year – > Jerry came from a chaotic family.

About a half year into the program he got into a major rule infraction and was taken back to court by his court counselor. The role of a teaching parent was to always be an advocate for the child, so the judge was petitioned to allow Jerry to return to the program, if, his father would go to counseling with him weekly. The father agreed, the judge agreed, and what a difference it made. Within three months the father was not drinking, was working overtime at his job, and had moved the family from a very shabby single-wide trailer to a nice, single-dwelling home in a totally different neighborhood.

Jerry's mother said, "He's gone from an alcoholic to a workaholic, but I like this better." Talking with some teaching-parent friends some three years later, they said that Jerry and his father were still doing well.

How far, or long, to get there?

Sometimes we ask someone who is familiar with a given route, how long it takes to reach a destination. Perspective can become a factor in the answer. My oldest son Ralph and I were discussing this idea as we hiked the Great Smoky Mountain National Park portion of the Appalachian Trail.

As we were going along we would occasionally meet someone coming the other direction, and sometimes would ask the question, "How far to the next shelter/marker/trail intersection?" – what ever we wanted to know about. It didn't take us long to discover that the answer always depended on whether the person was traveling uphill or downhill. We might be told such and such a destination was about three-quarters of a mile away and fairly easy walking. We discovered that when traveling downhill, a mile and a half might only seem like three-quarters. On the other hand, so might three-quarters of a mile stretch into a mile and a half when going uphill.

I think this same perspective distortion can also be a factor when discussing how long it takes to break certain behavior patterns.

29

Finding a Way; I Will Get It Done

One step at a time

Before embarking on my Vermont trip in mid-2001, I was devouring any and all "how-to" articles in *Backpacker* magazine. I read about the best rhythm patterns when hiking with trekking poles, tricks to "best rest breaks" while still carrying the pack, many cooking ideas, and more. One article in particular probably helped me more than anything else, on my 2001 trip, and since. The main point was that when climbing a mountain, break your "visual climb" into short sections comparable to something you are familiar with.

My example for that technique is as follows: say you live on a city block, and when you step out on to the sidewalk you see the newsstand where you get your paper just a short 100 yards away, then you recreate that image when climbing. Pick out a tree or rock that is an equivalent distance, and keep your focus within that range until you reach the designated point. Repeat as necessary until you have reached the top or other objective. I have found that whenever I resort to this while hiking a trail, I sometimes use variety in my motivators as trail conditions change. But the technique works!

And I have found it works in other situations when struggling to find a way to "get it done." In the chapter on perseverance I mention other things I have found that mentally and emotionally help in reaching a goal. We're familiar with the song and saying, "one day at a time," and when we can incorporate this into our daily living, sometimes even to the point of "five minutes at a time," or, maybe, "one step at a time" we are well on our way to success.

My wife's house in Tennessee has a very steep drive up to it. When I get the paper in the morning, I usually pick out an article to glance at on my way back up, and get to the house with much less exertion than when I am looking at the shutters, front door, or something else that only serves to remind me how far below it I am. When pulling the emptied trash can back up, I try to have some sort of counting game going on. Whatever the technique, it works in achieving the goal.

I read where Sir Edmund Hillary, first to reach the peak of Mt. Everest, was asked how he kept going, and he replied that he just kept plugging on … he persisted.

Ten-minute tasks

This tip I read may help in a wide variety of situations, and
May also apply to breaking patterns (especially if
The desired result seems too daunting and formidable.)
The tip; if you have ten minutes available,
Pick out a small task you can accomplish during that time period and do it.

The point was made that in many areas of our life
We will never have a chunk of time to get some things done all at one time.
Although it specifically had to do with organizing one's office
(You'd think twenty years after reading it, I would have made more headway)
It also has applications to most all situations we encounter.

I actually have been able to better apply it to many other areas of my life;
Much better than I have into office organization, but that's okay.
(We use our techniques in our areas of "best favorability".)
Patterns deeply ingrained take a long time to change, however,
A little at a time, we can find a way to get it done.

One pound at a time

In a play I wrote about the era of Dr. Record, an early administrator at what is now the University of Pikeville, I included the following story he used to tell students to encourage them not to get behind in their work.

"There was a man who had a young ox, still small enough that he could sling it over his shoulders. He did this every day, and even as the ox grew to full size the man could still lift it."

Now, I don't know if the ox story is true, or not, but I do know that when I was training for my backpack trip on the Long Trail in Vermont, I started carrying a backpack with just a few pounds in it, and slowly increased the weight until I was soon climbing the mountain near the house with more ease than the first time I tried it without a pack.

Abdul Samad "The greatest blessing of my life." (Really?)

Abdul Samad is another person we were able to invite to Pikeville College as a part of the Special Events Program. Back in the 1980's, as a young Afghan boy, the small village he lived in was destroyed, and Abdul had no idea where his family was, or if they were even alive. Later, he saw something shiny in a field, and, thinking it might be some kind of toy, picked it up. It was a landmine, which exploded, blowing off both of Abdul's hands. Eventually he wound up in the United States and enrolled in school. He was near graduation from a local community college the first time he spoke to our group.

Abdul didn't use prosthetics. Instead he learned how to do just about everything anyone else could do with his arm stubs. He drove with specially designed cups on the steering wheel, ate pizza slices as well as anyone, and told the audience that having his hands blown off was the greatest blessing of his life. He elaborated that he would never have received an education, or learned just how much he was capable of, had the incident never occurred.

Negative Motivators

(1) I will do it, in spite of you

Many years ago, while stationed in Germany, I went to a religious retreat in the Eagles Nest area in the Bavarian Alps. One of the speakers, Roger Brevard (not his real name), who was over the mission program in his denomination, was telling of when he first made a commitment to God as a young person. He said that he overheard two older ladies in the church talking, and one of them said, "That Roger, he'll never 'make it'; he'll 'backslide' soon."

Rev. Brevard then said, "I determined I would 'make it', if for no other reason than to spite those two old ladies."

Now, I'm not so sure that was a totally true statement on his part, or just a good line; and I'm not so sure it is such a pure motivation for "walking with God," but it can be a powerful motivator, and, in a situation of someone who has been abused, it sounds to me like a good motivator, "I'll just show you what I'm capable of" , or, perhaps, "Look what I've become, in spite of what you've done."

(2) Civil disobedience?

When I first came to teach at Pikeville College my division chair was Dr. Frank Jacks. Once, he was talking to me about one of my assignments I gave in my public speaking courses. I had students visit with someone who was primarily homebound (for whatever reasons) and then turn in a 2-3 page written response to the visit following given guidelines. Dr. Jacks told me that it was a nice assignment for, say, a course in interpersonal communication, but that it had "no 'f#@ng' place" in a public speaking course.

A short while later, as I walked back to my office, a certain part of me (for better or worse) was kicking in. I knew the premise of the assignment was good, so it was time to figure out how to engage in "civil disobedience" without getting into trouble, and/or putting my job in jeopardy. So, I thought, how do I make it have a place in my public speaking class? And then I was hit with my "Wow, could have had a V8" moment. Public Speaking – Speech – How about a "Shut-In Interview Review" speech? What a novel idea! Admittedly, that moment should have occurred when I started the written assignment a couple years earlier, but I never have claimed to be the sharpest knife in the drawer.

Anyway, a speech was "born," thanks to a "negative motivator." And, later, when I started teaching some interpersonal, and health communication courses, it also fit with them, and with the public speaking adjunct courses I taught for about five years, a few years back.

So, now, over the past twenty years I have heard over two thousand "Shut-In Interview Review" speeches (made with someone who is primarily homebound) dealing with issues of dignity, or lack thereof, loneliness, frustrations, overcoming obstacles, and often, words of challenge to young people, along with positive summations of their lives, and toward life in general.

There have also been a few cases, ten to twelve, over the years where the student made a visit (most cases of them to a grandparent), and it turned out to be the last time they ever saw them. I let students know when assigning the speech that if the assignment is "responsible" for their last visit to someone; I make no apologies for that.

Over my lifetime I have made some poor choices, and some good ones. I consider my implementation of this speech one of the better things I have ever done professionally. And, again, it basically was the result of a negative stimulus. If you believe in something you are doing, and others block that action, especially if it is something that is making a positive difference in another person's life, figure out a way to repackage it, and go with it.

Facing our fears

In public speaking, for many, the enemy is the lectern in the front of the room. I use the following example early in the course when talking about facing our fears, which are in fact, our enemies.

"We are all probably familiar with the story of David and Goliath in the Old Testament, but I want to advance the story to later, when the people of Israel started to give more attention and praise to David then to Saul, the king. They started saying things like, 'Saul has killed thousands, but David has killed ten thousands.' This aggravated Saul, he became insanely jealous, and tried on several occasions to kill David, to no avail. Then we read in I Samuel 18, verse 29, 'When Saul realized that the Lord was with David ..., Saul became still more afraid of him, and he remained his enemy the rest of his life.' When thinking about this verse, I am struck by the idea of 'if afraid; it remains an enemy'. As long as we fear someone or something, we can never become friends with that person or thing. There are some things we may never become 'bosom buddies' with, like this lectern up here, but we can move to a place beyond fear. If we are going to find a way to 'get it done', we have to control the fears. The move is ours."

Fears

For as long as you remain my
Enemy, you will
Always, always
Remain apart from me,
Separated by my worries.

Star Wars and the little red wagon

I was a graduate student at the University of Kentucky when Star Wars was starting to saturate our society. Ralph and Rocky were in the eight to ten age categories, and totally interested in collecting Star Wars figures. There was just one minor problem. It's the first part of the first sentence of this paragraph. We talked about a way they could earn money. Not from me, I didn't have any. We decided recycling would be good as there was a center nearby that paid for old newspapers and aluminum cans. I shuffled priorities, and purchased a little red wagon for them. We divided the Greg Paige Stadium View Apartment area we lived in into four sections and then scheduled pick-up days, Monday through Thursday, for each section. Flyers were made up, and the boys took one to every apartment in the housing complex.

A lot of students saved their papers, and more importantly, cans (partying can involve a lot of aluminum material), and Ralph and Rocky were "in business." After setting aside a tenth for giving, and some for savings, they were part of the Star Wars collectible craze. We built a paper-Mache base complete with paper towel cardboard roller towers, and "life was good in the universe."

We also laughed about the fact that I had a newspaper route, so I got paid for morning deliveries, and they got paid for taking those same papers away. Furthermore, if there was a coupon for something that we would need to buy anyway, we clipped, several times. There was even one item that had a free, try-out, coupon (not buy one, get one, just get one.) We stocked up!

The bottom line is there are ways to get things done. I still have to force myself to look for those ways sometimes, instead of complaining about what I don't have.

30
The Losses We Bear; I Can't Go On, but I Do

The loss of a child is something that just doesn't seem right, even if they are older. I remember after my older brother died of prostate cancer at the age of fifty-nine my mother saying to me, just as Jeff said in chapter ten, "This isn't right. The children are supposed to bury their parents; not the parents their children."

And, the loss of a child is near incomprehensible. I cannot envision the pain. I can imagine the sorrow and pain and inner wounding varies greatly from person to person, and is influenced by the relationship, the circumstances, and many other factors. And, words such as "Your child is now in the arms of God" may not offer much in the way of comfort at the moment. That may be true, but the knife of your loss is still penetrating deep into your heart.

How does one deal with getting rid of toys, books, clothing? One cannot know what is going through a parent's mind as they drop things off at, perhaps, Goodwill, a church yard sale, or some other "helping hands" organization. The fact is that most people aren't aware of when and how someone else is going through a particular rite of passage in the healing process, even if they have been through a similar experience. The bottom line is; each one has to "walk his or her valley alone," so to speak.

While trekking through the Gobi Desert after the death of one of his escapee companions, Slavomir Rawicz says in *The Long Walk* that the only thing on his mind was grief, which kept repeating itself over and over again.

It is also hard sometimes for a young person to comprehend loss, even for another. I recall when I was in the fourth grade; one of our class mates was absent and later we were told that her mother had died. When I got home that evening it was a topic of conversation at the dinner table; the illness, a hospital stay, what was next for the family, and so forth. I was familiar with death as my grandfather had died when I was six, but this was still the first encounter for me where it affected a friend. It stayed on my young mind for a long time as I wondered how my class mate could go on without her mother, and was my family in danger of this event.

It Started Out Like …

It started out like any other day. I was in the 4th grade.
Karen wasn't in school, and someone told the teacher that
Her mommy had said that Karen's mommy had died.
The teacher looked real sad, and said that it was true.

Her mother died? What's she going to do? What happened?
These and other questions slammed my mind.
I had never thought before about mothers dying.
And, although it started out like any other day, it wasn't.

The following was written based on comments by a friend about a loss
he experienced when in the 5th grade.

Billy Went Away

I was in the 5th grade when it happened.
The teacher took attendance,
And my best friend, Billy, wasn't there.
Later the principal came to the classroom
And said she had to talk to us.

She said that on the way to school
There had been an accident,
And Billy had been hurt
And taken to the hospital.

He died a few days later, and
Since that time, it hasn't been the same.
Why so young? He never had the chance to
Play on a team, go to dances,

Get married, have children, and do
All the other things I've done.
Maybe God knows what he's doing,
But I don't understand this one.

Traumatic events tend to replay in our minds with no way to hit the eject button, even if they did not end in tragedy.

My youngest son, Rocky, and I were rappelling off Half Moon Rock in the Red River Gorge in Eastern Kentucky. We decided to go off the "Whale's Tail," nearby. After our first drop of around eighty feet, we climbed back up the rocks to go down again. Rocky decided to go over "Aussie," which was face forward. He had done it off Half Moon a couple times, so we both figured this would work.

However, we couldn't get the rope into the notch before he started his lean. So he told me to just pull it down into place as he started forward (okay, stupid, I know.) He was leaning forward almost parallel to the ground, and I had the rope to within a couple inches of the notch when Rocky's balance shifted, and the rope was jerked out of my hand as he plunged downward. Fortunately he was able to brake himself, but he still slapped up against the side of the cliff enough to bleed some from his temple, but providentially, he maintained consciousness. He was down about six or seven feet, and between his scrambling and my pulling, we were able to be safely reunited on the top.

But his falling over the edge did not end immediately. For many nights after that, whenever I tried to drift off to sleep, I was sharply thrust back into fear as I saw Rocky once again plummeting off the "tail of the whale."

I can relate this to some situations out of the Infantry in Vietnam, and can only imagine that this is what some people go through with some of the losses they have borne.

Being Good Parents P/H

Being good parents leaves little room for rest
The hardest endeavor we humans can try.
And when even good parents have done their best,
There's still so many things that make them wonder "why?"
Like accidents, and other things that seem beyond control.

In-Country R&R's

With the Infantry in the First Air Cavalry in Vietnam, about every three months we had an "in-country R&R," which was a three stand-down on a base in the rear. We would come in from where we were out "humping" through the jungle to a firebase, a fortified area with sandbag bunkers and an artillery unit in a cleared out area in the jungle, and from there load onto the large CH 47 Chinook helicopters for transport back to a more secured, rear area. The Chinooks always "put me in mind of" large, flying, olive-drab school buses. The ride to the rear was always with mixed feelings, because, although there was "relax-time" coming up, there was also a keen awareness of those on the last flight who were not on this one, due to injuries or death,

Upon arrival at the R&R site, we would line up our packs and weapons in a heavily guarded location, and then head to our temporary barracks furnished with cots and, well, not much else, but getting to sleep on a cot; that was enough. The first sergeant would have a tub that looked large enough to take a stretched-out, luxurious bath in filled with ice, and a few cases of already cold beer in it; let the future headaches begin. Also, there was usually a stripper show lined up, and other activities designed for "helping people who were living and smelling like animals to feel like they were civilized." But somehow, the "cleansing" never did wash away the sadness over the absent ones.

Riding the Chinook

They looked like large, olive-drab school buses
With large blades on top that allowed them to fly.
Chinooks. It's what they used to fly us in from
An outlook firebase to the rear, for R&R; a bitter-sweet ride.

Sure, a three-day stand-down lay ahead with no rifles to carry,
Or Viet Cong to worry about, lots of beer, real showers,
And, good food served hot in a mess hall;
Overall, just a time to forget the war.

But in order to get there, you had to ride the Chinook.
And as I sat there on that noisy ride, blades whomping,
I used to look around at my traveling comrades,
And mourn the ones who were not there this time.

Loss of the future

Along with a physical loss of someone, we also bear the loss of future events that would have otherwise been, or might have been, shared with him or her. I have gotten together a couple times with a friend from Vietnam who lives in NW Nebraska. I can't do that with Rodney Evans, or Brian Morrow, or Fat Medic. Nor can a mother sit the child on her lap and sing, or tell a story. This is part of why pain comes round again, and again. And the triggers for the "absent-future-losses" lie all around, in many innocent places; walking past the play area in a shopping mall; a commercial; seeing a sunset like ones you and your spouse used to comment on; watching a movie; hearing a song; and, always the memories – memories that were being built to form a solid relationship – memories that suddenly become twisted and turned into knives that can stab emotions, and cut out hearts.

There may be a time period when one wonders if the potential is there for life to ever again "show a plus side." Questions that have no answers may bounce off one's mind like a barrage of ping pong balls I saw thrown off a twelve-story roof once by someone on the David Letterman Show.

There, then not there

The father of our 20th President, James A. Garfield, died when James was almost two. Garfield said he wasn't sure if what he knew of his father came from what others said about him, or infant memories. He said that he seemed to recall a man that played with him, and then he wasn't there anymore. There may not be a strong recollection, but there can still be the sense of loss.

Something Missing

When my oldest son's oldest son, Noah, was quite young, Ralph used to sing "The Unicorn Song" to him every night while putting him to bed. When Noah was around one, Ralph was gone for a few days for a speaking engagement. He was later telling me how his wife Linda, had called the first night and asked if he would sing "The Unicorn Song" over the phone to Noah, as she couldn't get him to relax and go to sleep. Ralph said every evening after that, he called and sang to Noah, and then, Linda said, he was ready to go to sleep.

One of those little stories we sometimes "ooh" and "aah" over, but the fact remains that Noah had something missing, his daddy, and his daddy singing to him, and without it, his bedtime ritual wasn't complete. This is a very poor analogy of what happens during permanent loss of another, but the truth to be garnered is, when something is missing, deep in our spirits we know things can't go on as before.

Loss of the family unit

I remember a friend rather jokingly commenting one time, "Divorce is like a death, except the person is still there." That could be good or bad, depending on the circumstances. However, if there are children in the family unit, there is a death, or destruction, of that particular structure. And, again, depending on the circumstances, that may be a good or a bad thing.

If both parents are concerned with the best interests of the child, then they will avoid the manipulation that so often takes place in an attempt to "get back" at the ex. But under even the "best" of circumstances, and usually regardless of age, the child is making some major adjustments.

Of course, beforehand, the world consists of both parents and the child, or children. Then it may seem like the world is being shattered right down the middle and torn apart. What most, although admittedly not all, children find out in time is they can go on, and there is room for both parents in their hearts, the parents just aren't together. The healing process for them has started, although the questions may long persist.

But for some, the inner wounding that has occurred leaves a permanent mark that they may never fully get over. As someone who is divorced and remarried, all I can say to parents is make sure that you don't use your children as weapons against the other; if you do, it may make a recovery process for the children much harder to attain.

Peace during the losses

Having said something earlier about words that mean well, I still firmly believe that we can find comfort from scriptures, and even having others offer those scriptures in a way of sincerely reaching out. Peace is offered through the words of Jesus in John 14:27, "Peace I leave with you; my peace I give you. I do not give you as the world gives."

There are some poems I wrote in the days following my mother's death in chapter fifty: "Peace like a River (or Maybe a Lake)," where I experienced the above first hand. Peace in difficult times can be hard to explain, but it definitely can exist.

Part of our healing has to come from milking all the enjoyment we can, right now; living in the present. Remember in chapter ten we saw Jeff, who enjoyed fishing with his son, and after Lamar died, "still fishing" became part of the healing process.

31

If God is Like a Father, Some Folks are Hurting

The Concept Question [P/H]

"God is like a father!" The preacher thundered out his words.

Jason tightened his jaws a little. "What am I doing here?" he asked himself.

The preacher continued, "It's all a matter of love, God's love."

"I may not understand it then," Jason muttered.

"The biggest problem in the world today," the thundering voice continued, "is those people who hear the message of God's love, but reject it."

It was snowing that Christmas Eve eight years ago when a nine-year-old Jason was pushed out the door by his drunk-again father.

"Yes," said the preacher, "willful rejection is dangerous."

Jason eased out of his back row seat and started for the door.

"Some here tonight may never have this opportunity again!" the preacher yelled.

It seemed that again bullets from his father's shotgun were hurtling his direction. Soon after, when his father passed out on the living room floor, Jason's mother sneaked him back into the house, past the Christmas tree and down the hall to his little trailer bedroom. The next morning, of course, the classic case of denial. Jason's father said he didn't recall any of it.

"He's standing at your heart's door!" pleaded the preacher. "Don't ignore Him!"

Jason closed the church door behind him. As he slowly walked down the front steps he could still hear the preacher's voice through an open window. "God is like a father! How well off we could be if we would only accept this!"

If God Is Like a Father ... ^{P/H}

It's said that God is like a father,
That concept works for some,
But don't try to force it on others,
For some that concept is really dumb.
For God would never take a child,
Shove him outside on Christmas Eve,
Shoot at him like a man gone wild,
Leave him out there 'til he starts to freeze.
So if your dad was good, be thankful.
Give him and God all their due praise.
But keep in mind before labeling,
Some saw their fathers in different ways.

Allen (not his real name)

"The Concept Question" and "If God Is Like a father ..." are based on an actual client I worked with while a teaching-parent in a group home. Allen (not his real name) had some very real issues. He was thirteen at the time I worked with him; only eight when his inebriated father shot a gun his direction.

When talking about communication misunderstandings in public speaking classes, I've used this example to demonstrate use of a real example/ hypothetical example combination to make a point.

Real example:
Allen's mother telling teaching-parents about the Christmas Eve he was shot at when he was eight.

Hypothetical example:
Let's say Allen has a friend named Dan, and one day when they are talking, Allen says, "I just don't know the way I feel sometimes; I mean, I get so angry, and I want to bust things, and hit people, and, I don't know, I'm just so mad sometimes."

So Dan says, "Well, you know, Allen, I know you don't go to church, but down where I go, the pastor is a real nice guy, and he's easy to talk to, and maybe it would help."

And Allen's reply is "Are you kidding me? I ain't never been to church; don't plan on ever going. I don't know nothing about preachers; don't want to know. I don't know nothing about God; don't plan on learning."

Over time, Dan keeps urging Allen to go, and so eventually (if for no other reason than to shut Dan up) Allen agrees to go see the preacher.

So as he walks through the door, Allen makes sure he lays the ground rules out right away. "Hi. I'm here because Dan said I ought to come, but, let me tell you right off, I ain't never been to church; don't plan on ever going. I don't know nothing about preachers (maybe pauses for dramatic effect, and to get the right 'spite tone'); don't want to know nothing about preachers. And I don't know nothing about God; don't plan … God … What is God like, anyway?"

And so our hypothetical preacher says (like hypothetical, and some real preachers do), "Allen, let me tell you; God is like a father."

At this point in my example I pause, get some chalk, go to the board, and write the word "Father" on it. Then I solicit from the class ideas about what "father" means to Allen. It generally has at least the following included:

Father
  Abusive
  Fear
  Anger
  Drunk
  Pain

Then, as I say, "All in all, not a really nice kind of guy." I add to the right side,

Father = S.O.B.
  Abusive
  Fear
  Anger
  Drunk
  Pain

Then I add, "Our hypothetical preacher just said that God is like a father. So, then, in our hypothetical example,

God = Father = S.O.B.

Abusive
Fear
Anger
Drunk
Pain

I go on to say that we no longer have a communication problem, we have a math problem. Did we not learn that if A=B, and B=C, then A=C; so, if God = Father, and Father = S.O.B. (not a really nice kind of guy), then God = S.O.B. (not a really nice kind of guy.)

Of course, there is follow-up to discuss how to turn this misunderstanding into a breakthrough (hypothetical preacher asking Allen what a good father is to him – Allen responding he doesn't know; never had one; but maybe he would take him fishing, wouldn't get drunk and yell at him, or hit his mother; maybe like that – and then how hypothetical preacher could tell Allen that God is kind of like this "good father" he just described.)

Once, in response to the example, a student commented about a friend Tom (not his real name) who had an abusive father while growing up. The student had invited Tom to church with him, and the invitation was accepted. However, at some point in the sermon, the preacher said that God was like a father. The student said Tom had a lot of trouble with the concept because of his own father-son relationship.

The bottom line is like the chapter title says, if God is like a father, **some folks are hurting!**

Along these lines, I am reminded of the words of William Paul Young, author of *The Shack*. He spoke during the Fall Semester 2012 in Booth Auditorium, at the University of Pikeville, and told how the book was, in effect, symbolically relating a several year struggle he went through as he "tore his father's face off the face of God." His situation with his father involved more of a strict, un-accepting, cold relationship, but, still, that transferred over to how he felt about God.

Danger (A pretty bad guy)

I believe that when we are faced with grief, or other horrific circumstances, there is a danger that we may draw the conclusion that God is, all in all, a pretty bad guy. I know that during my most prolific "war/tinnitus-writing phase" about 13-15 years after returning from Vietnam, this theme appeared at times for me. Two poetry examples follow:

God? P/H

Our world seems such a strange game that he plays,
Especially if he really saw ahead
And knew so many of the helpless strays
Would feel their lives much better if born dead.

The Truth? P/H

Just what's the truth about it all?
The Good Book says, lots called,
But few are chosen. According to the world
As is today, the Good Book and its God
Might be correct.
A God of Love, who knew all this would happen,
Went right ahead and made man just the same.
Heaven and Hell, a way lopsided ratio?
Now you tell me, Is that a God of Love?
And so-called spokesmen for this God
Get off on tangents rather odd.
We love the sinner, just don't let him
Get too close. Can't stand him really,
You know how it is. Be good like us,
And stop all of your sinning,
Oh, Blessed God, who chose to save our souls,
We thank Thee we won't go to hell.
Oh, damn this nonsense that I hear!

Of course, time and perspective have changed some of my thinking. Some of the same questions remain.

As I reflect, I realize that the long-term God-images I received from my father's actions were those of being a responsible family man and hard worker who provided for his children. My hope and prayer for myself is that I have been able to convey to my sons similar God-images.

But, again, **for far too many**, the image is like the one related below, conveyed during a recent interview where the man talked about his son-father relationship.

Roger (not his real name)

"I wish my father was alive to see me now. I'm 31, show up at work every day, and do my job, quite well I might add, and I'm proud of what I do."

"My father would go to the bar every night with his friends, and if I was still up when he got home, I was usually in trouble. I was never quite sure for what. I'm not even sure if he knew, but that still didn't stop him from knocking me around. He died when I was 10, and at his funeral all I could think of was that he wouldn't be hitting me, or my mother, anymore."

"They don't know at work how much I drink. I'm afraid to go out drinking with anyone, because after time people would probably start to talk about me, and it could hurt me at my job, so I drink at home alone. I've already been married and divorced three times. My drinking was always the problem."

"There's a woman at work I'd like to get to know better, but I'm afraid to. I know she's not going with anyone because I heard a couple of the other women at work teasing her one day. She turned red and said she just wasn't ready to settle down yet. I wonder if she thinks maybe no one is interested in her because she's quite a bit overweight, but I think she's real pretty too. Lately I find myself thinking of her when I'm drinking, but I'm afraid to start a conversation with her. I'm afraid she won't want anything to do with me. I'm too afraid I'm like my father. I hope not, but I don't know."

"I try to pray, but I'm afraid that's not working too well for me. Thirty-one years old and I drink at least two to three 6-packs a night, alone, and I don't like who I'm becoming. I'm also afraid this could start to affect my work; I'm afraid I might start missing. Recently it's been harder to get up, and I did wake up late not too long ago. Fortunately I was able to get going quickly and managed to hit the traffic lights in a good sequence. But I'm afraid I may not always be that lucky."

The one thing that struck me a lot, when talking with "Roger," was how often he used the words "I'm afraid." I think his fear is part of what keeps him trapped. And, it seems to me, that his biggest problem is not seeking professional help. That may be another fear, I don't know. I do feel quite strongly that, like William Paul Young, unless he can get his father's face ripped away from God, it is going to be hard for him to lose his fears.

32

Self Sufficiency (I think that I can go it alone)

Overall, I believe that being self-sufficient is a good thing to strive for. It is a good place to be as it strengthens, and teaches us to become more self-reliant.

When Rocky, my youngest son, was two, the boys and I were visiting the Red River Gorge area in eastern Kentucky and were climbing a somewhat difficult trail that led up to Natural Bridge. There were a few times where it seemed to me that it was extremely challenging, especially for a two-year old, and so I started to pick Rocky up to carry him on my shoulders. Every time I did this, he would wiggle and squirm and say, "No, by myself!" And in such manner he made it to the top. As a parent I am grateful for this trait in him.

But there is a pitfall to avoid that I believe can "tag along" with self-sufficiency. It becomes easy to feel like we don't ever need anyone else, and perhaps forget how we got to where we are, and let an unhealthy pride develop.

In Deuteronomy 8: 11 – 14, Moses warned the Hebrews, "Be careful that you do not forget the Lord your God ... otherwise, when you eat and are satisfied, when you build fine houses and settle down, and when your herds and flocks grow large and your gold and silver increase and all you have is multiplied, then your heart will become proud and you will forget the Lord your God, who brought you out of the land of Egypt, out of the land of slavery."

There is no such thing as a perfect analogy, but let's go back to Rocky and the Natural Bridge Trail for a moment. Rocky may have made it to the top by himself, but he never would have had that opportunity if I hadn't given it to him in the first place.

Emotionally and spiritually this sense of self-sufficiency could lead to withdrawal from others, isolation, coldness, and loneliness.

It becomes a continual tight-rope, like most things in life, to find the equilibrium that keeps us on a balanced path.

Sad and Lonely

In a "shut-in interview speech" a student told how many in her family lived up a hollow, and two aunts were among them. One aunt was rather poor, lived in an older trailer, but always had people coming in and out. The other one had quite a bit of money, and pretty much stayed aloof from the rest of the family, and had lived with her husband atop the mountain, in a large house they had built. This was the aunt the student chose to visit.

The student related words from her aunt to this effect. "I'm glad you came by to see me. Ever since your uncle died three years ago it's been especially lonely. Your uncle made a lot of money in his business, and we built this nice house, and didn't mix with the rest of the family; thought we didn't need them, and, to be honest, thought we were a little better because of our money. Since he's died, now I spend most of my days looking out this large window over the hollow. I watch people going in and out of my sister's trailer all day long, and I realize, I have money, but she has family with her all the time, so she has everything; she's the rich one."

Self Sufficiency (P/H – revised 2013)

I have a little fault, you see, labeled self-sufficiency.
I think that I can handle all my problems,
Whether they be big or small.

I think that I can go alone, and let my heart be hard as stone.
And keep inside where no one else
Can see the things that bother me.

So, Lord, help me turn myself around; to take this self-sufficient sound,
And turn it to a sound that's real,
And be a person who can feel, and rely on you, and others.

For I cannot stand it, nor can I make it, all alone,
And I can no longer tolerate this hardened heart of stone.
I need to reach out to a friend, so cold and lonely is not my end.

Another reason for the autonomous attitude may be slightly different than the tone set forth in the preceding poem. That implies a sort of pride; "I can do it on my own" because I don't need you; and may be a sort of arrogance. But there are other reasons why people don't want to reach out to others.

I had someone comment to me once about the poem, "Self Sufficiency," saying that she related to it, because as a single mother of two going to school, she knew that she needed more support, but she felt too ashamed to ask for assistance.

Ashamed

And even though I need assistance,
Something inside keeps me from asking for
Help. I think it is because I am
Ashamed to let others see that I'm not quite
Making it on my own; this applies
Especially for those who have expressed
Doubts about my "educational venture" in the first place.

The value of a good counselor comes in many aspects, one of them being helping to provide us understanding of why we feel, or behave, the way we do. Sometimes it may stem from those earlier patterns established by erroneous beliefs we have about God, beliefs we have allowed others to convince us are true, or beliefs that came as a result of the inner injuries we received from someone or something else.

In the *Apocrypha*, 'The Book of Baruch', Chapter 3, verse 14, we read, "Learn where wisdom is, where understanding is, so that you may at the same time learn where length of days are, where there is light for the eye, and peace."

Sometimes it takes someone "outside the circle" to point out what some of the misconceptions we hold are.

33

Once Upon a Mind Ago, Sanity Appeared

For some reason (perhaps PTSD), during the early to mid-80's, some 13+ years after returning from Vietnam, I went through a couple year period where I wasn't sure if I was wrestling with insanity in supposedly a sane world, or, rather sanely questioning things about a world that was, or had been – during the war, insane. Many of my poems (some published in *Poetic Healing*) about tinnitus, wars, sanity, and questions about God and patriotism were written during that time. In retrospect, I was making some sense of some 'insane areas' as I worked with ordered things. I believe this can be true for all of us, whether it's an activity putting us in touch with some of Nature's beauty and cyclic occurrences, cake decorating, sports or other games with ordered rules, talking, writing, making model cars or airplanes, auto body or mechanic work, or – you name it.

In some of the "other wars" mentioned elsewhere, we have to find something to cling to that helps us fight what seems total irrationality with something that appears, at least on the surface, to have rationality attached; we want things to add up to some sort of sense. And, again, I believe an important part of the healing process is to become involved with, and occupy ourselves with, the "ordered things."

Once Upon A Mind Ago P/H

Once upon a mind ago
Sanity appeared
And tried to ask a question
About something it feared
Didn't make much sense.
It was rebuffed,
It's life snuffed out.
It never reappeared.

Once Upon A Mind Ago II

Once upon what was
Nearly a mind ago, perhaps
Centuries, it seemed life had
Easier answers. But Sanity

Unexpectedly appeared one day.
Perhaps he was looking for
Other things, like a
Nice warm place to stay.

Alas, he asked a question.

Maybe you can explain, he said,
It doesn't make sense, this situation,
Not really.
Does it to you?

And of course Sanity was rebuffed, then
Gone forever, it's life snuffed
Out. It never reappeared.

To Be Sane, or Not To Be? That Is the Question While Searching for Sanity.

Three Straws Less Than a Bale P/H

Three straws less than a bale,
Two limbs less than a tree.
Always just a little short,
'Specially on my sanity.

Three Straws Less

Three straws less than a bale,
Higher than I ought to be.
Right now just a little short,
Especially on my sanity,
Eventually it will all be gone.

Sometimes wonder if the
Tinnitus is
Really the culprit;
Are there other factors
Weighing into the whole
Situation.

Last thing I checked on it was time to
Eat a banana split, and I
Suddenly realized I was two
Strawberries short there, too.

Know I Had It Somewhere P/H

Don't know where I put it,
Don't know where it lays.
Know I had it somewhere
In my yesterdays.
Maybe if it's gone for good
I can be set free.
No more wasted wondering
Where I lost my sanity.

Weight Loss

Weighed myself on the scales and
Even there
It was confirmed I was losing
Ground.
Hate to admit it, but
Time is against me. If the
Losses continue
Over too much time I'll be weightless as my
Sanity is draining out first, and really
Slipping off the pounds.

Thoughts Run Wild

Sometimes my thoughts run wild
As I sit and smoke.
What is this insane living all about?
And is dying a big Divine Joke?
What seem to be random patterns
Often make no sense at all to me.
But the longer I sit and watch this waterfall
It seems my thoughts flow more calmly.

Waterfalls

Wild run my thoughts
As I sit
Thinking about
Every little
Random pattern and if they all
Fall into any form of sense
At all. But the
Longer I sit and
Look at the water, the greater my
Sense of serenity

In chapter fifty, "Peace Like a River, or, Maybe a Lake," there are more poems and thoughts about the role water seems to play for many who are wrestling with internal questions. For now, we'll just get back to the questions.

Games

Guess the shadows I see
Are playing games with
My sanity, however, I am
Eating and have no time for nervous breaks.
See, I have to finish my corn flakes.

As I said at the start of this chapter, the early to mid 80's may have been my "PTSD period." I don't know, but I do know the following poem is another one of my favorites for reasons I'll explain after it.

Cheese Upon A Winter Yard P/H

> Cheese upon a winter yard
> And rug the textbook through.
> Mind is like a granite slate
> Which lets the whistle through.
> Hold upon sanity
> Engraved on golden strands.
> Sleeper with the water choke,
> And smoke upon the sands.

I have one wish for the preceding poem; that somewhere, someday, an English teacher will be trying to explain it to a class, explaining how all the lines are loaded with imagery and symbolism. If the truth be known, there wasn't much at all going on that day; I just felt like writing nonsense.

Math

> Math is stable, or so I've heard,
> And, even if you burn your brains out,
> Two and two still equal four. But I
> Haven't seen it happen lately in life.

If I Could Fly Like a Turtle P/H

> If I could fly like a turtle
> Or swim like a ten pound rock,
> I'd balance on my pointed head,
> Flap my wings and take a walk.

If I Could Fly

> If I could
> Fly like a turtle,
>
> It would be exhilarating. Or, If I
>
> Could swim like a ten pound rock,
> Or balance things from my mind
> Upon my pointed head, on the
> Level side, of course,
> Don't you know I would
>
> Flap my wings,
> Look around to make sure
> You were watching, and then take a walk.

Often one can feel like options are disappearing. This may be a result of having questions about whether or not things make sense.

Opt Out

> Often feel like the options are
> Perhaps running out,
> Time getting shorter, choices narrower.
>
> Only know for sure the ringing hammers
> Until I concede it is
> Trying to press my sanity.

Running Out

> Running out of options
> Ugly choices are
> Narrowing down and
> Nearly gone.
> I'm noticing rooms are getting darker;
> No relief from the mocking
> Going on in my foggy mind.

> On some days it feels like the world closes in
> Until I realize it's only
> Trying to press my sanity.

Five Parts Short

Five parts short
Is not quite a full measure.
Very close, but, not
Enough.

Perhaps I can work on being free.
All I need to do is shake off these
Rusty three chains. So maybe I can find a
Treasure. Nope, I'm six
Steps away from that possibility.

So, just what is
Holding me back?
Or, should I ask the question,
Really, what is keeping me paralyzed? Do I expect
Too much from myself?

The following was written in the same time period as "Cheese Upon a Winter Yard," and, I actually think there might even be some symbolism and imagery within. I just haven't figured it out yet.

Can't Quite Fit ᴾ/ᴴ

Can't quite fit the maze together.
Can't quite peer through the storm.
Burning up in this hazy weather
That's so cold lately I just can't get warm.

Trees are pushing roots up through the attic.
Mushrooms in the cellar fried in corn.
Acorns mixed with egg taste quite emphatic.
And horses envy cows who have no horn.

Goosebumps are my birthright for no reason.
Shame I gather, tossing it away.
Never changing, as I switch each season.
Never moving, plodding through each day.

Writing poems that never quite get readings.
Bits of jumbled mind that make no sense.
Letters hungry for some decent feedings.
Hungry for an author not so dense.

Times might even get a little leaner.
Common sense might stay away on strike.
Dirty hands might get a little cleaner.
Rubbing against trees on a long hike.

Suffice it to say, if you are writing as a method of healing and release, and you find that your poetry is coming out as a bunch of nonsense, hey, might as well keep on writing. You don't know what phase in the healing process you might be involved in.

34

Some Folks Kill Themselves

I think the following poem, though sad, is one of my "most favorites" capturing the idea that there is truly a difference between breathing – and living.

Some Folks Kill Themselves [P/H]

Some folks kill themselves by hanging.
Some folks use a gun.
Others kill themselves by living,
Waiting 'til it's done.

Suicide [P/H]

Seems like there are those
Unable to peer
Into the future enough to see
Clearly and realize that
Into each life troubles come and
Depression falls and
Evening shadows lengthen.

Feeding Forward

The following poem came from when someone once told me that in her imagination she had once thought of running her car off a steep mountain side, but was be drawn up short by the questions she imagined her two girls would ask, questions like, "Why did mommy want to die?," "Did I do something that made mommy mad enough to do this?" She said thoughts of those questions woke her up to the fact that she had two beautiful daughters to live for, and that gave her hope for the future.

Why Did Mommy Have to Die?

My imagination took a trip one day as I wallowed in self-pity.
Thoughts were running through my head, dangerous ones,
Like, time to drive away, and run my car off a mountain.

Then I thought of two little girls asking, "Why did Mommy have to die?"
I stopped thinking of myself and my problems; cried a little,
And then focused on a reason for living, my girls.

Permanent Solutions to Temporary Problems

Permanent solutions to
Temporary problems.
Sometimes people reach
A point where they feel
There's no reason to go on;
The wounds are too deep,
The shame too overwhelming,
Or, the pain too much to bear.
Usually time brings new perspective,
But only if we are around to note it.
Please don't try permanent solutions
For temporary problems!

Humanakinata

To what extent does it really matter in the overall universal picture
If there is one less life around?

It seemingly has its effect on those connected with that person
For some period of time, but does it even make a ripple
In the eonic span?

Is there an unknown result to the question, showing its face
Only after it's too late to change (if one is dissatisfied with the answer)?

It is true. We are born to die, but if we focus our life on waiting for the "hammer to fall," we'll miss a lot of joy and living in between the two events. Samuel Beckett also claims that although we are born to die, what happens in between matters. Too many, like those in the first poem in this chapter, aren't making the most of the time between those two checkpoints.

Waiting II

Waiting for an unknown execution date.
Time drags here on death row.
So I was born; born to die.
It's this living by waiting in between
That's killing me.

Waiting III

Waiting here on death row (some call it life)
Aware that
I face an unknown date and
Time of execution.
I wonder why time drags on. Why
Not get it over with,
God, and let me meet my fate?

People who take their own lives often leave those left behind wondering, "Why?" Sometimes there are no notes, no indicators. The poem "Uncle Mike" is not from personal experience, but there are those who can identify with the situation.

When Uncle Mike Left Earth

It was one of the hardest days of my life;
Finding out that Uncle Mike had killed himself.
A loving family, good guy, so, why?
What's happening with someone on the inside
Doesn't always show.

Frank

Frank was a member of our small, fundamental, ultra-conservative church, married, with two kids a few years younger than me, a son and daughter. Seemed like a real nice guy, talked to me after church sometimes, always friendly.

I was seventeen when the evangelist came to our church for a series of revival services. He sure knew how to preach hell-fire and damnation, and one evening he had an altar-call, and when everyone but his wife and I were down front to the rail, I turned and started to leave. As I walked out the back door, I heard him ending the "call."

Frank wasn't in church that evening, but he was for some of the other services. I recall after the Sunday morning service, walking out toward where our car was parked, and going past Frank, sitting in his car. "Hey," I said, "How're you doing?"

"I don't know, Basil. I just don't know." He shook his head. Then he went on. "If this guy is right, I don't think any of us are going to make it. I just don't know." He just looked real sad.

It was a couple years later and I was in the military when I got a letter from my mother saying Frank had killed himself. My mind immediately went back to his earlier words. And the questions; Why? I just don't know. As mentioned in an earlier chapter, patterns of how we think about, and feel about, ourselves can run very deep.

Living in the now

Living in the now is important for many reasons.

I was told by someone that she thought a lot about the fact that she would someday die; that the more she thought about it the sadder she got about her life as she wondered what her children would do after she was gone. For whatever reasons, she was caught in a "strange worry loop," and could not appreciate what she had, while she had it. Many can't enjoy today because of a focus on tomorrow, and that may well be another negative cycle, or "strange loop" that one needs to get out of.

Schedule

So I think about what
Comes to all.
Have to die
Even if we
Don't want to. Now,
Usually I can stay busy with
Lingering pains, but even that will still
Eventually will give way to Mr. D.

35

Death; or Is That Rest?

When Mark Huglen and I were working out how to arrange poems for *Poetic Healing: A Vietnam Veteran's Journey from a Communication Perspective*, I became aware for the first time just how much of my poetry up to that point dealt with burning, and death. In that book, Mark theoretically delves into was going on inside me. I just knew I had to write and get thoughts down on paper.

Eight Hours or Forever P/H

Sleep I need you for awhile
Do me as is best
Eight hours or forever
Either way brings rest.

Time and death are interesting concepts. Outside our solar system, time as we know it is irrelevant, and death means this; life here is over, but, what does that really mean?

Living Life; Facing Death

My childhood is gone; how long ago depends on the age you say it left.
Was it when I became a teenager?
Or turned eighteen?
Or when at the age of nineteen, in Vietnam, in the Infantry, I observed
War casualties for the first time – and later contributed to the count?

No matter how you measure, in my case, it's been awhile.
And yet I love the question,
"How old would you be if you didn't know how old you were?"
If that's the criteria used to ponder the question,
Then sometimes – my childhood isn't gone.

But in the standard way of looking at things, my childhood's gone.
But I don't miss it, not really. Actually, it's still here,
Lurking in my memory, mostly bringing smiles from days gone by.
Funny how time seems to take the edges off the "bad" times,
Gives perspective.

Do I want to go back? No. I wouldn't change anything,
Because it all has brought me to where I am today,
And, for the most part, in most areas, that means smarter, wiser,
A more mature perspective that has learned,
Often the hard way, the difference between fun and foolishness.

Most of my scars, seen and hidden, come from the latter.
But if we learn from experience, then I'm a learned man,
And, wondering, more frequently these days,
About the phases past
And phases yet to come.

I truly believe that one of those phases will involve
A major transition, passage from the flesh I'm familiar with
To something else, quite different, where I believe I'll say,
"Do I want to go back? No. I wouldn't change anything,
Because it has all brought me to where I am today."

And echoes from some distant past will say,
A segment of my life is gone; how long ago depends on when you say it left.
Was it when I "died" on earth? Left that phase?
Or does the question still apply,
"How old would you be if you didn't know how old you were?"

This Frame of Mind P/H

Just what the hell put me
Into this frame of mind.
Guess I'll have to roll
Back the years of time.
That damned war left its mark
And somehow stayed with me.
Now I fight this frame of mind
And hope to soon be free.

The Bottom Line P/H

When it comes right down
To the bottom line,
The old man straightened and said, "The harsh reality that dictates,
Is someday we'll all be dead."

The Bottom Line II

The bottom line,
He said, that
Everyone has to

Be aware
Of, is
That no matter how we
Try to avoid, or
Otherwise get out of it,
Mr. Death

Lives, and lingers
In the shadows. He's
Not going
Easy into night.

The Dog Dug Deep ^{P/H}

The dog dug deep to bury his bone.
He thought he smelled some more.
The years had shifted sands, so soon
He scratched a coffin door.
The wood was rotten, he fell on through
With little choice but to linger.
Rover soon found himself quite content
Gnawing on my ex-finger.

I don't know why, but I've always liked the imagery in the preceding poem. Maybe the fact I plan on being cremated enters into the equation. Sorry, Rover.

I'll Finally Relax

I' wonder sometimes how
Long I must run, how many
Lengthy miles before I am

Finally set free.
I only know that the memories
Never stop; they keep coming
After me. Just how
Long before this stops? How
Long before I can rest?
Years? Months? Each breath

Reminds me of the past.
Even though I have tried, I seem to have
Left something undone.
And so I may never relax
X-cept when caught by sweet death.

Noise Screaming Like a Banshee 4/2/11

> Noise screaming like a banshee,
> Slapping pain into my mind.
> Depression falling like a fog.
> The only thing I know to do,
> Is do, something, anything to
> Keep me occupied and
> Functioning as I plod onwards
> To the day when its existence,
> The noise's, will cease.
> Perhaps at last, sweet rest.

Let Us Go

> Let's take a closer look at
> Exactly what it is in mortal bodies
> That seems to hold us so.
>
> Usually people want to be free from trouble,
> So why can't we soar like the birds,
>
> Go winging it through the air, telling that
> Old earthen clay to just let us go?

Grass Will Go

> The blades of grass are waving at me, trying to get my attention.
> All they want to do is say, "Hi."
> Just like the rest of us, they only
> Want to be recognized before it is their time to die.
> I guess in them we see a microcosm of our own lives.
>
> Grass comes and goes, and has limitations
> On how high it can grow; we say the sky's the limit.
> But grass "really wants" to be noticed for what
> It is before it fades and dies away.
> In this regard, I guess it's just like you and me.

The Squeeze P/H

When they put me in this coffin,
They didn't leave much room to move.
Elbows tight against my side,
I'm sure locked into a groove.
Hoped that I would go to heaven,
Feared that I would go to hell,
But I'm squeezed instead in limbo,
Trapped with this decaying smell.
Can't believe my spirit left me,
Left this old clay far behind.
I can't walk. I can't run.
(I can't even change my mind.)

There were two occasions in Vietnam when I thought I was dead, with only seconds, if that, to live. One was when the explosion occurred on April 26, 1969. I distinctly recall thinking, This is it, Mom's going to get a notice I'm dead. That was all, until I started thinking about the dead body that I had "just helped make" (see poem, Questions, Chapter Four.)

The other time was on July 18th, 1969, when during a process of Medevac, Vietcong hiding in tree lines shot and killed the pilot of the helicopter. The co-pilot took over, but not before the helicopter which was hovering some 25-30 feet overhead started to "rock and roll" from side to side. Those of us directly beneath thought we were goners. Obviously, we weren't.

I think about those two times occasionally, and ask myself, why am I not even more aware that every moment is a gift? Shouldn't I be doing even more productive things with my life than I (hopefully) am now? I guess it is easy to get lulled right back into the old thinking that we will be around in this life forever. Well, we may actually be around forever, but we know that in this particular stage of whatever we are in, while we are getting to wherever we are going to for the next round, life as we know it will end. So, yes, Lord, help me to recognize even more that every day is a special gift from you, and help me not to "fritter" it away; and especially help me to recognize that just "goofing off" with a loved one is NOT frittering time away.

Each Day, a Gift

Every moment of each new day
And every breath I take should help me
Cherish life, and realize, that as far as I know, it's all I
Have. You'd think I'd know that by now.

Death has stared me straight in the face
And let me understand he could come any minute, any
Year. So why do I have to keep re-learning this

Again and again. Oh, yeah, I

Guess it's because I'm human, or maybe
It's just that I'm a little slow. Either way, I
Find my prayer (as I get older – I wonder why)
To be, Help me, Lord, to realize each day is your gift.

Bigger Picture

Blasts and explosions entered
Into my existence,
Gutting me to the core,
Giving me new direction.
Expecting to die; I didn't.
Reserved for another day.

Perhaps someday
I will understand –
Comprehend just what
The bigger picture is.
Until then I'll be
Really thankful for
Every day.

Perhaps I can summarize my thoughts on death with a poem I originally planned to include in the chapter on "Paradoxes." However, after some thought, I believe it is better suited here.

A few days after the taking of some twenty aspirin (October 1979), as mentioned in chapter two, I was going from where I lived in Breathitt County, to Lexington, KY. As I was walking out of the house I looked over the Eastern Kentucky hills bathed in Fall colors, and the following lines came to me, "The rolling hills lie ravished in their robes of rusty red, And softly slithering leaves invite all wanderers to their bed."

At the time I lived on the campus of Oakdale Christian High School, and I stopped for a moment in the office. While at the counter, I asked for a pen and paper, told the school secretary the above two lines, and said that I was going to write a poem. Before I left the office to get in the car, I had penned the first stanza. In an English Literature class I was taking at the time we had just finished reading some of John Milton's works, and I recalled he talked of his Muse helping him. A couple minutes later as I turned left to take War Creek Road over to KY 15, I said out loud, "May John Milton's Muse help me with this poem." (I don't know if that actually happened or not but ...)

The second stanza came to me shortly after I said that and I pulled off to the side of the narrow, curvy road to record it. I drove on, and about a half hour later on the Mountain Parkway, I jotted down the rest, copying them over as soon as I got to Lexington as my scribbling was almost unreadable (at 70 mph you can't really look at what you are writing.) So, regardless of what all did or didn't transpire in the writing of the following poem, it is the one I want to close this chapter with.

Puzzling Paradoxes P/H (October 1979)

The rolling hills lie ravished in their robes of rusty red,
And softly slithering leaves invite all wanderers to their bed.
The wind softly whispers, then arms gently sway,
And seem to beckon me to come to a new world, far away.

I climb these rusty, rolling hills and feel within me rise
A newer, freer spirit, somehow closer to the skies.
The burdens of the day grow light, I know that God above,
Upon these reddened rises, showers shadows of his love.

For is not beauty here because some leaves go to their grave?
And is this not like Jesus, God's Son who came to save?
And how can death give way to life? It seems a battle won.
Perhaps these trees give insight to the Resurrected One.

In mind I climb another hill; its sides are bathed in red.
Upon its crown a mangled man is hanging, grotesque, dead.
Yet all my hopes are bound in him, that as in his third day,
I live to die, but die to live in a new world, far away.

So fear not when the autumn comes; O Death, where is your sting?
Because of rolling, reddened hills my heart within does sing.
No longer feared, Death drops his head and slowly slips away,
His biting poison neutralized in the light of that new day.

36
Feelings of Loneliness and/or Rejection

John Powell, in his book *Why Am I Afraid to Tell You Who I Am?* says that we are afraid to tell someone who (we often erroneously think) we really are because, if that person rejects who we are, what else do we have to offer? I think he is on to something, and because of this fact, we wrestle alone with many subjective areas. We could paraphrase what Powell said something to the effect of, "If I tell you what's bothering me, or what's running through my mind right now, I'm afraid you'll start running the other way, and then where am I?"

The following poems may be extended to touch many areas; abuse, illness, injuries, and the like. Some things we can look back and see how we got to where we are in feeling a certain way; some things are a part of the whole "Life happens arena."

Lonely Inside

Hiding behind the ever-ready smile
And bubbly personality,
Telling everyone, "It's okay,
I'm fine." But also keeping them

At enough of a distance so
They can't peer over the
Wall and catch a glimpse of the
Lonely inside.

My Damnable Fate P/H

Storms brewing in my head,
Raising tensions higher.
Paralyzed emotions
Stifling desire.
Pushing me to strike out
At those who can't relate.
And, therefore, gaps are widened.
My lonely curse, this damnable fate.

It seems like some of us have been loners since as far back as we can recall. I know I spent a lot of time as a child playing alone, walking through the woods near the house, dreaming of creating my own little village – even country, one time, or, climbing as high as I could go without the branches breaking in the "chokecherry" tree near the house, dreaming I was a sailor up in the ship's crow's nest. And I was overall content in my little world. Now, I can't tell you how much of that behavior was part of my "DNA-scripted" personality and how much came from the circumstances I was born into.

I do know, have known from early years that my mother was very depressed when carrying me in the womb, and at one point, was getting ready to take an aspirin overdose when one of her sisters called "just to tell her she loved her." That call changed Mom's life, and soon after she had a dramatic, possibly even fanatic, conversion. My understanding from psychology courses I had in college leads me to believe that the baby in the womb can still pick up on depression and rejection, therefore, possibly setting the stage for a "loner lifestyle."

I don't think there is much value in trying to over-analyze the past, or even to somehow correct it, the past is just that, the past. We should try to understand how it might have affected us, and realize the future is ours to move into and conquer.

Past II

Perhaps we shouldn't try to over-analyze,
And try to make the past be what it wasn't. Instead, maybe we
Should thank God for everything that has brought us
To where we are, and "trek on" from here.

Lonely Place

Let's be clear. There's
Only one place
No one else can
Enter; one place to
Live all by
Yourself.

Perhaps it is
Lonely there. Not
A problem. Elsewhere they
Can find (and maybe even bother) you. So I'll
Escape to the safeness of my mind.

Lonely Bit

Looks like the
Only place to resist this
Never-ending loneliness
Eventually winds up in my mind.
Lengthy battles ahead, some
Yet unknown.

Battles that must remain
Inside as I prepare for
The lonely bit ahead.

All Have

All have their problems and
Loads of things that
Linger in minds and

Hearts. Seems like no one cares
And loneliness is the
Very best they can muster as they wonder if they
Ever can communicate how they feel.

This Lonely Bout P/H

Tears seem poised near the surface
Wanting to spill out.
But tears can't wash this noise away
Or help me in this lonely bout
I'm fighting.

How Much Should One?

How much should
One keep locked inside?
Where does one draw the line?

Maybe he does know that
Unless he
Communicates it will just get
Harder.

Still, even knowing that internal
Heartaches are bubbling
Over, he
Usually believes the
Lie that absolutely no one gives a
Damn. If

Only he could start
New patterns and
Eventually change directions.

Why Not Stay Here?

Why shouldn't I stay here,
Inside these lonely walls,
Sheltered from the storms of hurtfulness,
And the winds of criticism?

I may be alone here,
But at least I know the territory.
I've walked these grounds many times,
And know where all the traps are.

So leave me to my little "It's all right" smile,
And my quiet, withdrawn ways. There's a
Certain safeness accompanying the loneliness,
So, again, why shouldn't I stay here?

Just lying here, wondering if I dare break out of the lonely shell and see if survival is possible. I'm following through my mind, the twisted, rocky pathway that leads to my current place in life. It seems, like the Israelites in the desert, I've circled this mountain before. Two comforts (I guess): I'm not the first to travel this road, and there is a Promised Land ahead.

37

If Guilt and Fear Are So Useless, Why Do I Keep Them Around?

Guilt is included in this section as I think one of the things some of us war veterans wrestle, or have wrestled, with is the question of why we are here while our fallen comrades aren't. This especially is driven home for me every time I pay homage on Veterans Day as I realize that although many of us feel like we gave our best efforts, and made sacrifices, we are also aware that we didn't give our all, or in the words of President Abraham Lincoln, our "last full measure of devotion."

So, why is there guilt? We served our country well, did our part. And so did Rodney Evans, and Brian Morrow, and Larry Parr, and – _____ you fill in the names – but they came home in a flag-draped coffin 40 years, or 5 years, or 5 months ago, and we're still here. Why?

In my case I can say … I am glad it wasn't me in the coffin, but, still, why … wasn't … it me? And I believe there comes a point where we have to submit this, and all the other questions we have, to a Power that is larger and greater than us, and find, and take, our place.

Another factor that I believe also enters into inside wrestling matches is, an awareness that it is not all, nor should it be, "all about me." We don't want to keep focus on "me and my problems" – therefore, we keep them inside.

The Simon Peter in all of us

Three of the four Gospels present Simon Peter's betrayal of Jesus. In Luke's version, Chapter 22, verses 61 and 62 we read, "The Lord turned and

looked straight at Peter. Then Peter remembered the word the Lord had spoken to him, 'Before the rooster crows today, you will disown me three times.' And he went outside and wept bitterly."

Some may criticize Peter, but all in all, how human he was. How often have we found ourselves in the same position, aware that we have failed again, maybe repeated a negative pattern, exhibited unkind traits toward others, or just fallen way short of some important goals set for ourselves?

But we also know that later Peter found peace in God's vast acceptance, forgiveness, and peace.

As I Struggle

As I struggle through the long night trying to see another dawn,
Help me hold on, Lord, not give up as I wrestle once again
With this earthen clay. I've let others, and myself, down, once again.
Please help me hold on long enough to see the sun rise.

I Wrassled Victor the Bear, and Won
(Did it in 1983; wrote this in 1988)

"Think I could do that?" I asked as I looked down at my two sons, ages eight and ten.

"Yeah!" both Ralph and Rocky replied excitedly. Their responses let me know I had just backed myself into a corner.

We were watching a sideshow attraction at the Lexington (KY) Bluegrass Fair where men could sign up to get into the ring and wrestle with Victor, a "wrassling" bear who was trained to respond to over thirty voice commands. Since I had never wrestled anything but my older brother, and had always lost those bouts, I was really becoming quite aware of a knot beginning to form in my stomach as I realized I may have really "blown it" by asking my sons the question.

"Are you going to do it, Daddy?" Rocky tugged at my hand and looked up at me with wide hazel eyes.

"Well," I hesitated, "sure, why not?"

I moved to the desk where I not only signed up to wrestle, but also to sign the Release of Liability form. That in itself should have sent me a message, but it didn't, and a few minutes later I found myself waiting outside the ring with nervous tension mounting. It wasn't helped by the fact that the man in the ring before me outweighed me by probably some fifty pounds, and Victor had just "whupped" him soundly.

"Ladies and gentlemen," the bear's trainer spoke into the microphone to announce my entrance. "Another challenger to Victor the Wrassling Bear!" He laughed as he continued, "Some folks never learn, do they?"

I weakly laughed with the crowd, and then warily started moving my 180 pound, 5' 8" body toward Victor's 650 pound, 9' 6" grizzly bear frame.

I put my arms slowly forward and Victor countered with his front legs and paws. We linked up and moved around facing and eyeing each other. After what seemed awhile, but I'm sure was just a few seconds, the trainer said something to the effect of, "Take it easy, Victor." and I immediately found myself on my back staring up at Victor from the canvas floor, having second thoughts.

Victor had his head on my upper left arm and was trying to bite. Fortunately the muzzle he was wearing prevented him from doing so (and I was black and blue in that area for only about a week.) But the partial weight of the grizzly started to give me some kind of bear phobia * and I desperately struggled to get free, to no avail.

"I give up! Get him off me!" I hollered.

"Come on, Victor. Behave yourself," said the trainer, and Victor obediently backed away, allowing me to get up.

I grinned in relief and climbed out of the ring to the applause of the audience and the "worship-full" eyes of my two sons. Their daddy had wrassled a bear!

I've thought about that incident many times since then, and actually, the memory has helped me through some rough spots. Two of us faced each other in the ring that day. To Victor (if he could think) I was just another foolish human (idiot?) climbing into the ring with him; just another ordinary encounter like he faced several times a day. But for me, it was an entirely different story. I had faced off with a real, live grizzly.

But maybe the story for me wasn't so different. I feel like I face a bear every day as I awaken to the sound of a ringing in my ears; tinnitus, from nerve damage caused by an explosion in Vietnam. As of this writing there is no real cure for it, and I know I must listen to it during all my waking hours; it even awakens me at night sometimes and it is hard to get back to sleep, and there are times when I feel like I just can't take it anymore.

But I take hope in my recollections of Victor. That day I faced a 650 pound bear, knowing I would lose, knowing there weren't any odds in my favor, knowing it was an insurmountable challenge. But I didn't back away.

I left that ring with a new confidence in myself, and more self-assurance about the unknowns in my future, even the continual ringing.

I wrassled Victor the Bear – and won!

A bear on the back porch. Photo by Ralph Clark

*The phobia in the ring turned to fascination. I love bears. I've hiked in "bear territory" a few times and always kept my camera packed in a quickly available spot. I really envy one of my sons getting this picture of a bear coming onto his back porch.

Fear flees from reason

We hear the expression "irrational fears." I'm not sure if that means there are rational fears, or what. Perhaps a "rational fear" is not so much fear as just good common sense, like, I'm afraid if I put my hand on that hot stove I will get burned. Well, yeah.

This idea is addressed in the *Apocrypha* in the 'Wisdom of Solomon', Chapter 17, verse 12, where it says, "For fear is nothing but giving up the reinforcements that come from reason."

So perhaps some of the questions we wrestle with should be approached as Victors, insurmountable challenges that we don't back away from, but, reinforced by reason, take them on, then leave them in the ring.

My Place P/H

Sometimes when I write
It's for an audience of one
As I try to tell myself
That no battle's ever won (until it's over.)

So I can't say I'm defeated
And I can't give into strife,
For there's still some unknown time left
To struggle in this life (and I like to fight.)

For it seems I am a human and we all were given spark
To keep struggling 'gainst the odds,
To keep searching in the dark
For rays of light (no matter how small.)

Seems the hardest part of battle
Is before the breakthroughs come,
And we want to give up
For all senses seem to numb (and slow their pace.)

But back off darkness, look out odds.
I'm too proud and dumb to quit.
Somewhere in the universe
I will find my spot to fit (and take my place.)

38
What Does It Mean? (If Anything)

What Ship Carries Us?

What ship carries us across the rugged way?
It bumps against the molehills and the sticks
That seem to crop up day by day,
As flying through the universe it picks
A path for us, to see us somewhere.
Umm; is that really true?

Just because we may have a firm belief that there is a larger picture, and things are working together in some way for our good, doesn't take away from the fact that there are times where we may ask questions about the meaning of it all. This may be especially true during those circumstances where our worlds have been turned upside down. A fairly common phrase we used in the Infantry in Vietnam was "don't mean nuthin'."

Don't Mean Nuthin'

Days tumble into days
Over and over again,
N'ever slowing down enough
To let us find out what the

Message is they're bringing.
Evaluating them can be depressing,
And if you are dealing with war,
Nothing really adds up.

Nor do some of the other non-
Understandable events
That occur along life's
Highway. So in summing it all up,
I'll borrow a favorite phrase from the
Nam; "Don't mean nothin'."

Actually, some forty years later, if something is not going the way I planned or hoped, I still find myself shrugging and saying, "Don't mean nuthin'."

Just Lying Here 5/17/09

Just lying here, recently awakened, and wondering about
The purpose of life and why and where we find ourselves
After we arrive there one choice at a time,
Sometimes, so deliberately, so consciously.

Is there a place of belonging?
Don't know why, but sometimes
Feel the overwhelming
Urge to run back to loneliness.

Hiding behind those shells
And self-built walls,
What's so attractive about it?
Freedom from responsibility?

But in the long run
Wondering – Why? Who? Where?
What? When? And,
Does any of it matter?

I guess the above poem shows that for all of us who wrestle, or have wrestled, with something traumatic, there will never be a complete ending to the questions. That's okay. I personally believe that the answer to the last question of the poem, "Does any of it matter?" is, "Yes!" It may take a while and a lot of questioning moments to arrive at that conclusion, but, for me, the alternative is inconceivable.

There is a parable from Matthew in the New Testament about seeds being choked by worries and cares of this life. It does seem to ring true that sometimes we get so caught up in the everyday things involved in making a living we forget to live, but more importantly, sometimes fail to remember, or realize, that we are put here for a purpose.

The Circumstance P/H

The old man looked at God and said,
I only wish that I weren't dead
Before I fulfilled a lifelong goal
To become someone who gave his soul
To writing.

But you put me into such a rough life
Where circumstances cut like a knife
And I never could find the chance to write
As I struggled and looked for a little light
In my miserable existence.

God grinned at him and said, Don't you see
That a true writer can be set free
From the problems of life with a flick of the pen
So I gave you a chance, but saw then
That you wouldn't take it.

In a former life you wanted to write
So I put you in circumstances that would
Ignite a flame of an author, if it was
Within, but you wasted your chance
The deepest sin you could ever commit
Against me--or yourself.

(Okay, Mom, so you don't go along with the reincarnation idea. Maybe not, but I seem ... to ... remember ... you ... from somewhere....)

"If we're here to help others ..."

I remember reading on a t-shirt, "If we're here to help others; what are the others here for?"

Not long after, I jokingly referred that question to a pastor friend. He rather indignantly rejected what he called "a flippant attitude" on my part. I specifically recall thinking (but not saying), Hey, man, lighten up. Where's your sense of humor?

Actually, I do believe there is an answer to the t-shirt question. We are here to help others get to the place where they can help others. I listen to the Dave Ramsey Show sometimes, when it and my driving coincide, and, I think he is a good example of helping others get to where they can help others.

Joanne (not her real name)

"I often have questions when it comes to thinking about life in general. Often, in this life we're dealt a hand of cards that we just don't know how to play. We're so frequently left with more questions than answers and sometimes we get so frustrated with our obstacles that we just ask God, 'WHY?' This is certainly true in my life; there have been so many times that I've just broken down and cried over certain things and I still continue to search for the answer of 'Why?' "

I Stand Against P/H

I stand against a universe
That doesn't seem to care,
And vow to fight with all my might
To show that I can persevere against
Whatever trials come my way,
Whatever pain hits me,
And smile at little cracks of sun
Until the day I'm free.

Does the universe we see care about us?

Probably the most common place for people to ask questions about the "whys and wherefores" of life is out under the stars, especially with a full moon out. Questions may even be asked of the moon, like, "Do you care what's going on?" We know she can't reply, but somehow, we still wonder. The answer to this question follows.

She Doesn't Give a Damn [P/H]

Looking through my telescope
Wondering if there's any hope.
Moon looks down so silently,
She pretends she doesn't see
And doesn't give a damn.

She Doesn't Give a Damn II

Silently looking down from the
Heavens
Every night, she

Doesn't give a damn.
Oh, you may say,
Ever so wrong;
She cares (what about the songs?)
No she doesn't. She can't
Talk, and doesn't want to.

Give me a telescope and
I will examine the moon
Very closely for any
Evidence of hope.

A close scrutiny will

Doubtless reveal none.
And to make it worse, the
Moon will pretend she does
Not even see us.

In *Discovery On the Katmandu Trail*, Marc Mailloux states that as a young person, he moved into the time period where he started to ask questions about the meaning of his life while looking up at the stars; he said that gazing at them, one has to ask these questions.

I am in total agreement with him on the "star statement." When I was seventeen, I often slipped out of the house around midnight and would go walking, and smoking. At the time, we lived on Grove Street, in Clinton, Massachusetts, so I would go down Grove Street toward the Wachusett Dam, pick up River Street around the fountain at the base of the dam, and at the end of River, connect to Nashua Street, back to Grove, and back to the house. I usually stretched this into an at least forty-five minute, several ciga-rette*, walk. It would not have taken near that length of time, except I walked slowly, and spent a lot of time looking upwards at the stars, wondering about the aforementioned questions of meaning.

I spent fourteen months in Vietnam in the Infantry, and except during monsoon season, drifted off to sleep looking at the Southern Cross and other constellations. There, more than ever, the questions persisted. Because of be-ing in the Infantry, and seeing what seemed to be on some occasions, needless deaths, I guess I wondered even more, and adopted an attitude of, "ain't going to live to be twenty-five anyway, so what does it matter." It actually took a while to get over that, but after twenty-five came and went, it became easier. However, the "what does it matter" questions persisted.

Later, especially during spring 1985, I often left the house to smoke* in the driveway, and look upwards, trying to determine if there was any meaning to anything. Looking back, I was probably in the middle of some level of post-traumatic stress disorder. But at the time, I just felt compelled to go outside and ask the questions.

*After twenty-five years of smoking, I quit in 1989; it may have helped my breathing; the questions lingered.

Star Gazing; Just Asking Questions

Just wondering sometimes as I walk along under the stars,
What am I doing here? Oh, I know I chose this particular road to walk on,
But, what am I doing here, as in, on earth?
Yeah, so my parents got together one night and made a baby,
But that still doesn't answer the fundamental question,
What am I doing here?

Even switched hemispheres for a while, decided to take
A vacation(?) in exotic Vietnam, backpacked it for a year or so,
Wandered wherever I wanted to, as long it fit the orders for the day;
Saw some beautiful sights in the jungle, horrible ones, too,
And occasionally an interesting animal, or snake, and still, the question,
What am I doing here?

My tour in Vietnam was ended early by a log flying through the air,
Catapulted by an explosion in a bunker, deciding that my face
Was a good place to come to a halt, breaking my lower jaw, crushing
Sinuses, and puncturing an eardrum. I saw stars again, and then felt pain.
So all that led to stays in three different hospitals, and along with me,
Came the question, what am I doing here?

Fifteen years after the afore-mentioned Vietnam-vacation (?),
It seemed (maybe that's not a strong enough word), that the
Noises were getting louder. Not just the ringing ones in my ears;
They had become a given, but the Noises from the questions.
More of them since I had also become a creator-in-part of two boys,
Done before I knew the answer to the question, what am I doing here?

Of course, with regards to my sons, I can only say, with the poorest grammar I can muster up, "I done a good thing!" Actually, I can't quite wrap my head around what life would have been like without Ralph and Rocky, and then, their wives and the children out of those unions. We have had so many good times together, and I like to think they mean something.

Angry at myself, God, anyone

I have related to a few people about the time when I was twenty, recently returned from the Infantry in Vietnam, and driving down a road in my 1964 fire-engine red, GTO convertible. I was disillusioned, frustrated, feeling worthless, and angry with God, for starters. The following two poems, "Self-Pity Serenade" and "This Game of Life," were written a day or two prior to this "GTO incident."

Self-Pity Serenade P/H (1970)

Things go good for a while.
Folks are friendly; give a smile.
The inevitable must always be,
It's like a hex that follows me.
We kind of like you, but we think
That your habits kind of stink.
So I'll move on, wandering, lonely.
Damn this plague that curses me.

This Game of Life P/H (1970)

This game of life is such a tedious thing?
Put out what's wanted, but who really cares?
A few folks amazed at achievements that I've had,
But most just give the good old animal treatment.
Who gives a damn about this flea-filled dog?

As I said, I was driving in my car, top down, and I vividly recall looking up at the sky as I was flying down a rural two-lane road, and throwing up my middle finger and hollering out loud, "F*%# you, God!" I thought I was telling him off, but good, with all the rejection I could muster. I now honestly believe that somewhere he was looking down laughing, or at least with a smile on his face, saying something to the effect of, "Well, it's about time; you're finally getting angry at all the false concepts you have been taught about me. Now you can start learning about who I really am."

I think we live at times in our own little worlds of false concepts, otherwise known as an "unreal reality," and I also contend that the realm of fantasies could also be labeled the realm of "reality vs. the ideal," or, maybe, just "reality vs. unreality."

Something that happens during times of war, other separations, and/or other traumatic situations is there may be an ideal built up in the mind that actually helps in survival, or at least, making it through a certain situation or time period of our lives that may not be the most pleasant. In fact, for prisoners of war, combat personnel, victims of abuse, and other situations, this "ideal creation" may be the only thing that keeps us holding on.

In combat it could go like this. I'm over here serving and fighting for my country, and back home, my spouse, my children, they are so wonderful – or, he, or she, is off in service for the country, who could ask for anyone better. And we, or they, come home … and … sometimes people change a lot in a year; that's not bad, it is called reality. So we have this conflict in our minds; the perfect person we created that lives there, and the very real person that we live with. So we can either accept that growth involves change; or fight to make the other person try to fit our ideal image (and that probably isn't going to happen.) If we hold on to the ideal and reject the reality, we can really find ourselves in a lonely place (but, of course, at least we have our fantasy.)

Fantasies

Fantastic, we say, Look
At that house. Isn't she
Nearly perfect? Look at
Those large pillars in the front, standing
As if they were holding invitations to enter.
Shuttered windows are adding to the lovely.
Inside of her walls, laughter is no stranger.
Even heaven can be seen reflected there.
So, why does she have to burn for reality to enter?

Bodies [P/H]

Bodies come and bodies go.
Don't it make you wonder though,
What the people in them mean.
Is it more than just a race?
Is there meaning in the pace?
My thoughts take philosophical trips
When I eat potato chips.

Journals, diaries, and other types of notebooks are filled with expressions by authors who feel the need to just "get it out" and down on paper, or more recently, an electronic equivalent. Much of this activity is a form of self-therapy, but the question, "Does it really matter what I think?" still can enter in. We may wonder if, not only what we do, but, also, what we don't do, really counts for anything. I happen to believe that someday we will see how it all fits into the big picture.

Writing [P/H]

S'long as they're unwritten,
Lots of thoughts are dead.
But ingredients for their lives
Are paper topped with lead.
Wonder what the difference
At my trumpet call
If I never wrote a line,
Or had a thought at all.

How often have we gone past someone in a car sitting in a ditch or involved in some other kind of accident, and thought, I'll bet that wasn't on their list of things to do today. Or, even at the end of one of our days, perhaps numbly thinking back over the events of the day, still reeling from shock from a phone call, or other traumatic incident, we ask, why? How did this happen?

Sifting Through Ashes

Haze-filled minds trying to sort through shadows of days past,
Hoping to find some gold in the ashes.
It started out like any other day, and then the phone call,
And now life will never be the same, although they're
Sorting through the ashes looking for the memories,
And maybe something that will make sense;
Some kind of reason for any of this.

I did it, but, did it mean anything?

I am willing "to bet the farm" that in the big picture we will find out that there have been a lot of beneficial actions committed by those with good hearts that were bogged down with habits and ruts, and other forms of internal woundings, who maybe lived a lot of their lives wondering what any of it meant. The idea for the following short story could also go in the chapter about things that seem minor to the one who does them, but major to someone else.

'The Town Drunk' is a story I had printed in 2001 in a Quality Paperback Book Club compilation of *The World's Best Shortest Stories*. Criteria for the stories included a fifty-five word limit.

The Town Drunk (2001)

Tom squinted through his drunken haze at someone flailing in the river.

Joe felt someone pull him out, but was choking badly. When he could look up, his rescuer was gone.

Two weeks later, obituaries carried news of Tom's death.

"What a shame," Joe told his wife, "to have lived a life so utterly useless."

My thoughts on the preceding:

Actually, the idea for this story came from a time when my dad was driving home from work and went through a flooded area and drove the car into a ditch where it started to sink. He couldn't open the driver's door, and decided to try and get out the hatchback door. It only opened from the outside, and, to this day, Dad still doesn't know how it got opened. He thinks someone may have seen the car going down in the water, and opened it for him, but when he got out, he didn't see anyone.

Of course, my "overactive writer's imagination" kicked into gear, and I wrote an initially longer, short story about a drunk rescuing someone from drowning, and taking off because, in his befuddled mind, he was afraid that somehow he would be blamed for the person starting to drown in the first place.

Long Lines of People [P/H]

Long lines of people
Through this life do pass.
Some seem to help,
Others play the horse's ass.
Some sit and watch,
Others up and do.
All the rest are wondering
What the hell they're going through.

Sometimes we like to start lists of all the "important" things we need to work on. Then we may ask ourselves if our list really matters.

Lists

Lying here thinking of all the
Items and things I will
Start as soon as I finish
This list. But, sometimes,
So much listing-making makes me tired.

Fires Within

Fires within, covered with sheets of
Ice. Layers of cold followed by
Really hot. I know
Eventually some sort of
Sense may come out of all this.

Wishful thinking?
I hope not.
The struggles in my mind and
Heart go on, and some days
I'd rather
Not try and figure it all out.

Oops

So, there are times when we feel like we have no clue,
Yet for some reason we strongly desire to see things through,
And so we learn in these times the value of patience and perseverance.
If in the middle of the above we start to get impatient, and start to take
Things out on others, then we alienate our brothers, and sisters
And may even shave years off of our own lives.
So, I'm wondering if five minutes after it is all said and done,
And the next phase of life, or death, I have won, will I hear
"Well done," or, "Didn't matter anyway," or, perhaps,
"Oops, Mr. Clark, I see you have to go back and do it all over again."

39

"What's Going On, Lord?"
(The Not-So-Good Stuff)

While discussing the Sandy Hook Elementary School nightmare (December 14, 2012 – 26 people killed, 20 of them young children), I told my wife, Cora, that for the parents, families, and friends that this was, in my opinion, worse than military war. We go into combat expecting that there will be appalling situations. We are not expecting young innocents to be gunned down. It is almost beyond comprehension, what those parents went, and are, going through; the anger, questioning, not understanding why, etc. And, naturally, the media focus on events like this is going to be huge.

And, yet, we must also be aware of the fact that there are parents faced with these same questions everyday with children who die in accidents, stricken with cancer, violent deaths, and so forth. Now, the national media generally overlooks these individual situations, but the pain, wounding, and sorrow is no less for these individuals facing a "small scale tragedy/traumatic event" than the more publicized ones.

Paradoxically, there may, in fact, be an advantage to this lack of coverage. I personally believe some of the media coverage may be so intrusive into families' lives at these times to the extent that it is a form of "journalistic pornography." Why is it so necessary to explicitly display on the front pages people at a most private and vulnerable moment, a time of grief, or shock?

And yet, another spin-off paradox may be that those lesser known situations may have family or friends asking why their moment of tragedy isn't "just as important" as the others, even as they know that the other event is a much bigger deal to society as a whole.

But it still raises the individual feeling of why the "other" generates such a larger outpouring of sympathy, and even sometimes financial assistance, while those with "individual woundings" go through it alone or seemingly so. I recall when the hostages held in Iran were released in 1981; I was watching celebrations for them being held, and while I was glad for them, there was still a small sense of depression because it seemed like no one in the country as a whole much cared when we (Vietnam veterans) returned.

And, actually, watching news a couple days later I saw a report that said that counseling hotlines nationwide had been flooded with Vietnam veterans expressing those same feelings. It appears that there may be additional wounding when we feel like we are facing a tragedy alone.

You call that justice?

Another circumstance where insult may be added to the already inner injury is when there is a loss caused by someone else, and it seems that the life of the person who did the damage goes on as normal, or seemingly so, while the victim is struggling with the pain of loss. I read in the paper not too long ago of someone who spent a whole 24 days in jail after being convicted on a DUI manslaughter charge. I can't imagine how those who suffered loss feel, but it sure doesn't seem like justice was even close to being served.

Why was that, again?

I believe that sometimes the search for meaning, or at least giving our interpretations of why something happened, can be done erroneously, perhaps even self-righteously, as in the example of some folks in the church I grew up in regarding an accident my father had.

I like his version better

When I was a young boy, my dad worked on a duck farm in Sterling, Massachusetts. One time a tree he and others were cutting fell the wrong way, and one of the branches took dad to the ground and broke his collarbone. As I recall, because of this dad was off work for about six weeks.

Now, the little church I grew up in, granted, did not have a large congregation, but some managed to make up for the lack of size with extra doses of smugness and "know-it-all," and my dad was criticized by some as "sheltering some sin in his life," or "holding back on God," and these were "touted" as reasons why he had been injured.

A few days after the incident, at church on a Sunday evening, during "testimony time," my dad stood up, his arm in a sling. His "testimony" went something like this. "I want to share something that happened a while back. One day I had this awful feeling come over me that something bad was going to happen to someone in the family, and I couldn't get away from it. This feeling continued for weeks, and I just couldn't shake it. Every day I came home expecting to find out something had happened to Marvel, or one of the children. I didn't know what to do, and even though I tried to rid myself of the dread, I couldn't. So a couple weeks ago, when the tree fell and broke my collarbone, the men I was working with came rushing over to see if I was all right. I can honestly say I felt no pain, and was flooded with an indescribable peace." My dad's eyes brimmed over with tears and he choked up as he continued. "I felt the burden that had been hanging over me disappear, and all I said back to my co-workers was, 'I'm okay, I'm okay, it's all right.'" Then he sat back down.

Now, I do know that there were still some in the small congregation who said he must have done something wrong, and the accident was an attempt by God to get his attention, but I'd rather remember the story the way my dad told it.

In the Gospel of John, Chapter 9, Verse 3b, Jesus was replying to a question his disciples had asked. They wanted to know why a certain man had been blind from birth; if it was because the man, or his parents, had sinned. Verse 3b says "… this happened so that the work of God might be displayed in his life."

Why Me, Lord?

When difficult things
Happen in our lives
(Yet again),

Many times we quickly, in
Exasperation, ask, Why me,

Lord? And sometimes (maybe quite a while later),
On down the
Road, we hear the words of our Lord saying,
Don't you want me to use you?

Supporting this idea, in II Corinthians 1: 4 we read, " Who (God) comforts us in all our troubles, so that we can comfort those in any trouble with the same comfort we ourselves have received …"

I'm trying to ask myself the following questions these days when I find myself flopping around in some sort of trouble, or suffering;

(1) Did I put myself here, and, if so, what can I learn to avoid doing it again?

(2) Is there something else I need to be gleaning from these circumstances which seem out of my control?

Or, perhaps most importantly:

(3) **Is there someone on down the road I am going to be able to help as a result of all this?**

Part Three:
From Impediments to Peace

40
Hope Found in Coffee Filters
(and a Few Other Places)

Sometimes as I am preparing coffee for the next morning I think about this: it seems like the package of newly bought coffee filters should last forever, but, in a matter of weeks (or months, depending on the package count) I am done with them – tiny little items which are ticking away the days of my life, and a constant reminder time waits for no one. But this does not have to be a 'downer,' it can be a continual reminder of just how fleeting – and precious – time is, a wake-up call to relish each day, and, maybe, maybe, try to spend more time with the world all around me.

Days by Minutes; the Coffee Filters of Our Lives

Each day slowly ticks into another,
And another pack of coffee filters disappear
One by one, carefully laid into place the night before.

Morning ploddings into the kitchen.
Push the button, start another pot.
My life is measured by coffee filters;
Almost a depressing thought, until …

Epiphany!

Every night I ready the coffee pot
In anticipation of morning;
My statement of faith, hope, and perseverance!

Coffee Filters

Counting them
Out, daily
Finding my
Faith in belief that, as
Every night I ready for it,
Each new day awaits.

Filters are simple,
Intended to hold coffee.
Little do
They know they also
Express anticipation of tomorrow.
Resurrection in a daily cycle,
Simple, but also, hopeful.

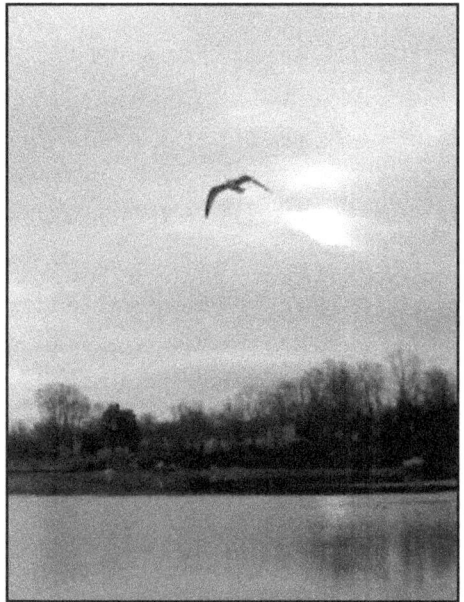

Emily Dickinson in her poem *Hope is the Thing With Feathers* says in the first stanza:

"Hope is the thing with feathers
That perches in the soul,
And sings the tune without the words,
And never stops at all."

I believe there is a place we can reach where we understand what she is talking about. The problem is, we have to embrace the unseen with something called faith. The Apostle Paul addresses this in his letter to the Romans, Chapter 8, verses 24 and 25. "But hope that is seen is no hope at all. Who hopes for what he already has? But if we hope for what we do not have, we wait for it patiently."

Hope

How can one explain the
Overwhelming, deep-seated
Peace from knowing there is a larger,
Eternal picture unfolding.

Hope II

Having assurance that
Over the long haul the
Purposes will
Eventually be revealed

Hope and Babies

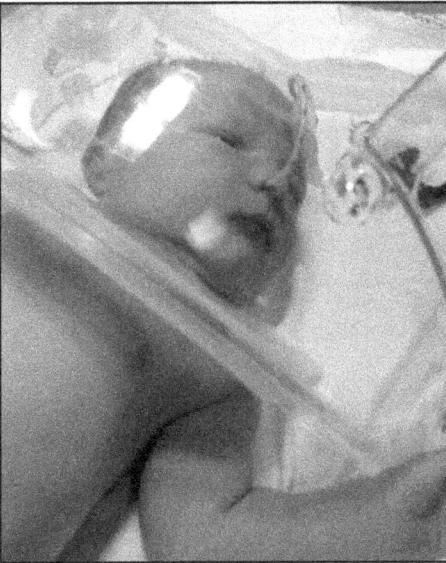

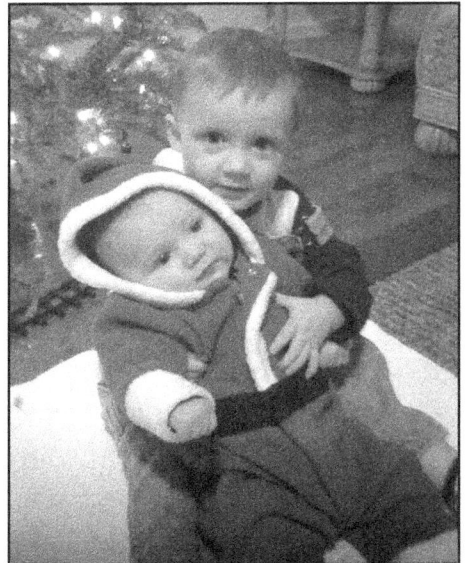

Zeke's first hospital hours, and, about three months later, with big brother Zack, breathing easier.

I have heard it said that each new baby is God's way of saying he hasn't quite given up on the human race yet. This may be true, but it is also a bit troubling when you think of all the babies born into families and conditions where it seems like they already have "two strikes against them" before they even start the game. But there is a certain amount of hope and promise when you look at a newborn, and even though God may not favor the conditions under which some babies are conceived (irresponsible behavior, drunk, rape, etc.), you cannot help but feel when the new life is conceived, and then later "pops out," that God is up there somewhere saying, "Wow, look at how cute that one is; let's see if we can help her reach full potential, and change the world."

Babies

Beautiful little "critters,"
Always spark hope
Because we see
In each and
Every one the potential to
Somehow change the world.

Hope when being swept under

In the early to mid-90's, near the end of May, my two sons and I went to a family reunion at my sister's in Littleton, Colorado. We arrived about three days early so we could spend time hiking in some nearby mountains on a trail section my oldest son, Ralph, had read about. On the second day we reached a spot where the trail crossed a rushing stream with waters too deep and turbulent to wade. Due to the time of year, the melting snow from higher altitudes also made them quite cold. There was, however, a log that had been cut and laid across from bank to bank, and although it was not wide enough to walk across, we figured we could hold onto it and edge ourselves along through the water.

Rocky started out, got partway over, and fortunately turned to wait on me. I eased into the freezing water and started out. When I got to the spot where the water was deeper than I was tall, I tightly gripped the log, but the waters were just too swift. I lost my hold, and under the log I went. I've never been much of a swimmer, and I panicked. Rocky was close enough that he reached out and grabbed my clothing and pulled me back, and then towed me to the other side. I am grateful that I have sons who are stronger than me, and to this day I am certain that if Rocky had not been close enough, quick enough, and strong enough, my boys would have found my drowned body further downstream. There have been a couple times in my life where my life was saved by someone else's actions, and this is one of them.

Now what if I had fought Rocky as he tried to help me? Instead, I put my hope in the only help available. I heard a preacher talk about a life-changing experience he had during World War II, and how some people later told him it was only "foxhole religion." The preacher said he had thought about that statement, and that he came to realize that there probably is no other kind of religion. When we are being swept under by the mountain stream, or the sometimes raging currents of life, we turn to the available source of hope and help.

Swept Under

The waters were too much for me and
I couldn't maintain my hold on
The log over the stream and a split second later
Panic set in; that overwhelming feeling.

It's like we know in a split-second span
That things are beyond our control and
Even though we struggle and resist,
We are going to be carried downstream.

But another force intervened (my youngest son).
Rocky was nearby and quickly reached out
And grabbed me and pulled me back
To where life once more awaited.

Can you imagine if I fought him?
Tried to break loose to do it on my own?
Rejected my only hope?
T'would have been quite foolish.

But Lord, do I really "deserve" to hope?

Again some of us may find ourselves wondering if we are really deserving of the love of God. Let's face it, we're in a "broken world." Not only do we see evidence of this all around, we find we are very much a part of that brokenness at times. The good news we read in II Chronicles 30: 18 and 19 is, "May the Lord, who is good, pardon everyone who sets his heart on seeking God – the Lord, the God of his fathers – even if he is not clean according to the rules of the sanctuary."

Since we do not know what is going on in someone else's heart, this is probably good news for more of us than we think.

But it doesn't look like it is happening

However, we can find further hope in Psalm 27: 13 and 14. "I am still confident of this: I will see the goodness of the Lord in the land of the living. Wait for the Lord; be strong and take heart and wait for the Lord."

And in Habakkuk 3: 17 and 18. "Though the fig tree does not bud and there are no grapes on the vine, though the olive crop fails and the fields produce no food, though there are no sheep in the pen and no cattle in the stalls, yet I will rejoice in the Lord, I will be joyful in God my Savior."

Even a live dog

I've always liked the phrasing of Ecclesiastes 9, verse 4, "Anyone who is among the living has hope – even a live dog is better off than a dead lion!"

So, let's tie animals into (along with people in need) the following statement. Ecclesiastes 3: 7b says there is a time to be silent, and a time to speak up.

One time we are told for sure to speak up is in Proverbs 31: 8 and 9. "Speak up for those who cannot speak for themselves, for the rights of all who are destitute. Speak up and judge fairly; defend the rights of the poor and the needy." I think this applies to people, but there are implications toward animals as well, as in Proverbs 12: 10 we find, "A righteous man cares for the needs of his animal."

I don't know if animals feel hope the same way we do, but we do know they feel, and love, and are grateful. So why not assume that when rescued from dire circumstances, they also feel hope.

Let's close out this chapter, but hopefully not the discussion, with thoughts on just how to harness this thing called hope, and (just kidding), turn it into a business.

Hope is Seeing Things

I think I have figured out a way
To become a millionaire, no,
Make that billionaire. All I
Have to do is capture Hope,

Analyze her, break down each
Of her ingredients, and then
Build a factory; one that will
Manufacture Hope.

The problem is, you can't
Quite wrap your arms around her,
It seems she lies hidden within
Each of us, sometimes dormant.

So maybe I should start a school,
Have a curriculum loaded down
With all the ways and means and
Methods to fan her into life.

That's a problem, too. It seems
There are no formulas, except, maybe one.
Hope is seeing things that aren't yet there,
But we know they can be, will be … … are (?)

41

Wine of Nature; Drink Deeply

I wrote the following poem near midnight, April 26, 1989, at an overlook on the Blue Ridge Parkway near Boone, North Carolina. It had been

twenty years since the April 26, 1969 incident I wrote about in Chapter Two, and so I was "celebrating and reflecting" on my life after that point. In other words, I had taken the day off to spend it driving around alone and climbing around Grandfather Mountain.

Wine of Nature

Wine of Nature

Scrub me softly with the wine of Nature;
Let it wash over my wounds and start the healing.
Let me soak until it permeates my pores
And slowly seeps inward to intoxicate me,
Leisurely, gently, cleansing.

Where the wine comes flowing
Over rocks,
Spraying in the wind;
Let me drink and play until my head and heart
Are under her influence –
As the inner healing continues.

As mentioned in the chapter on hope, I think most would agree that despite its sometimes destructiveness, Nature provides a multitude of opportunities to find hope and peace and an underlying sense of contentment. And I'm a firm believer one should try to communicate with Nature wherever and whenever possible. And watching baby animals, we almost have to ask ourselves why in the world there is a need for any other entertainment activities.

Baby Animals

There are just so many times the photos and videos,
Or just the simple observation of,
Bring smiles to our faces, and make us feel good.
So maybe there is a cure to some of the evils and
Other problems in the world. Spend less time

Envying and fighting, and trying to claw our way to the top;
Less time talking about others and putting them down;
And spend more time just watching the baby animals
(Doing all this with our own babies, of course.)
Oh, and one other thing, I'm being too simplistic, aren't I?

Baby Animals II

Bet you can't watch without a smile,
A couple kittens at play,
Batting each other around, and,
Yes, looking very serious

About it all;
No, hiding behind a mask
Is not allowed.
Maybe we would
All be a little better off in our
Lives if we would just
Spend a little more time watching the babies.

And, take a garden, for instance. I think we discover a lot about ourselves (and God) there.

Something in a Garden [P/H]

Something in a garden shows that miracles occur;
Giving daily lessons on how to persevere,
On death, on rebirth, and on not enough care.
Droughts make roots go deeper, dry too long can kill,
Water transforms into growth, too much destroys still.
Yes, miracles are still around, in the garden they are caught,
With balances and cycles ever being taught.

Cultivating a child to appreciate nature

I still remember childhood days with Mom and Dad in the garden across the road from our house in Sterling, Massachusetts. That triggered an early love for growing that endures to this day. If someone were to ask me my particular religious denomination, I might be inclined to answer, I have a theological degree in gardening (by the way, want to see my failures?) I have worked with children in the garden. Nothing beats the wonder of watching a child daily check on the zucchini, or sunflowers and exhibit delight in the growth process. It is such a wonderful place to teach the things mentioned in the preceding poem; death, rebirth, roots, watering, balance, cycles, hard work, payoffs, and more. "So children if you will just open your scriptures with me to the seed packets of beets and carrots, to be followed by a lesson from spinach."

Garden

Getting my hands really dirty
As I bury the seeds – and
Reflect on life – that is as necessary as the
Dirt. Both put me in touch with
Everything important; seeing
New growth, and thinking about it.

I also believe that we can learn something about the ways of a Higher Power, Creator, if you will, in a garden. Since it takes a varying time period for different plants to come to maturity, I think we can also learn not to put "God in a box" as far as how or why he puts certain processes in place, or how long it takes, or has taken, to see them come to fruition.

Garden II

Gardening is one way to see
A wonderful microcosm of all life.
Really. The seed's responses to
Dirt show us a lot about Higher Ways.
Enough occurs in the growth cycle that
No one can plead ignorance of God.

Following up on, "no one can plead ignorance"

Romans 1: verses 19 and 20 say, "… Since what may be known about God is plain to them, because God has made it plain to them. For since the creation of the world God's invisible qualities – his eternal power and divine nature – have been clearly seen, being understood from what has been made, so that men are without excuse."

Of course we can look at all the visible garden lessons and make this case, but one may ask, "What about all the discoveries since that was written, microscopic, subatomic, and so forth?" It is my belief that as we discover more about the complexities of nature, so we more clearly realize the complexity of God; we cannot fit him into the proverbial box. The following deals with more than nature (although maybe we can find garden growth applications.)

God, We Put Him in a Box

Guess we are all "victims" of
Our circumstances as far as the
Daily patterns and influences

Which rear their heads
Every now and again,

Pushing things we learned,
Usually in the early years
To the forefront.

How often do we allow God an
Inch when we should give him a
Mile. Sometimes we try to limit him

In areas where we don't want to grow.
Naturally, it's easier to cite "His will"

And then attempt to blockade the

Bridge he wants to try and take us
Over and the next place he wants to "plant us." Why can't we
Xccept he knows our soil (or is that our dirt) better than we do?

How to Find Wisdom Using Gardening Approach

In the *Apocrypha*, Wisdom of Sirach 6:19, in reference to finding and nurturing Wisdom, and caring for your soul, the writer says, "Approach her like a man who plows and sows, and wait for her abundant crops. For in cultivating her, you will toil but little, and soon you will let her produce."

This is similar imagery espoused by the writer of Isaiah 61: 11; "… soil makes the sprouts come up and a garden causes seeds to grow…" I think Isaiah might have done a little gardening, and a lot of observing nature, along with his writing.

The Lessons Nature Teaches

I was climbing down the rock stairway leading to the waterfalls at Linville Falls, NC, and paused to reflect on a tree growing atop a large rock.

The Little Seed ^(Originally P/H; revised 2013)

The little seed fell by accident between a rock and a hard place,
Really, between two rocks, and odds for survival were pretty slim.
But tiny roots took hold; a twig started, and then grew into a tree,
And the tree roots strained to force rocks apart to make room for him.

The rocks didn't give too easily, but the tree still held its ground, and,
Beauty soon became of both, and the pain of growth diminished; grew dim.
Many people pass them by now, and I wonder how many pause and think
On those lessons nature teaches when the odds of life look grim.

Nature Wonders About Me

Nature takes a look at me from outside my window
And wonders why I'm in here
Just sitting on my duff, drinking coffee, one cup after another,
Writing furiously as if my life depended on it,
Instead of doing something more eternally oriented,
Like, walking o'er God's land.

The erotic side of nature

If we want to go there, I think we can find some erotic comparisons to make in the natural realm.

Nature's Erotica [P/H]

Fog like a nightgown
Piled up high
Flirtation with earth
By a quiet night sky.
Sun comes up and
Starts to caress
Then sits back to watch
The meadow undress.

Nature's Erotica II [P/H]

As always her lover turns to leave
And she's left to watch him fade away.
A chill creeps over her, darkness falls, and
She starts to dress in her nightgown of fog-gray.
Nights without him seem long and drear; she
Misses the warmth of his smile, touch of his rays.
Ah! He's returning, drawing nearer,
It looks like another one of those days.
Her nightwear moves aside in response
To his caress. And soon again she
Lies, fully undressed.
He frolics with fair meadow,
Kisses moistness from her lines.
He causes heat to rise in her
Giving fruitful times.
She milks all the pleasure she can from him,
For all too quickly it seems,
The evening shadows come; again,
He leaves her with her dreams.

The spider chiding

Yes, I have to admit, sometimes it takes a spider to get my attention and "give me the on down the road" I deserve. I'm trying to do a better job of listening to them.

I Saw a Spider

I saw a spider peeking through the windowpane.
"What are you?" he asked, "Crazy? Insane?
You sit there foolishly, wasting time at your computer,
Yeah, that's right; I'm calling you a time-looter."
He started to climb his strand, and then dropped back down.
"Nature," he said. "Nature, look, fool, it's all around,"
He swung sideways, and laughed. "See? You could be having fun
Swinging on a vine like me, or just walking in the sun."
"Well," I answered, "You could come in; there's solitaire, or we could play ..."
"You're a bigger fool than I thought," he snickered, as he up and swung away.
I sat and stared at the screen, then stared and stared some more.
Am I really listening to a spider? I asked, as I headed toward the door.

Life Sustaining Fluid P/H

Cutting through the water,
The swimmer sets his pace,
Straining 'gainst the flow
As if he's in a race
Against himself.

Head below the surface, vision
Not so clear as when above.
Coming up for air and sight
And seeing that his love for life
Still lingers.

Ice on a Tree

After an ice storm, when
We see tree branches coated,
And light sparkles
Shimmering in a new day,
We marvel at the beauty,
Although the ice on the pavement

May prove a bit more dangerous,
Sending us sliding places we don't want to go.
But the ice will melt and fade away in the light,
And heat, of the sun; and that feels good.
Paradoxes reign throughout Nature as
Lessons are taught in the strangest way.

Lessons like,
Slow down;
Look out the window at how pretty;
Watch where you're walking;
I can provide you with inexpensive splendor;
Or, I can cause all this to disappear.

A great ride. If you are near the Cherohala Skyway in Western North Carolina, it is a great ride with beautiful scenery. The following two poems were written on 9/5/09 from the Skyway.

Mountains Protruding

Mountains protruding through the skull of the earth,
Bearing secrets we will never know;
And even if we did,
Would it make us any better?

Cherohala Skyway at Dusk

Cherohala Skyway at dusk,
Overlook on a cloudy evening,
Ear noise still circling mind and spirit,
However, up here, it's as close as it gets to peace.

42

Everybody's Best Friend
(and a Stray Cat or Two)

Several years ago while preparing a section of a health communication workbook dedicated to the health effect benefits of pets, I ran across a statement by a doctor which in effect said that if a drug was found that potentially offered all the health benefits of pets, Congress would probably be willing to pour millions of dollars into more research, however, because we're just "talking about dogs and cats," that doesn't call for further investigation. But the good news is we don't need congressional approval to appreciate just how much pets can contribute (if not allergic to them) to our well-being. And, lately, good news, there has been more research into the "pet benefit" in health-related areas.

Companions, Companions, Companions

In chapter eight Ronnie Hylton mentioned that he "was happy with a small house and an old truck, as long as I can find a good spot to fish and a place to go walking with my dog in the woods. You can't put a price on those things."

In chapter eleven Elisha Taylor stated that her four dogs. "have helped me a lot, just being there; that the support a pet can offer is irreplaceable."

And in chapter twenty-two Todd McLean said that, years after it occurred, he still recalls his best day in Iraq as the one he got to spend with his friend's German Shepherd dog.

Reading Assistance from Dogs

Another form of inner wounding can take place when someone does not learn how to read on pace with his or her peers. The reasons for this are varied, and sometimes complicated, and are not the focus of this segment. But there is increasing evidence that pets can offer assistance in this area also.

A December 24th, 2012 article in the *Chattanooga Times Free Press* told about a program at Wheeless Road Elementary School in Augusta, Georgia where volunteers with therapy dogs take part in a reading assistance program put in place for children in kindergarten through third grade who need help with reading skills.

Nationally, research is limited in this area, but initial studies are showing that literacy can be impacted by the presence of animals. Part of this comes from the fact that animals, specifically dogs in this article, don't care if a child misses, or mispronounces, a word. That creates a more relaxed atmosphere where children gain more confidence.

One study in 2010 by the University of California Davis Veterinary Medicine Extension showed reading fluency improvements varying from 12% to 30% on the part of third-grade students and home-schooled students who read aloud to dogs only once a week over a ten week period.

My Angel Friend

Years back I had a collie named Angel that seemed to sense my moods. Lots of times if the ringing was overwhelming, or I was just feeling down, I would go sit on the back porch steps where I could see the hills around me. Angel would come beside me, sit back on her haunches, and flop her head sideways on my shoulder. She would stay there beside me until I got up. Obviously we didn't talk, but the communication was awesome. She never failed to offer comfort.

Angel

Angels come to us in many ways. I
Never suspected that the
Gentle old ragged-looking collie
Entering my
Life was a creature from a higher dimension.

A Stray Cat or Two

My dad and mom had a cat, Tootsie, which they got from a shelter, via a friend, in 2005. Tootsie immediately took up with Mom, but shied away from Dad for some time, and they concluded that, in her past, she might have been mistreated by a man. Over time she warmed up some to Dad, but she was still primarily Mom's cat.

Mom died last year, and I talked with Dad recently about Tootsie, and what having her around means to him since Mom's death. "She's a companion," he said, "I'm not alone. She needs to be taken care of; you have a responsibility."

He added that caring for his cat gave him something to do "beyond himself." Dad said that although Tootsie wouldn't have much to do with him when Mom was still living, after her death, the cat perhaps sensed that she had a new caregiver (and, maybe then, that she had better be nicer to him.)

"I noticed that when I was coming up the front walk she was sitting on the windowsill, and by the time I got to the front door she was there, and she stayed with me as I did things. Before, after I got in bed and was reading, she might have come into my room for a couple minutes, and then she left to be with your mother. Now, when I'm reading, she lays down at the foot of the bed."

Dad chuckled. "When I'm ready to sleep, as soon as I lay down my glasses and start to put in my eye drops, she comes right up by my head, waiting to be petted. She stays there about five minutes and then leaves. Sometime around two a.m. she comes back and spends the rest of the night at my feet." He laughed again, and then continued. "The other morning I slept a little later than usual and she was up on my shoulder pummeling me."

I am grateful for Tootsie in my Dad's life. I have a brother that lives half a block from him, and a sister in Littleton, CO, a couple hours way. They are there for basic needs and transportation if Dad needs to go somewhere, but, at ninety-one, Dad still wants to live in his own place, and I am so glad he has his cat to keep him company.

And Don't Overlook the Birds

Several years ago my mother worked at a nursing home that followed the Eden Alternative guidelines. These included allowing interaction between the residents and animals. The particular home my mother worked at had an aviary in the middle of a common room with park bench-type seats nearby. The aviary was around ten feet high and had a diameter of "six-plus" feet.

Because it housed several exotic birds, it had cost around $15,000, and had been donated by someone whose mother had received excellent care at that home during her final years.

You could constantly find people sitting in the aviary area, reminding you of a scene from a park. Having to face up to one's mortality is another form of subjective battle, and it looked like having a park-like atmosphere made it more enjoyable for many of the people who resided there.

43

Automatic Writing; Order from Disarray

One evening in 1984 I was listening to the 11 PM news and there was a story about the remains of a pilot that had just been found in Vietnam. The report mentioned the relief of his family knowing that he could finally "be put to rest." However, after the newscast, I started to become a bit depressed, and then picked up a pen, and wrote the following – nonstop. The only changes I have made to the typed copy are to separate into paragraphs, and, correct a couple of typos from the original.

A Father's Prayer

What toll the wars when one stops to think about it makes no sense when realized there are ways and means to overcome there seemed to be no pattern or reason for the deaths some through their own foolishness or trying to show courage and then there were some who wanted glory and received it after a fashion at the expense of other lives and I wonder how well they sleep at night now and some part of my brain tells me some of those dead would have died during the same time period anyhow if they had been home but somehow senseless deaths are easier to take when there are accidents involved then when engaging in games designed to kill one another but maybe I just don't have the right perspective and sometimes I even wonder about any I killed and who gave me the power and right to exercise that kind of control over another human being and especially with the one that I knew was wounded but that is all in the past and yet the ringing from nerve damage done to my ears due to that loud explosion links me to him and I guess even to others because whenever I read an article about someone who died there is a sense of sorrow and loss and depression comes over me and feelings surface from somewhere so I wonder about some of the guys from the unit and what they are doing now and does the war ever bother them if they are still alive and if they ever think of Rodney or Brian or Fat Medic and I guess there is a special feeling of remorse over him because he was wounded when I left him and then the volley of gunfire so without thinking I reacted and dove for cover and yet he was still out there and dead from a bullet in the chest when we went back later and I cried that night and dreamt of him and others as the need arose and things like that made it difficult walking down a street in Boston when some demonstrators hollered baby-killer, baby-killer and I knew I hadn't done that and yet there were deaths and blood on my hands and I wanted to scream shut up you bastards but instead walked on in my uniform in honor or shame or whatever it was we came back with from wherever it was we went because I think they renamed it after we lost and left or left and lost I forget which sequence it was in or maybe it was that the losers went over there to finish that part of their lives

I'm not sure but either way we weren't consider winners and if you don't win then you lose and if you lose you lost but I guess one doesn't have to stay that way and it's really not too hard except that fifteen years later the country is still kind of embarrassed but there were good times too so don't let me fool you like on an in-country R & R getting drunk so you wouldn't remember where you were and I remember waking up the CO at four AM one morning during a stand down drunk out of my skull looking for another bottle of whiskey and I guess he was mad because I probably woke him out of a dream about the girl who had danced for us the night before slowly taking off her clothes until she was totally naked in that small Vietnamese body and she paid special attention to the captain because he was the captain and even asked for his watch and rubbed it all over and even into her body and then gave it back to him and maybe I awakened him as he re-lived that but anyhow he was mad and I even felt a little guilty about it when he died in a chopper crash a couple months later but not too guilty because he was a real bastard but I guess he was still a person whether more or less of one than the Vietnamese I split apart with bullets but either way they are both dead and I made it back so I guess that's all that counts except that sometimes the hours tick by too slowly especially sometimes at night and then there is always the fear of waking up and finding out that it was all a reality and really did happen, and I remember blacking out in a hospital in Saigon and coming too just a few moments later but already I had been transferred to bed and already they were pumping on more blood and the color of the hospital walls were a light green like the color of the walls in the living room of the house we lived in when I was thirteen and for a few seconds I thought I was back there on the couch awakening from a long and horrible nightmare and then it sunk in that it had indeed been my life and I couldn't forget it away like most dreams and I felt real bad and kind of sorry for myself as I walked along the hospital walkway and then this guy wheeled past me and I realized how fortunate I was because he had both legs amputated above the knees and I talked to the chaplain about later when he was making his rounds and he related how he had just come from a guy with bad kidneys who depended on a machine to clean his system out and how he the chaplain had never realized before just what a blessing it was to pull it out and take a leak and that happened to me twice once on stand-down after the first sergeant had shown the usual array of porno flicks for us poor fools who had to live like animals so he was giving us something civilized to absorb into the mind but anyway Little John who was over six feet tall came in drunk and pissed on my bunk and something splattering on my face woke me up and I pulled my poncho liner over my face and the next morning I awakened him by throwing the wet liner in his face and he was mad until I told him why I did it and then he was embarrassed and apologetic and we became the best of friends and I never did get mad at Jackie when he peed on me because it was in the middle of the night in the jungle and out there there were worse things than being pissed on and he had just gotten off guard duty and had to take a leak and thought I was a log but I still do say it's better to be pissed off than pissed on but that wasn't as bad to me as the night I had planted my body down for its rest along what I later realized was the main trail some rats were using and they didn't even bother going around just up and over but I managed to catch one the next day and tied a little rope around its little neck and pulled on it until I killed it and then hung it from a tree limb and that was kind of like the head of a Vietcong some of us put on a small stake and then popped a purple smoke grenade under it and it sure looked strange but if it weren't for things like that to do occasionally I guess a person could have gone insane but it wasn't all that way because fortunately there were some more civilized things to do like that time with the girl in Saigon and I was on leave and stayed with her several days and I wonder when I see pictures of rejected Viet American kids if one of them might be mine and you should have seen the look on my mother's face when I mentioned the girl and I guess it was kind of a shock because after all there I was doing something like that in the midst of the noble act of fighting for my God and my country but the girl next door got married while I was away and I like pumpkin pie better than apple anyway so that chapter of my life or whatever I'm involved in here on this planet was doomed to become as so many other things around they're just a tumbling memory falling slowly about like the brightly colored geometric shaped I saw as I tripped out on some grass laced with opium that I bought for five dollars for twenty joints near the Cambodian and everything was so laid back that when we got mortared and they were landing all around us someone had to pull me into a bunker because I thought the explosions were beautiful to watch and I didn't care because I was angry with the captain because the week before he had been mad at our lieutenant for something or other and transferred him to Alpha company with orders handwritten on a C-ration box to embarrass him and the LT was one heck of a guy and two days later he died from a bullet in the head while trying to rescue a guy who was pinned down and the captain of the unit he was sent to had written him up for the Distinguished Service Cross and I grieved when I heard of his death and I still have his faded picture in my possession and I wonder if in whatever afterlife he is involved in if the medal is worth anything to him because I know I even got a Silver Star once for going out through a so-called wall of bullets for some guys who were pinned down and brought them all back in safely and yet I doubt I could even buy a cup of coffee with it unless I had at least thirty-five cents to go along with it and some places even more depending on whether I wanted large or not yet it was kind of strange because the night before we got hit the platoon leader had taken me aside and said that if anything were to happen to him and the platoon sergeant then I was the squad leader he wanted to take over and the next night the only two from our platoon to get wounded and later medevaced were him and the platoon sergeant but we couldn't get them or the ten from the other platoons needing to be medevaced out until the next morning because the Vietnamese kept hitting us all night and once when Jon and I were sitting on the edge of the foxhole waiting for daylight so he could get to the hospital by way of helicopter he grabbed my arm and whispered did I see that bush over there and I did and he said the bush had just scratched its nose and we threw a hand grenade and the bush disappeared with a little cry and the next morning when we went to the spot there were blood trails and marks where someone had dragged one dead bush who thought he could cause a certain pandemonium if he could sneak all camouflaged into our perimeter but that was a mistake on his part and Jon was in the hospital for almost a month because the shrapnel had securely lodged next to his jugular vein and when I extended for a second tour of sunny Vietnam he and I were in a recon platoon where he was the platoon leader and I was the platoon sergeant and later he was the best man at my wedding in Germany and also star witness at my trial when the battalion commander was trying to bust me because I had gotten mad at my company commander and taken my staff sergeant stripes off my shirt collar and gave them to him as I told him what part of his anatomy I thought they would go good with but there was that good old Vietnam to back me up and the colonel did his best to see me busted but NCO Academy honor graduate and Silver Star and two Bronze Stars, a Combat Infantryman Badge, and a Combat Air Medal were too much for him and probably too much for me but those look better on my uniform than say a shovel to honor the time I had to dig a 6X6 foot hole in the middle of the firebase because the CO caught me with a bottle of rice whiskey or maybe a match to commemorate the hooches burned down in one little village but the VC that lived in them had all fled to hide in the jungle and I guess they could build some more and besides I was there for some reason even if it was only to watch the blood trickle down Jose's face from the two bullet holes in his head and he only had a couple months to go and he didn't even want to be there in the first place but that was a category a lot of people fit into and Larry wasn't even old enough to be there in the first place being just barely seventeen but he had lied and it didn't really seem to matter because he died just as easy as if he had been older and one of the hardest ones was Brian because he and I decided to extend together and see if we could survive another six months in the field but he was killed just five days after we signed the extension papers, but I had to still go back after my leave in the States which fortunately was over Christmas so after I got back then I went to the recon platoon and went out with small reconnaissance and ambush teams and while I was there I was given the nickname of Crazy Horse although one of the guys wanted to know if he could just call me Crazy for short and later I find that's true if crazy means irrational then there are times I act crazy and feel torn but maybe that's the way it's got to be and when it really boils down to it who really cares about a link to the past of my own making for after all the choice was there to shoot or not to shoot and I shot him and hit those damn grenades that made that nerve-damaging explosion and the choice was there to go or not to go and I went and chose Infantry and probably would again because if you make a choice don't waver but give it your all and that sounds so nice and high and lofty but sometimes the consequences of that stick with you long after the high and lofty has worn off at least throughout this life and hopefully not into the next because if I have to listen to it there I don't want to go and yet I don't want to stay with it here so again a choice but at least the more recent ones have been in a trend that seem to be more positive and I can't go back and change the earlier ones and I have to live with the consequences anyway so I might as well try to make the best of it and hopefully make some choices that will help my sons in their decisions so that they can stand up for whatever is right and feel some sense of obligation to help those who are oppressed but God I pray that they will never feel the urge to sit down some night and write about what toll the wars when one stops to think about it ...

Automatic Writing

As it appears to me,
Unless I'm wrong (and
That is always a possibility),
Often we find ourselves
Mulling over something from
A time, (or
Times) past, and
Into our spirits
Creep the "ugly ghosts."

Writing is a way to find
Relief. Let words flow
In and through the pen (without
Thinking.) All
In all, you usually find a
New perspective, a new way to
Grasp onto and deal with the issue.

One thing I find interesting, just a short time ago, as I re-typed the entire "A Father's Prayer" into this script, I found some sadness occurring as I recalled the time of burning huts (we called them hooches) but I also realized that the inner healing has long since taken place and there is the realization that I truly cannot change the past, and it is useless to live with guilt; all I can and should do is learn from the past and do what I can to be positive in the lives of others now. And I am aware the perspective from writing has been a part of that.

How can we work toward healing in a practical way with automatic (stream of consciousness) writing? The following is an assignment I have given to communication theory and interpersonal communication classes after the class has read the preceding section ("A Father's Prayer".)

Assignment:
This should be handwritten as "stream of consciousness."

After reading A FATHER'S PRAYER spend a few moments thinking about something you wonder about, or fear, or hope for, etc. Then on a blank sheet of paper engage in "stream of consciousness" writing about what you were thinking about. Just write wherever your thoughts take you – don't worry about grammatical rules – just write. If you draw a blank then write the word or phrase of wonder, fear, or hope, then take off writing again. Fill at least a page (Write all you want – but for this assignment only turn in 1-3 pages of it.) Okay, go for it.

I have read some writings where people dealt with some heavy issues ranging from abuse to drinking and/or drug issues, to questions about career choices, and questions about relationships they were in, or thinking about getting deeper into (marriage, for example.) The general feedback always has been that the writing helped in gaining a new perspective on things, and, in some cases, brought to the surface some questions or fears that the person was not consciously aware of.

So, grab a pen, or get on your keyboard or keypad, and let 'er rip. Don't worry about spelling, grammar, or logical patterns; just write, write, write.

44

Sidetracked Dreams with Excellent Endings; A Bigger Picture

Even though I like to think (and do actually believe) that somehow everything that happens is all part of a bigger picture being painted, there are still so many things that happen which make no sense whatsoever, especially in the areas of abuse of children, the elderly, or other weaker victims; mass murders; animal cruelty; and so forth.

When it comes to these, and many other areas, and trying to fit them into some sort of bigger picture, sometimes all I can say is, "I don't know a lot more than I know." But I am still trying to learn and understand.

Quirky Minds

Along with my accepting the premise of a bigger picture, I find I also have to accept what I will call "quirky minds," along with other things, as a part of the larger scenario.

Several years ago in one of my public speaking classes a student was giving a speech about his "shut-in interview" visit with his grandmother. He shared one of his discoveries made during the visit. He described it as "something from my grandmother's quirky mind." Once she was old enough to start thinking about having a family, she decided that she wanted two children, believing it would be best for a child to have a sibling to play with, so after her first child was born she was anxious to get pregnant again. She did, and later twins were born.

This was when the student said his grandmother's "quirky mind" kicked in. Three children were an uneven number; she wanted an even number of children, so she wanted another child to "balance things out." And so she got pregnant again, and had another child, his mother. Of course, he waxed a bit philosophical as he shared the fact that he only existed as a result of "grandma's quirky mind."

The Tipping point

While assigned to the 1st Armored Division Non-Commissioned Officer Academy, my oldest son, Ralph, was born on October 18th, 1973, in the Nurnberg Army Hospital in Nuremburg, Germany, and three days later he and his mother were home in our military base housing apartment. October 18th, 1973 was also the beginning of what became known as "The Yom Kippur War" between Israel and Egypt and Syria. On the 22nd, as Israel was closing in on Ismailia, a United Nations truce was negotiated. It started to fall apart on October 23rd when Israel was well on its way to surrounding the Egyptian 3rd Army.

United States military units in Europe were put on alert, and I had to report to mine with all my field gear packed, ready to go wherever, whenever. After everything was ready to go, just before leaving the apartment, I took one last look at my five-day-old son sleeping in his crib. Tears welled up and I just shook my head, said, "I can't take this," and then went to my unit. I decided enroute that when three more years were up, I was getting out. I never changed my mind, and after eight and a half years' service, got out, never looked back, and, have never regretted the decision. This has created in me, though, the utmost respect for all of our men and women in uniform who do "take this." I still tear up over the memory of looking down at Ralph, and pay honor to all those who make these sacrifices.

My Sons

I cannot begin to comprehend what my life
Would have been without them.
The Psalmist once wrote (Psalm 127:3),
"Children are a gift from God; they are his reward."

I think he was right, and I also think
A special tribute is due for
All those who make sacrifices for us
At a cost of time with their own children.

Looking at My Son

Looking down at my five-day-old first-born son in his crib
Created feelings I had never experienced before.
As I got my military gear out of the closet so I could
Take it into my unit to wait for further instructions,

I thought of the past few days. Ralph was born, and
I was there throughout the entire process. Indescribable;
Something I would encourage every father to be a part of.
And then, bringing that "miniature adult" home.

Now my unit in Katterbach, Germany was a part of a
Military world-wide alert. It was October 1973 and
What became known as "The Yom Kippur War" was underway.
If we had to ship out, what the future held was unknown.

Before leaving the apartment, I picked up my sleeping son.
I had been in the Infantry in Vietnam; I was not uneducated
To the ways of the world of war. I knew there was a chance
Once I left, I would never see him again; nor him, me.

Holding my five-day-old first-born son in my arms
Created a new feeling that ran cross-grain to existing ones.
I looked down at him with tears in my eyes, first thinking,
And then, saying, "I can't take this; I just can't take this."

I still had three years left on my enlistment, and I served
Them out honorably, and proudly. I was raised that way.
But after 8 ½ years, when my chance came round, I got out.
I left, and have never looked back, have had no regrets.

But I am filled with respect for those who have, and still do,
Serve, answering the calls of duty, honor, country. Time and
Time again our military personnel have looked down on
Sleeping babies, then turned, and ventured out to the unknown.

God bless them, every one!

Theatre and the Infantry

I didn't start college until I was 27, and then at the age of thirty switched my major to Speech and Theatre. The first production at Eastern Kentucky University that I was involved in was CABERET. I was working as a stage hand changing sets between scenes.

The night of our final rehearsal I was overwhelmed with an "almost spiritual" experience as I was working, and reflecting on how everyone counted on each other, on and off stage, and how the error of one person could, and most likely, would, affect everyone else. What was "getting to me" was that it had not been since I had been in the Infantry in Vietnam that I had been involved in a group that had this kind of dependency on each other. The consequences of someone's failure weren't near as significant, but, still, I realized I liked that kind of reliance on each other.

Where you wind up

As I earlier mentioned in chapter one about going out on a field problem in Germany that I didn't want to go on, but then meeting Cpt. Beer and getting an assignment that dramatically changed the direction of my life, sometimes we wind up in places we did not originally intend to go to. This may work out to be either positive or negative for us, but the fact remains, we didn't initially have this place in mind. In the Old Testament we find Joseph wrestling with this issue after he found himself in Egypt.

Joseph and slavery

In the latter part of Genesis we read the story of how Joseph was betrayed by his brothers and sold into slavery in Egypt. After some time, through a series of providential circumstances, he became an assistant to the Pharaoh, and was put in charge of food distribution. Later his own family was in need, and the brothers who betrayed him were forced to seek him out for help. They were worried that due to Joseph's power and control, he might seek revenge.

But Joseph saw that the initially unpleasant turning point in his life was fitting into a larger picture. He replied in Genesis 45, verses 5 – 8, "And now, do not be distressed and do not be angry with yourselves for selling me here, because it was to save lives that God sent me ahead of you. ... So, then, it was not you who sent me here, but God."

Working where you work

I do not know the percentages, but I think we can all agree that a lot of people complain about where they are working, the bosses, conditions, pay-check amounts, co-workers, etc. If these things sound familiar to anyone, try praying. I've always liked the thoughts of C. S. Lewis on prayer; that it doesn't change God, it changes us. But we can find other reasons for praying for our workplace, too.

Pray for your place of business

One of my favorite verses is Jeremiah 29:7, "Also, seek the peace and prosperity of the city to which I have carried you (into exile.) Pray to the Lord for it, because if it prospers, you too will prosper." Here the writer was speaking to people who had been carried into captivity to another country, and then enslaved. I would speculate that they were not necessarily under the best working conditions. But they were being encouraged to want the best for their city, and by extension, place of work, for the most logical of reasons; if it did well, they would benefit also.

I have a handwritten note in my Bible next to this verse; "University of Pikeville." No, I'm not in exile (or enslavement); I choose to be there; and working conditions are downright tolerable, even good. Upike is doing well, and I believe I am too.

A truly life-changing climb

I saw an article about Seneca Rocks, WV, in a *Backpacker* magazine, and knew from that moment on I was going to get there someday. My opportunity came while coming back from a trip to Vermont the summer of 2008. I not only was able to get this picture, but I knew that as soon as I got to the

top I would be able to get a photo similar to another rock depicted in the article that caught my attention. There was an observation platform near the pinnacle where I took a few more pictures.

As I left the observation area to continue my climb I encountered the following sign.

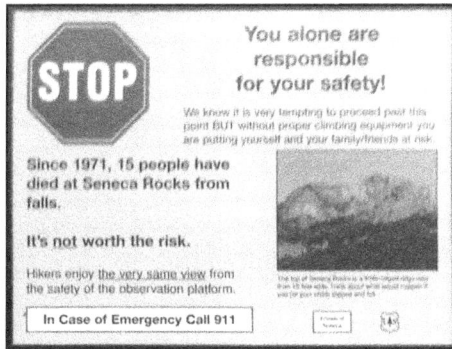

Along with a warning not to climb to the highest point, it said that the view from the observation platform was just as good as the view from the top. They lied; the view from the top was much better!

However, I could not see the rock pictured in the *Backpacker* article. I decided to have a snack, and then after eating, I looked around the summit a

bit more. While peering over an edge I inadvertently relaxed the grip on one of my trekking poles and it slipped out of my hand and fell downwards. My frustration was short-lived though, as I saw the pole lying on a ledge just a few feet below my location. I climbed down to where it was and recovered it.

I had a clear view of the rock from the article; a picture I could never have gotten had I not climbed to the top and then accidently lost my trekking pole over the edge.

And from my new location I saw it ->

However, the most significant "trivial event" occurred as I was leaving the top of Seneca Rocks. In a spur-of-the-moment decision, I decided to hold my camera phone at arm's length and take a self-portrait.

A few months later when I decided to go on e-Harmony.com, I used the image for my profile picture. Cora said the picture was what caught her eye, she read my info, and decided she wanted to "get to know this guy a little better." The rest is history.

From Above; the Arrangement

Summer of 2008, sitting atop Seneca Rocks, WV,
Reflecting, pondering, a bit lonely,
But also used to the loner role.
I'd spent most of my life there.

Little did I know that the self-portrait camera pic
I took before descending, four months later to be
Posted on e-Harmony.com, would be
The thing that caught her eye.

It did. She decided to take a chance,
Come out from her "loner-shell-role",
Contacted me with e-Harmony guided communications;
And then the lengthy phone calls.

January 2009 was the first face-to-face.
Then over two years of six-hundred-mile
Round trip weekends. Then marriage.
Two loners, Cora and I, now connected,

And definitely, no longer lonely.

Cora II

Captured my heart
On E-harmony
"Reeled me in"
And that has made all the difference.

Cora III

Concerned about me and I really feel
  like she wants what is best for me.
Organized and efficient and fun to work with,
  and just fun to hang out with.
Retains dignity, when necessary, and knows how
  to let her hair down, whether necessary or not.
And I love her and want to hold on to her, and hope
  I mean as much to her as she does to me.

Cora IV

She entered into my life by way of e-Harmony.com;
Took me somewhat by surprise. But I soon
Came to my senses and went through the
Guided Communication with her, and …
Then, later, the 600 mile round- trips back and forth,
And back and forth, and, back and … you get the point.

Building our relationship, and really giving
My Elvis Gospel CD's a workout.
I thank God daily for the most
Incredible blessing he has given me,
And, since she contacted me first, I guess
I really can say, indeed, she is a gift from God.

The Missy Mae

One of the things we enjoy when the weather allows is taking the Mazda Miata out for a ride with the top down. My first time driving it was over "The Tail of the Dragon" in western North Carolina, touted as "318 curves in 11 miles"; fun. The following was written shortly after a get-together with some family, Easter 2010. Cora drove over.

The Missy Mae

The Missy Mae
Is the name we have given her;
Our Burgandy ragtop.
With the top down, as
She shifts through
The six gears, Cora
Looks over at me and says,
"You'd think we'd get
Too old for this,
But we don't."

With Cora

Car doing 80 as we roll along
Over the Interstate; sharing moments,
Really enjoying good laughs,
And sometimes, just quietly, enjoying each other's presence.

Convertibles

Missy Mae, our Mazda Miata;
Five years old now, but enjoyed just
As much as if we had driven it
Out of the showroom yesterday.

There's nothing to compare to
Driving down the road,
Wind blowing through your hair,
Or in my case,
Swirling and sliding
Over my bald spot.

Even if it's 50 degrees (Fahrenheit),
(Not raining (you think I'm crazy?)),
The top is usually down. At 50 degrees,
Windows up, heater on, naturally.

Roll bars behind seats, of course,
Not really sure what
Difference they would make.

In hardtop cars we live
In a world of illusion,
Thinking we are protected at
Seventy miles per hour by the roof;
That covering which must be
All of 1/16th of an inch thick,
Or less.

In a convertible you know what's
Between you and the road,
And realizing that, each wind-swept breath
Is chock full of life and all it offers.

It's true; you feel more alive when driving down
The road, wind blowing through your hair,
Or, in my case,
Well, you know.

So your sons will marry you

This is taking a verse out of context, but sometimes that can be fun when it fits something else (and it isn't any significant "point of doctrine".) The NIV translation of Isaiah 62:5 includes, "… so will your sons marry you." Cora and I have to smile at that one because between us we have three sons; Troy gave her away; Rocky was my best man; and Ralph officiated at his first wedding. What can we say?

45
Nudges (Slight Pushes in the Direction to Go)

Nudges

It's the morning of February 2, 2013. Cora and I are visiting relatives in Graham County, Western North Carolina, I was up and reading earlier, and, now, along with more coffee, to this.

We were told last night that the forecast was for snow to be starting midday, possibly two to five inches accumulation. It is now 10 a.m., and looking out the window to the north, mixed with sun, I can see some dark clouds on the mountainous horizon.

We slept in a room last night where the window shades kept it quite dark, even after daylight. We got to bed rather late, so, as long as Cora can sleep, I'm "letting" her do so. However, I also know we don't want to get our trip back to Chattanooga started too late; there are some potentially slick mountain roads to maneuver. So when I went into the room to get my laptop, I was totally quiet, except, when closing the door behind me, I let it make "just the edge of noise," figuring that it might serve as a "small nudge" in the awakening process.

I'm a firm believer that God uses "nudges" in our life most of the time. Of course, in my case (and possibly some of yours), he has to occasionally weigh in a little "more strongly." But I have found over and over again, as I am sensitive to the nudges, I start to get a clear vision of the direction I should be going.

In Proverbs 10:8 we read, "The wise in heart accept commands." I have a handwritten note alongside this verse, "Thanks for all my advice from Cora." I truly have come to realize she provides many useful suggestions, or nudges.

Time to lighten the load, and focus

For a long time I walked around with a yellow backpack slung over one shoulder. In it I carried several folders containing draft manuscripts to some eight or nine "book projects." The evening of March 22, 2009, Cora and I were discussing all these unfinished scripts, and she suggested that maybe it was time to prioritize, and complete some. She wondered if maybe I kept working piecemeal on different ones (and listing ideas for new ones) because I was afraid of success. I agreed, but also knew it was hard to just set old habits aside. The next morning I was reading my Bible, and in Isaiah 28: 24, 28 saw "When a farmer plows for planting, does he plow continually?" and, "Grain must be ground to make bread; so one does not go on threshing it forever."

I immediately made a note beside them with the date, and that, to me, was just a confirmation of what Cora had been saying the night before. I stopped carrying all the folders around, and started to concentrate on *Marvel's Mistake*, and *Barabbas*, two short stories that would be the easiest to complete. They are both publisher-ready (looking, in-between work on this one.) And there are drafts on a shelf now that I truly want to get to in the future; but, one at a time (thank you Cora.)

Daily reminders

I have a marker in my Bible I turn to as a part of my daily readings. On that page I have written:

Cora:

I love you
I accept you
I care about you
I forgive you
I appreciate you
I will listen to you

I find the listening part helps with the nudges (plus she knows I feel free to say "no" if necessary.) I also know that "half of being smart – is knowing what you're dumb at." For example, that is why, recently, I did not want to talk to an agent about refinancing my home unless Cora was there. As a retired mortgage banker, I just knew she would provide nudges as to which way to go.

Nudges

Now and again
Under many
Different circumstances
God gives me a gentle push,
Enough to turn me in the right direction.
Shoves only happen if necessary.

Reminders to "keep me nudged in the right direction"

I suppose there are some responsibilities I have to keep up with in order to be open to receiving nudges (otherwise it might take a body-slam.) The following are some guidelines I try to keep in mind. I do not know if these are all recorded together somewhere, or not.

Lord, help me to live so that it won't hurt much to die;

To love my wife so that no backtracking is needed;

To love my children so they'll be sad when I'm gone, not bitter and relieved I'm out of the picture, or even guilty because they don't feel anything;

To always be engaged in activities such that in any given moment I wouldn't be ashamed to be found dead;

To drive in such a way that my chances of dying on the highway are reduced;

To find out what you want me to be doing in this life so that you can review things with me instead of reveal things to me;

To eat sensibly and, also, to learn more about times of refreshment from you;

And, help me not to be too afraid of the unknown so that I can enjoy the discovery of new things in your creation.

I guess in summation, all I'm saying is, "Lord, let the words of my mouth and the meditations of my heart be acceptable in your sight, Oh Lord, my God, forever." (Psalm 19:14)

46

Paradoxes Make the World Go 'Round

I made a statement which drew a surprised and questioning look from a colleague. We were talking about things involving the concepts of good and evil and I said (not an original statement or thought), "I believe I am the best person and the worst person I know." I think if we are honest with ourselves we may all have to admit that. It's just one of the paradoxes of the human condition.

As time goes on, and I have the opportunity to observe more of life, I'm coming to believe that somehow, life works on the "Paradox System." Not only do we have those times where things co-exist side by side that seemingly couldn't, or shouldn't, but there are also just those moments where we realize that things might not always be what they seem to be. Take the pictures below, snapped by Cora on I-75 S, for example. They could leave the impression that a head-on collision was inevitable.

"I think a problem is coming my way."

"No, I'm just being towed."

I teach public speaking courses and tell my students one of my goals is for them to become more comfortable speaking in front of others. I point out, that for many, behind the lectern is the "uncomfortable place." They are then introduced to the paradox that the only way to become more comfortable is to keep coming up to the "uncomfortable place." It's the same with many (maybe all) other areas in life. Want a new parking garage for more parking in your town? You're going to have to put up with less parking for a while. That's the way it works.

The Mess

Across the street from the college (where we used to park)
They blocked off traffic, brought in bulldozers,
And cranes, and cement trucks, and,
All sorts of building materials (and made a real big mess.)
Took away a lot of our places where we could park,
But now that it's finished, the three story building, plus the
Roof, provide plenty of spaces for parking (all we need.)

Several years ago I was helping a friend renovate a room and made the comment that, for a room we were supposed to be fixing up, we were sure making a big mess. My friend replied with something I will never forget. "Remember, it always looks worse before it looks better." I have learned it is not only true of building or renovation; it is frequently that way in life also. So, don't quit – the mess you're in now may in fact be part of a "renovation" going on.

Paradoxes

Personally speaking,
A principle I see making our world go
'Round is the "Paradox Principle,"
Always two things co-existing that
Don't seem like they could. So
Often we see this happening.
"X"cellence, for example, doesn't
Ever occur without
Some failure along the way (Case closed.)

Paradoxes II

Such paradoxes; even after forty plus years
I can't stand the ringing, but I've learned to accept it.
I want to scream and holler about it,
But I don't want to aggravate others with my problems.
I want to have moments of complete silence,
To hear nothing,
But I realize I have forgotten what that sounds like,
And I don't think I'd recognize it if it occurred.

I realize my life now is in large measure
A consequence of earlier choices.
I can't stand this ringing,
But I'm at such a good place in my life.

War Paradoxes

One problem with war is, there is a
Certain amount of exhilaration at times.
Every time a Huey Medevac helicopter flies
Overhead to land at the nearby Medical Center,

A part of me wants to go for a ride,
Side doors off, sitting with legs hanging over the edge,
And upon descent, at about 300 feet,
Sliding out to ride the skids down.

Fun, thrilling, and something
I would never have enjoyed, except
For, the First Air Cavalry, Infantry,
And over fifty combat air assault missions.

This Sucks, But It's Ok (4/26/10 - 41st "anniversary" of "Uncle Tinn")

The fact is sometimes I
Have to realize we are all
In our own little
Space, which by its very nature is

Subjective, and our battles continue
Until we find the place where we
Can accept that no one else can really
Know – but it's okay – they love and
Show they care, and, they have their own

Battles that they wish others would
Understand. Despite all the
Trying we do to reach out to

Include others; sometimes it's just a case of
Touching whenever possible and
'Sending out the message – we

Often fail as humans, but please
Know, we're in this "fight of life" together.

Looking For the Better Life

Bottle took him to the skids,
Eventually ruined him.
The irony of it all was
That he thought,
Eureka! I know how to
Really have a better life. So he

Left his wife and kids
In spite of their tears. Played the
Fool, and after a while,
Even wound up begging for bread.

Anyone familiar with the poem, *To an Athlete Dying Young* by A. E.
Housman may recognize a similar idea in the following.

Space Shuttle Challenger Crew [P/H]

It seems they died before their time
The day the shuttle blew.
Yet death is what must come to all,
Let's stop and think it through.
Their interest levels at their peaks,
Their happiness at a new high,
Not much warning, shortened fears,
An almost perfect way to die.
Immortalized they will become,
From here on have their praises sung.
An inevitable tragedy gave to them
A beautiful way to go out young.

Icicles

Icicles adding fuel to the fire,
Chill dripping into each day,
Inching along and fanning
Cold flames. They wonder if they should
Let go, and stop the angry fires,
Except, the ice is so sugary
Sweet it makes the heat go sour.

Lord, Grant Me Patience, and Give It to Me Now

We're probably all familiar with the above. The paradox about patience is that we have to experience some situations where we are usually impatient in order to develop patience (Sorry, God's laboratory procedures.)

Patience

I want it, and I want it now! Lord grant me patience,
But don't make me wait on it!
We do get frustrated sometimes as we wait for
The loan officer to call us in so we can apply for the money to

Complete a home renovation project, or
For the line to move at McDonald's (Why did I come here at noon?),
Or for this cold to get better, or the, oh,
You know what I'm talking about.

And, please Lord; don't make me
Have to wait for signs of progress
In my everyday living,
Overcoming obstacles, *ad nauseum*.

Because, as you can see, Lord, I'm busy right now;
I have been looking over my list
Of all the things I need to get to today,
So please don't make me have to explain this to you all over again.

47

Things That Make You Go Hmmm.

The Power of the Mind

In another speech from the Shut-in Interview Review assignment, earlier referenced, a student told of visiting a member of her church who was over a hundred years old. He had been born late in the nineteenth century, around 1898 if I remember correctly, and her assignment and subsequent visit with him occurred during the fall semester 1999. In the course of her speech she told of a goal he shared with her. He said he really wanted to see, and be able to say, he had lived in, three centuries.

I again had this student in another class the following semester, spring 2000. The first day of class I asked her how the man she had visited was doing. "Oh," she replied, "He died January 5th, but he was happy because he had reached his targeted date."

Since it was an interpersonal communication class, we included the rest of the students as we talked briefly about the power of the mind in reaching goals.

It All Depends On What the Definition of Magnificent Is

Slavomir Rawicz, in *The Long Walk* tells of the first meal he and six others fixed eight or nine days after their escape from Camp 303 in Siberia. They felt they were finally far enough away, well over two hundred miles, that they could safely light a fire for warmth, and cooking, for the first time. He describes a meal of Kasha gruel made with heated water, pearl barley, flour, and salt, and then sipped while eating a piece of bread. Rawicz says that afterward they sat around and congratulated themselves on such a magnificent meal.

This should be something that makes me go "Hmmm" the next time I'm evaluating my barbecued chicken dinner at, say, Smokey Bones so I know how to answer the waitress when she asks, "Is everything all right?" I should probably start answering, "Magnificent, just magnificent!"

The Starlight Scope

On the night of September 17th, 1969, after the attack mentioned in the prologue, we were all either down in or sitting on the edge of, our foxholes, on high alert. One of my squad members came up to where I was sitting and told me that earlier he thought he had made out the outline of someone sitting in a tree, but a few minutes later it was gone, so he wondered if maybe his eyes were playing tricks with him. Then he added that what he had seen was back again. He pointed out to me the area, some 50 yards or so away. I had a starlight scope so I looked through it to where he was pointing.

I was startled to "zero in" on a VC soldier sitting in a tree looking right back at me with what appeared to be his starlight scope. My hands were a little shaky as I put mine down and had my RTO (radio-telephone operator) call for artillery. Hmmm, I wonder why after a few artillery rounds we noticed the person had disappeared. In the bigger picture, I also wonder sometimes why he wasn't able to do something to me before I was able to do it to him.

Starlight Scope

Sometimes I think about
That night after the
Attack. We were waiting on
Real high alert, feeling
Like daylight would be nice.
In the dark it's hard to see. I
Guess I never figured I would
Have to stare straight back at
The figure of a man who could kill me.

So, maybe You
Could help me Lord to
Overcome the dangers that want to
Pull me away from my purpose. Let me
Ever be looking through your starlight scope.

Before you call, I will answer

While a graduate student in theatre at the University of Kentucky I took a couple playwriting courses. In one that I took during fall semester 1983, the instructor kept bringing in playwriting contests she was aware of, and encouraging the class to enter scripts in them. I submitted to several, including one for short plays with the Performing Arts Repertory Theatre (now TheatreWorks USA.) The day before the deadline I decided to do a double-check of the criteria before I mailed out the short, twenty-minute play I had just written, and to my great chagrin realized that as I "got to following my characters around and recording their dialogue," I allowed them to expand to nine, and the rules said no more than six. After an initial sinking feeling in the stomach, I decided to take what I felt was a good idea and merge some of the characters to meet the criteria, and, the deadline. The play, Change of Exchanges, was mailed the following afternoon, with a timely postmark.

Meantime, I was starting to hear back from some of the other contests I had entered; the form letters thanking me for my submission, letting me know that I had not won, and encouraging me to pursue my interest in writing.

For several reasons, I sat out of school for a semester and did pencil-sketch portraits and home-schooled my two sons while their mother worked at a bank in Lexington. My pencil sketch business was basically hovering between slow and slower, and the amount of money going out was not in balance with the money coming, or, more to the point, not coming, in. A loan application for two thousand dollars at a local bank was understandably not approved, probably because they really like you to show you don't really need the money before they will lend you any. So, anyway, a few days after the refusal, I sat down with Ralph (10) and Rocky (8) and told them that we needed to pray about something. I told them that things were getting a little hard money-wise, and so we needed to pray that I would be able to start doing better with my pencil sketch sales. We prayed, and then went about some of their school assignments.

The very next day, I received letter in the mail from Performing Arts Repertory Theatre. I opened it figuring that I was about to read another rejection form letter. Imagine my surprise when the letter started out; "Dear Basil, the enclosed check for two thousand dollars is your award for winning grand prize in our playwriting contest." And this was not a loan; it did not have to be paid back!

Of course, Ralph and Rocky were strongly reinforced in the belief that prayer works, but I also explained to them that when we had prayed, the contest-winners had already been determined, and the check was already in the mail. I did tell them, though, that there was a verse in Matthew 6, from the Sermon on the Mount, that said, "Your Father knows what you need before you ask him." But, hmmm; it still makes me go hmmm.

Something that was of interest to me was Ralph and Rocky's responses to the situation. After the check was cashed, some of the money was set aside for tithe, some to pay off a few bills, and some to get a professional mat-cutter, which was, in part, why I had applied for the loan. I told the boys that after we all went out for a nice dinner at a Western Sizzling, then we were going to go do some necessary shopping for a few staples, clothes, and one new toy for each of them. I honestly cannot recall what they picked for their toys, but I vividly remember how excited the boys were picking out new clothes, including underwear and socks.

48

In For a Long Haul; the Twin Trekking Poles of Faith and Perseverance

I'll struggle to stay

How many times does someone who has gotten into trouble (gotten drunk or high/had a reckless sexual fling/succumbed to some negative pattern or habit/etc.) swear that it will be his last time? But after a while, in a paraphrase of President Ronald Reagan, "There he goes again."

Here I Go Again

Here I go again, flat on my face,
Ashamed that I'm as weak as I am,
Don't feel there's anyone I can talk to,
Just don't know what to do.
Guess I need to pick myself back up,
And keep on going.

"Unsung Heroes?"

But many people who find themselves in in these negative cycles still show a tremendous amount of perseverance and hope. These folks may turn out to be some of the "unsung heroes" of our time as they pick themselves up and head out into the world to try again. I've heard the saying, "Some people succeed because they were too dumb to quit." If that's the case, I hope I always maintain a certain dose of dumbness.

Perseverance Leads to Hope

I do believe perseverance comes from hope. If we are not looking for something better to come our way, why bother going on? In days past (when I did more hiking than these days) I named my trekking poles "Faith" and "Perseverance"; Faith in myself, others, and God, and, Perseverance to reach my goals.

My Twin Trekking Poles

Faith, and Perseverance; I chose their names in winter 2000 when I was training to do the Long Trail in Vermont. I knew I wanted to hike it from the moment I read an article in *Backpacker* magazine about the Readers' Choice for the ten most difficult trails in the United States. The Vermont Long Trail was rated number six. I was born in Vermont, and the trail seemed to reach out of the magazine and grab me, so, of course, I had to go along. Obviously, to me, the next step was to start getting into shape. There was a reclaimed surface coal mining site behind where I lived at the time, so I decided to train there.

The first day I climbed the hill I had no pack, just two trekking poles, and I was so out of breath by the time I reached the top of the rather steep hill, which was only a little over ¼ mile, I decided to call it a day and go back down (okay – so I was 51 and quite a bit out of shape.) The next day I went back up, and then started across the field at the top. Then it was over the field and start up on the trail that went up again. After a few more days I tackled the next reclaimed hill with a very steep gravel road up the side. This trek eventually added up to a three-mile round trip, and I decided I had my training route established.

A couple weeks after my initial out-of-breath attempt it was time to add a backpack with a little weight. I added ten pounds a week until I was hiking the route with forty pounds, and running, while on sections of level ground. It was during this time of preparation that I named my poles Faith and Perseverance.

I knew I would need both of these if I was to do a longer hike. Six months after I started training, I headed out for Vermont and completed the southern half, 145 miles. My pack on the trail weighed around sixty pounds, and I totally enjoyed the trip; I still look back on it with pleasant memories, and, pride in what I was able to accomplish. This would never have been possible without the early morning, or late night, daily three-mile training sessions that were carried out through winter and early spring, 2000 and 2001. And the side benefit was the time I had during this hikes to reflect on the "subjects in hand," faith and perseverance.

Trekking Poles, Not Crutches

Some may say, I would guess non-hikers, that trekking poles are just a crutch. I beg to differ. If I get injured, a doctor may put me on crutches for a while with the express purpose being to assist me in preventing further injury while my foot or leg heals. But the end goal is for me to be able to eventually cast away the crutches, and walk normally again.

Trekking poles are different. When backpacking, poles provide balance, and relief from a load that you must carry; it's just a necessary part of this journey. And who in life doesn't have some sort of load to carry; that's the way it is. When you sit down, you can rest and get relief from the load, sometimes even take the pack off and walk around without it for a few moments, but when you are ready to continue down, or up, the trail, you must put the pack on again. And the trekking poles help you get back upright. As you walk along, you can look around and enjoy the views, large and small, even more because you have those two poles acting as an additional sense of balance.

A Great Weight Lifted

I read an article several years ago in *Backpacker* magazine (fortunately before I left for the Vermont Long Trail) about the load-lightening value of trekking poles. When you have a pack on your back, every time you push down on the trekking poles as you walk along, the load is lessened, which means less weight bearing down on your back, and particularly, knees; the article said over 200 cumulative tons! The cumulative load reduction for a day is astounding, and my calculations which follow, line up with those put forth in the article. In order to verify this, I stood on scales with a fifty pound pack, a trekking pole in each hand, and just lightly pushed down on the pole the same as I would while walking along. The scale weight dropped some 20 to 25 pounds.

It's time to do the math. If I walk along at a normal pace I will be pushing down on the poles at the rate of about one per second. That multiplies out to 20 lbs. X 60 seconds which comes out to 1200 lbs. /minute. I lowered the 1200 to 1000 for easier computation, and occasional distractions such as glancing at squirrels or rhododendron. With a ten minute break every hour, I will go for 50 minutes, and 1000 lbs. X 50 min. = 50,000 lbs. Now I'm going to stop for lunch, but all in all, put in a good 8 hr. day, which is not at all uncommon; serious backpackers often do more. So, 50,000 lbs. X 8 hrs. = 400,000 lbs. To determine this in tons, I must divide 400,000 lbs. by 2000 lbs. and come up with 200 TONS. That is a lot of cumulative weight kept off knees in the course of a day! Go trekking poles!

At the Stratton Shelter on the Long Trail, I encountered a woman and her fourteen-year-old son who were averaging 18-25 miles per day. They each used trekking poles, and their cumulative weight lessening would have been much more than what I achieved in my little 10-12 mile days.

It's the Trekking Poles, Stupid

After four days hiking and about forty miles I took a side trail into Manchester, Vermont to spend a night at a Bed and Breakfast, and get resupplied. That evening I called my sons to update them on my progress. When talking with my oldest son, Ralph, I asked him if he remembered how difficult our twenty-nine mile day had been on the northern section of the Great Smoky Mountain National Park. Naturally, he responded that he did. I then said, "Ralph, in a paraphrase of one of the 1992 Bill Clinton presidential campaign slogans, 'It's the trekking poles, stupid!'" We did not use any, and I now know our hike that day would have been a lot easier if we had. I'm trying to use the trekking poles of Faith and Perseverance more in daily living.

Four Hundred Sunday Papers

Perseverance is a factor in the healing process. One area where I was forced to think about perseverance quite a bit was in 1990 when for a period of time I had an early morning Lexington-Herald paper delivery route that during the week was about 190 miles long with around 350 customers, and on Sundays, around 210 miles, with 425 customers. On Sunday mornings, around two AM, I would get to the paper drop-off spot in front of the Jackson Inn, and, paper by paper, insert the weekend supplements, and then load the car. I had a small GEO Spectrum, so by the time the task was completed, I only had a clear view to the front. But as I went along, I measured my progress by which windows I could start to see out of, then which seats emptied, and, eventually, around nine a.m., by the "emptiness" of the car. At two a.m., what seemed nearly insurmountable had been accomplished, by persevering, and dropping off one paper at a time. I've related that to life many times.

Another factor that enters in as far as persevering, is the reason it may be taking so long to "rid ourselves of the demons" we wrestle with. Total, immediate healing of our inner woundings might be more than we could handle at one time. I'll explain by way of an Old Testament example. Moses was receiving information from God about when the Israelites would be going into "the promised land."

Exodus 23: 29 and 30 reads, "But I will not drive them (their enemies) out in a single year, because the land would become desolate and the wild animals too numerous for you. Little by little I will drive them out before you, until you have increased enough to take possession of the land."

In other words, if they had taken over the whole territory at one time they wouldn't have been strong enough to hold on to it. They had to slowly increase their strength and capabilities to match the new territory they were conquering. And trust me, when we move into areas of inner healing in our lives, it is moving into a whole new world which carries with it, new responsibilities. We have to expand our capacities to cope, and that does not, cannot, and should not, happen too quickly.

Faith and Perseverance

Forwardly looking
And believing
In the certainty of the
Things not seen and being sure of the things
Hoped for.

All in all, I
Need to have my
Daily reminders (trekking poles, perhaps?)

Perhaps I should quit
Except there is something
Really deep inside that keeps
Saying I should (once again)
Extract myself from another
(Very predictable) mess and
Examine the
Road I'm on
And look for
New strategies and ways to
Cope with my
Ever-developing life.

It "Ain't" Over 'Til the Checkered Flag Falls

In the Goody's 500 NASCAR race in late August, 1995, Terry Labonte was in the lead, headed toward the checkered flag. He was bumped by Dale Earnhardt, and his car went into a spin. Labonte said he kept his foot on the gas, and because of this was able to say, "This is the first race I have won sliding backwards across the line." Every driver's nightmare turned into every driver's dream.

But, this stinks

On some days while driving from my house to Pikeville, there is an area where there is frequently a "sewer smell." This is especially noticeable if driving in the Miata with the top down. There is only one thing to do; keep driving; the smell eventually becomes a part of the past.

Exodus 6, tells of the difficulty Moses had when trying to convince the Hebrews in Egypt that they are about to be delivered. In verse 9 we read, "… but they did not listen to him because of their discouragement and cruel bondage." It is hard to feel hope in the midst of bondage, abuse, or illness. I think that what we can only see in retrospect is, "To hang in there; the story is not over yet."

This is reinforced by the Apostle Paul in Philippians 3: verses 13 and 14; "But one thing I do: Forgetting what is behind and straining toward what is ahead, I press on toward the goal …"

I think quicker than I do

Cora and I were talking about some sabbatical deadlines I had set, and I said, "My problem is, I *think* accomplishment quicker than I *do* accomplishment."

This is probably true for many of us, and thinking about it, can be a place of discouragement. It becomes important when we encounter these times to persevere. Faith might be in the thinking, but we must follow through with "do" to increase faith and bring the desired goal to fruition.

I have found a boost in my faith at various times in Psalm 27: 13 and 14. "I am still confident of this: I will see the goodness of the Lord in the land of the living. Wait for the Lord; be strong and take heart and wait for the Lord." Somehow this does help me see more clearly what I must set out to do, or continue to do, to accomplish my desired objective.

49

Proverbs 17:22 – A Cheerful Heart is Good Medicine

Like the plaque I have of the Panda Bear trying to stand on her head says, "Life is too important to be taken seriously."

But some may say, there are times when it just doesn't feel good to laugh; times to be serious. After all, life is not a joke.

Laughter; Good Medicine?

Yeah, so I've heard it said, that
Laughter is good medicine.
And maybe it is; for some people,
Some circumstances.

So why don't you walk a mile
In my shoes, experience what
I'm going through, and, maybe,
Just maybe, you'll sing a different tune.

Thankfulness, Praise, Laughter (similar effects from each)

Sometimes when we are really down, it is difficult to laugh or be cheerful. Although we can multi-task in some areas, emotionally, this one just might be too hard to do. The closest we may come to it is a "certain poignancy" at times; a feeling that may be best described as a "sweet and sour pork" moment. And we can't rule out that there are times where laughter or "excessive bubbliness" might not be altogether appropriate.

I recall watching a show years ago (can't recall details of date, network, etc.) where a woman was talking about the comic actor, Eddie Murphy. She said that some time earlier her only child, a son, had been killed under tragic circumstances, and the afternoon after the funeral, she went home to an empty house, overwhelmed with the events of recent days, wondering about the meaning of her life, and whether there was any reason for her to even go on.

She said after a while she turned on the television and flipped through channels. There was an Eddie Murphy movie starting, and she numbly started to watch it. She recounted how there were some places where she couldn't stop herself from laughing, and when the movie was over, she felt a sense that she could go on, that she could hope, and that her life was worth living after all.

Some may wonder how all that could come out of an Eddie Murphy, or any, comedy; I'm not sure as it did; it may have come out of the laughter.

Laughter in Extreme Conditions

I know I have referred to *The Long Walk* by Slavomir Rawicz several times, but it is such a good story about inner wounding, perseverance, etc., and, also, laughter. One of the six other escapees with him from the Siberian prison camp was a man called Zaro. One night when they were a few days distance from the camp, they were particularly exhausted, and forcing their muscles to scrape snow up for a sheltering wall, when Zaro squatted down in the snow, put his hands on his hips, and started kicking his feet forward as he did a Russian dance. Rawicz said that they all started laughing at the sight, and that Zaro taught them that even when life seemed most unpleasant and dark, that one could still find humor.

Rawicz also said that sometimes watching Zaro and another escapee joke around that it was hard to remember that they were in such a difficult situation, with barely any food, and the hardest part of their journey ahead of them.

Smile Anyway [2013]

I don't know if I can get through this; it is just too much to bear.
And you don't know what to say because you don't understand.
Life doesn't seem fair; what are we? Like C.S. Lewis questioned,
"Rats in the cosmic laboratory, with God as the vivisectionist?"

Lord, help me to be like Zaro in *The Long Walk*,
Exhausted, sore, cold, no fire, and snow falling.
Not really in the best of circumstances; but anyway,
Let me, like him, laugh and "play in the snow."

Easier to act your way ...

I have told acting classes on occasion that I read somewhere that it is easier to act your way into feeling good than to feel your way into acting good. I say the same thing if talking to a class about job interviews. Someone may not feel on top of the world, or may be nervous or anxious about an interview, but if he or she can walk through the door looking confident and professional, and greet the interviewer with a firm handshake, that will go a lot further than shuffling through the door, head down, and extending a "limp fish."

Try walking around for a minute or so with shoulders slumped, mouth in a half-frown, and dragging your feet along. Then change to upright shoulders, smiling, or at least a hint thereof, and a brisk walk. You look different, you feel different, and in time you can change to a different attitude. It seems that's the way God has put our system together; we can change the way we feel.

Smile, in Hope of Better Things to Come

We read that faith is the substance of things hoped for,
The evidence of things not seen. Is that what, in court,
They call circumstantial evidence? I mean, if you knew
What I knew, or, you felt what I'm feeling, you would agree,
It is not a smiley kind of day.

But there seems to be a place where we have to trust
In the bigger picture, and in the one we believe is being painted,
So, in spite of the noise in my ears, or the noise in my spirit,
Or all the other pains, help me, Lord to smile, and trust,
In hope of better things to come.

Not good; or, maybe, if this isn't funny, then why does it make me smile?

I guess maybe it makes me smile in part due to the "sick" sense of humor and irony developed while in the Infantry in Vietnam.

I remember reading in 1992 about a flight in Russia where the pilot had brought his two young children into the cockpit with him. The plane crashed, and all seventy-four people on board were killed. When the black box was recovered, among the last words spoken was a child's voice asking, "Daddy, what does this knob do?"

Now, it was not established whether the child turned the knob or not, but those were the last words recorded. So, like I said as a heading for this, "Not good; or, maybe, if this isn't funny, then why does it make me smile?"

Made Sense to Me

Trying to make the numbers add up can be a difficult task sometimes. The following incident basically shows that even when they don't (add up), one can still have a sense of humor about it all; as a matter of fact, I think an underlying sense of humor is what helps us survive in many situations.

I earlier mentioned my nickname, and squad leader call-sign for the radio, was Crazy Horse. When I came back from stateside leave to start my second tour of Vietnam duty, I was assigned as Platoon Sergeant for our Battalion's Reconnaissance Platoon. When our Platoon Leader went on a thirty day leave I was appointed to fill his position until his return. One of our missions was to recon an area where the day before Alpha Company had been in a firefight and suffered thirty-two wounded; thankfully, no one killed. Just before we were to board the helicopters to fly us out, one of the men in the platoon came to me with the following concern.

"Sarge," he asked, "Got something bothering me," and, of course, I asked him what it was.

"Well," he continued, "I'm wondering, we're going into the same area where Alpha Company had thirty-two men wounded yesterday, and we only have twenty-five in our platoon. Isn't that a bit of a problem?"

I'm sure I set his fears at ease as I replied, "Well, I can guarantee you one thing, we know for sure we won't get thirty-two wounded."

(Just stating the facts, sir, just stating the facts.)

50
Peace Like a River(or Maybe a Lake)

Picture taken and poem written, July 2012

Prairie Lake, MN

The two days spent there were a taste of heaven.
Surely heaven will consist of peace, hummingbirds, lakes
Family, friends, and gentle dogs.

Prairie Lake, MN; a taste of heaven.

In Isaiah 66:12 we read in part, "I will extend peace to her like a river."
I believe "peace like a river" is no accidental choice of words. Of course, we
all know there are times of flooding and destruction connected to rivers, but
by and large, peace is a word associated with rivers and lakes. Fishing may be
fun and relaxing, and even provide good eating, but it is done in conjunction
with water and most people I know who fish say they enjoy it because it is so
peaceful.

My mother's death, and, South River, Riva, MD

I called my folks every Sunday evening; usually it was Mom who answered the phone and talked. On March 25th, 2012, we talked for quite a

while, including in our conversation the fact that her 87th birthday was coming up in a few days, on the 31st. A nice talk, like so many before. The next day I received a call from my sister telling me that she and my brother Dan, and my father were with Mom; that the night before, she had fallen and had been taken to the hospital. They told me they would keep me posted on what was going on. Another call later in the day revealed that the doctor wanted to keep her for observation as something "wasn't right." The next afternoon my brother Dan called and said the tests showed that Mom had cancer in her liver and spleen and had been told she had a few days to a few months to live. I made plans to leave for Colorado the following week as the University of Pikeville had no classes on Good Friday. I received permission from my Division Chair and Academic Dean to take the days before and after the Easter Break, so I figured I would leave Wednesday after classes, drive through the night to Bartlesville, OK, pick up Rocky, and then go with him to Sterling, CO. We could spend Friday and Saturday with Mom, leave Sunday to go back to Bartlesville, and then Monday I could drive back to Pikeville.

I was able to talk on the phone with my mother briefly on her birthday, but I could tell she was not feeling well. On Monday, April 2nd, my sister called and said Mom was going downhill fast. Paula and I talked for several minutes and she told me if I left right then I still might not get there before Mom died, and that even if I did, she doubted Mom would know who I was. That confirmed plans I had talked about earlier with both Paula and Dan. Christmas 2011, I was visiting Mom and Dad, and Mom and I had talked what I should do if she died before her sister Beverly who resides in an assisted living home in Brattleboro, Vermont. Mom and I agreed that if she departed this life before her sister, instead of going out to Colorado to the funeral, I would go be with my Aunt Bev, for a few days.

I notified my Division Chair and Academic Dean that I wanted to follow the same time schedule, but I planned on going to Vermont instead of Colorado. On Wednesday, April 4th, I had classes at 9, 10, and 11 a.m., so I packed everything I would need so I could leave from the school at noon. I had told my students that if my cell vibrated and it was from one of my siblings that I would step out of the room to take the call. Shortly after 9 a.m. my brother called to tell me Mom had just died. I finished that class, and on the break between my next classes called Aunt Bev to let her know I was leaving at noon and that I would be with her in Brattleboro the next morning.

I drove "Missy Mae," our 2008 Burgundy Miata ragtop. It was a beautiful sunny afternoon, and especially driving on I-68 from Morgantown, WV, to I-81 N, it was a wonderful time of reflection on Mom's life, while drinking in the beautiful scenery and sky. I wasn't with Mom, but it was almost heaven.

It was also a good choice to go be with Aunt Bev. She and Mom were the last of seven siblings, and losing Mom was especially hard on her. I was able to spend Thursday and most of Friday with her, and we were together Friday the 6th at the time the burial took place two time zones away. Later I headed back toward Kentucky by way of Riva, MD, where I was going to spend a day resting at the home of Bob and Nellie Cunningham, a sister-in-law and her husband. I arrived at their place shortly after midnight and was able to catch up on some sleep. Their home sits where the following picture is a typical view of a sunrise over the South River.

The evening of the 7th I spent a couple of hours on a dock on the river, reflecting, and feeling peace like a river.

Peace Like A River April 7th, 2012

Pondering, reflecting over links to
Eternity. Mom was buried yesterday, just
A day ago, and I had made the
Choice to go spend time with her only remaining sibling.
Every choice has consequences; these were good. Now I'm

Looking out over South River
In Riva, MD, and I
Know that the trip to Vermont to spend
Extra time with Aunt Bev had been the right thing to do.

Although the circumstances were sad, we

Really took a lot of comfort in the fact that Mom had entered
Into another realm, one she was
Very much ready to go to, and so
Even as I sit on a dock on the South River,
Reflecting, pondering, I know everything is okay.

The first time I cried after hearing Mom was dying was when it struck me she would never meet my wife Cora. We were planning a trip to Colorado summer of 2012, but Mom wouldn't be there. They would have liked each other.

I'll also miss Mom's "Check-up calls." "I saw on the news there was a bad storm in Kentucky; are you guys okay?" "Sure; Louisville's over 200 miles away." "Okay; just checking. Mothers worry, you know." I'll miss those calls.

I was hanging by the seat of my pants on a small stub of a broken branch up the tree near our house in Sterling, Massachusetts. Mom said I was four or five. This is one of my earliest memories of tree climbing. Apparently I had slipped; the rear of my pants got caught on the stub. Mom heard me hollering for help, and came to my rescue.

Henrietta Marvel Clark

Hanging by the seat of my pants,
Enough broken branch stub to catch my
Nearly new four-year-old body from
Really getting hurt.
I remember Mom saying she wasn't real
Excited about climbing
The tree, but
There was no
Alternative. And,

Moms do what they gotta do
And so she donned pants, took a
Real deep breath, and started the
Vertical trip to rescue me.
Eventually, back on the ground, she said she
Laughed long and hard about it. I

Could write many stories,
Long and short,
And a few best forgotten, about a
Really wonderful Mom who
Knew exactly what I needed.

Don't you dare try

About three and a half months after my mother died I was visiting with my brother Dan, who along with my sister Paula, was with Mom most of the time during her final days. He was telling Cora and me that after her initial diagnosis and being informed by the doctor that she had maybe three days to six months to live, her doctor then told Mom they had a couple options. One was to keep her as comfortable as possible while nature ran its course; the other was to hook her up to systems that would prolong her life. Upon hearing the second option, Dan said Mom immediately told her doctor, "Don't you dare try and slow me down from meeting Jesus!"

Mom's Faith

Me; I have to admit,
Over the years I have had a few
Moments where I thought that surely
'**S**he was being somewhat naive. However,

Finally, the day came for
A journey for her from this world and
Its problems to
The next realm.
How well she took it!

I am at peace with God ...

Mom's leaving this world puts me in mind of the last page of *A Grief Observed* when C. S. Lewis writes of his wife, Joy's, last words; that she said she was at peace with God.

You Ain't Seen Nothing, Yet

Mom died on April 4th, and a week later, the 11th, I was with one of my appreciation of theatre classes at the Prestonsburg campus of Big Sandy Community and Technical College for some "heritage presentations." While there, we were also treated to a laser light show in their planetarium. I can't recall the songs that the displays were timed with, but they had nice, strong beats. I laid back in the reclining chair and thoroughly enjoyed. And, afterward, I told my class that it was almost as if I could hear my mother saying, "This is cool, son, but, trust me, you ain't seen nothing yet!"

Nettie Hyde; my "surrogate mother-in-law"

My wife lost her mother at the age of twelve, and, Nettie, a neighbor, with children of her own, tried to be a mother as much as she could for Cora and her siblings. I met Nettie shortly after Cora and I started dating, and we took to each other right away. Every time we visited family in Robbinsville, we also stopped to see Nettie. Recently she went to the hospital in a lot of pain, doctors discovered she was "loaded with cancer," so she went into a nursing home for what everyone knew, Nettie included, were her final days. On May 7th, 2013, Cora and I went to Robbinsville for the day to see her, feeling quite certain it would be our last time, at least in this realm. It was; Nettie died a few days later, at the age of ninety-one. Cora's comments on Nettie's passing were, "I can't feel sad for her; she was in so much pain, and she was ready to go. I almost feel bad, not feeling sad for her; but I do feel at peace."

Like the river rolling in what seems to be an eternal cycle, Cora found peace in her loss because she knew Nettie was also at peace, and, as a part of the sequences of life, had transitioned to the next realm. It's calming for me to observe, that most folks, when it's time, seem ready to move on and join all the other "people-molecules" that have already entered the flow of the eternal river.

```
WWW      WWW         OOOO
WWW      WWW        OOO  OOO
WWWWWWWWW         OOO    OOO
WWW      WWW       OOO    OOO
WWWWWWWWW         OOO     OOO
WWWWWWWWW         OOO     OOO
WWW      WWW       OOO   OOO
WWW      WWW        OOOOOO
WWW      WWW    2    OOOO
```

Peace Like A River II April 7th, 2012

Possibly the most relaxing thing
Ever is to sit on the bank of
A river – or stream –
Contemplating things – temporal, or
Eternal.

Looking at the waters flowing
Into their next phase, one
Knows, senses deep inside,
Every trouble is being soothed.

A river offers

Repair for the soul; how
It happens is beyond me.
Very often I'm not
Even aware of how much I've
Really settled, until I stand up to leave.

Rivers April 2012

What is it about rivers and streams that reaches into the very depths of my soul and overwhelms it with peace; a settling effect?

I think that there is somehow a link to a larger process that pulls me out of myself and connects me to an eternal flow, and lets me be flooded with the awareness that I am a very small part of a larger picture being painted.

Possibly the best thing to do after sitting by waters is go work in a garden so I can reflect even more on just how it is that the Artist works the brush.

Wet 'Artism'

Water and I don't even speak the same language.
As a matter of fact, as far as I know, it can't even
Think like I do. And, yet, why is it, that when it comes to
Etching a beautiful piece of artwork on a
Rock, it will always surpass me, even with all its supposed limitations?

Wet 'Artism' II

Narrow at places, though in other spots it spreads to a fan
As it slowly, powerfully, carves out the land. We sometimes can ob-
serve
The immediate effects of water over the rock; other times it takes years
for the
Mystical force, which no one can block, to complete its artwork.

Water; Let Me Try to Gain

There is plenty of transparency, and it is easy to see through
(unless you are overwhelmed.)
It is a life sustaining fluid which washes out impurities
(unless you're under.)
Water is totally refreshing and brings unparalleled invigoration
(unless, of course, it is contaminated.)
However, though there's negative to find, let me
(try to) gain its qualities.

Location Shift

On almost any given day we can look at parking lots of
Drugstores, bar rooms, and, even churches, and
Find them full, or almost so.

And yet I wonder if some of these spots would see a
Reduction of cars outside, and, therefore, less people inside,
Maybe even go out of business

Because of a location shift. With new activities, we might even see
The sales of pens go up as poets flourish, and, probably an increase in
The sale of softballs, and Frisbees.

Yes, if only more people would go out, by themselves,
Or with their families, to play, enjoy God's world, and be by
The streams and the waterfalls.

Peace in the Absence of a River

In the final reference in this book to *The Long Walk*, Slavomir Rawicz tells of a period of time when another escapee from a different location, a young, seventeen-year-old girl, joined and traveled with them for some time. He says that she saw them all as either older brothers, or in the case of the oldest escapee, a father figure. Rawicz wrote that even if all the men were restless due to worry over travel conditions, lack of food, etc., Kristina would be able to sleep comfortably because her trust in them was so complete. What a tribute to peace of mind through trust. My prayer is that we may all find this kind of trust in One who sees the bigger picture.

Another Conclusion (of sorts)
or Maybe a Beginning

So perhaps we can conclude that although there may have been, or still may be, some really rough or negative times in our lives, the paradox is that, as in Nature, we may find our scars are part of an etching being turned into a beautiful picture.

APPENDIX A

From the writings in this book, and other places, we can see that there are many who feel the answer to the problems facing them is to end it all. But, what would it be like for someone who was then chained to the consequences of his actions? The following short story explores this idea.

To Choose or Not To Choose, That is the Consequence

Ted Dixon's fingers recoiled slightly as they touched the barrel of the .22 caliber Derringer pistol, but he forced them on to close over the weapon and lift it up. Slowly reaching down with his free right hand, he firmly grasped the handle and lightly felt the trigger with his index finger. He lifted it up and away so that the open end of the barrel was pointed at the off-white spackled ceiling. Ted deliberated a few seconds while rolling his lower lip into his mouth, biting on it. His eyelids lowered to shut out light from eyes that already ached too much. Then with a deep breath he opened them again. Looking slightly away so he could barely see what was happening in his line of peripheral vision, he brought the barrel perpendicular to his temple. He paused again and his thoughts flashed to Joanna.

"It'll hurt, but only for a while ... there are others ... better off without me ... Dad won't care ... my car's out ... I've got no money ... nothing going right. Who cares?"

Taking another deep breath, Ted edged the barrel end closer to his head.

The deafening roar settled down to a buzzing sound that was somewhat like their lawn mower. Then Ted experienced a feeling similar to what he had when he rode up an elevator.

"Strange. I should be dead," he thought. "So what went wrong?" As he rose higher, he looked down and saw someone lying in a crumpled heap on the floor with blood spurting from a gaping wound in his right temple.

"I've got a shirt like that. And pants." Ted strained to make sense out of this dream, and felt like he was looking at someone unusually familiar.

"That gun. That's my Derringer. How'd it? That's me! But what--?"

The door to his bedroom flew open as his mother took one look at the bloody pile in the middle of the floor and let out a piercing scream. She collapsed to her knees next to his twisted body, and threw her arms around him. "Oh, dear God! Teddy! Teddy! Teddy!"

"It's all right, Mom! I'm right here!" Ted called loudly. Funny. He remembered calling out the same thing some fourteen years earlier from the shelf corner of the closet in this same room. He was four then, and playing hide-and-seek with Mommy. She stayed downstairs in the kitchen for five minutes and then came looking for him. After "looking" for a few moments, she started calling for him. But this time she didn't respond to his reassurances to her.

"Oh, Teddy, what did you do? Oh God, my baby! my baby! my baby! Oh God!" Clutching his corpse to her breasts, she rocked the upper half of her body back and forth.

Again Ted hollered to his mother, but to no avail. "She can't hear me. I'm really dead. I can see and hear her, but she's not even aware that I'm here." Unable to bear the spectacle of his mother's heartbreak any longer, Ted turned to leave, but no matter how he tried, couldn't. As he puzzled over this, he became aware of a slight crackling sound, like Rice Crispies right after the milk is poured over them. Then he observed its source coming into focus. It was some sort of energy field, pinpointed flakes of light that appeared to be a series of circles, a chain that ran from right in front of him, wherever he was, down to his mother, where for some illogical reason he could see its penetration into her body where the innermost link was lodged into a spot centered between her breasts and shoulder blades.

Ted thought maybe he could yank the chain loose, but he couldn't get hold of it.

"So here I am, stuck in my spirit, no body, full of emotions. How can-- no! Hell is just a joke, besides there's no fire, no one else is here. But I can't leave and I can't talk to Mom and I can't go back to my body!"

Again Ted ineffectively tried to grasp the chain.

Still sobbing heavily, Mrs. Dixon released her grip on his body, lurched back on her hands and knees, and turned so she could use the chair near Ted's cluttered desk to pull herself up. She looked as though each rise and fall off her chest, in rhythm with her breathing, was forcing the last traces of energy out of her. She blindly felt for the phone on his desk and fumbled as she picked it up. She automatically dialed her husband's office while staring through and beyond the numbers.

Ted's mind felt like it was breaking with the new feeling washing over him, for not only was he linked to and fully aware of his mother, but he was also completely confronted with his blood-smeared heap of a body lying life-less on his bedroom floor. Then a third energy chain shot out from his spirit and he was also watching his father push the button on his desk intercom and tell his secretary, "Put her through, Tricia, thank you." Then, "Hi, Joyce ... Joyce? ... Joyce! What's wrong? ... Ted? What? Joyce! Calm down and tell me what's wrong!"

Ted watched his father's face freeze into shocked disbelief. "Oh, no! Oh, God, no! Joyce, he didn't! I'll be right home. Call Dr. Raynor, and have him come right over. I'll be right there, Joyce. I'll be right there."

Theodore Dixon dazedly hung up the phone and stared long and hard for a moment at his desk, as his eyes misted over, then tears started flowing. Ted felt a choking sensation as he called, "Dad, I'm, sorry! I didn't mean to, Dad! I really didn't mean to!" The same earlier frustration swept over him as again he realized he was not being heard. Then he watched as his father raced into action, grabbed his jacket from the back of the chair, and flew out the door. As he passed his startled secretary, he gasped, "Emergency at home! I'll call later!"

Meanwhile Ted was also registering his mother's call to the doctor and the accompanying expressed shock on Bud Raynor's face as he too prepared to rush to the Dixon's. Ted put all his efforts one more time into trying to return to his body, but soon realized it was useless. The same energy that linked him to those finding out about his crumpled body also prevented him from rejoining it.

As his mother hesitantly dialed Joanna's number, Ted realized he had to concentrate hard to even remember what last night's argument was about. The anger he had felt at the end of the evening when Joanna insinuated he was being childish had been fueled by the self-pity he felt while he was sulking.

"Hello?" Joanna cheerfully responded as she picked up her white and gold Classic style phone from the white Colonial nightstand next to her bed. The pages closed on the Penguin paperback she had been reading, and Ted's spirit ached with a smile as he observed the title, *Piers the Plowman*. Joanna loved Langland, Chaucer, and other Middle English authors. As a freshman at Vine Oaks Community College, she often spoke of the various literature courses she would be able to take after her transfer to Tyson University.

"It was a mistake, Joanna! A foolish mistake!" Ted screamed out as loudly as he could, but knew as he started that there was no awareness on her part of anything but what she was hearing from Joyce Dixon on the other end of her phone. For Joanna, plans and dreams of a week ago came crashing down on the bed beside her, and mingled with her shock and disbelief was the very obvious sense of loss of someone dear to her.

Shaking her head, Joanna cried out, "But why? Why'd he do it?" She broke down, her body wracked with large sobs as her mother rushed into the room asking, "Joanna? What's wrong, dear? What's the matter?"

Ted felt chain after chain fly out from him as the news was relayed to family and friends, and the agony of being intimately linked to them in their sorrow and confusion was becoming more than he could bear. The reality of his action was sinking in as the clay that once housed him was removed to the Vine Oaks Funeral Home for burial preparations. Howard Watson had assured his parents he was confident that he could repair the head so that there could be an open casket funeral. Ted watched as Howard and his assistant, Jason, prepared the body.

Jason spoke. "I've seen these before, but I guess I'll never get over it. It seems that a lot less people would do this if they could be around for the aftermath."

"Yeah," Howard answered. "You never get used to it. I guess if they ever hint at it, most people think they're just kidding. I don't know. It seems like a lot of this could be avoided if we could all learn to love just a little bit more."

"Love," Jason sighed. "Easy to say--and sing about, but it really boils down to a lot of effort--and perseverance."

"I think you've got that right," Howard responded. "Now if you'll hand me that scalpel, I'll start the incision near this wound."

Ted wished he could look away, but his focus was riveted to the mortician's right hand as it firmly grasped the scalpel handle and brought the blade toward the right temple of Ted's lifeless head. As the metal touched his skin, the cold steel of the barrel startled him, and after slowly lowering the pistol and placing it on the desk, Ted sat down in his chair, picked up the phone, and dialed Joanna's number.

Speaking generally here, the human race as a whole might be better off if we would all do more of what the character Ted did in the story, where he obviously took a trip in his mind, feeding forward if you will, thinking about aftermaths. How much heartache and pain could be avoided if we seriously considered how our choices might affect others.

The problem is, as expressed in other places in this book, when we are in the middle of our very subjective woundings, it is hard to see clearly through the fog that is encompassing us. But it is something we must strive to do on the pathway to peace. And my general conclusion and belief is that, as so many pointed out in their stories, the spiritual realm enters into the equation.

John 14:27a says, "Peace I leave with you; my peace I give you."

APPENDIX B

Rodney Evans; Then and Now

As mentioned in the Introduction and in Chapter Two, Appendices B and C are about an event that occurred some 40 years ago, and a dramatic re-creation of that event just recently on a stage at the University of Minnesota, Crookston Campus.

First, the original; Rodney Evans was a squad leader in 3rd platoon, Company D, 1/12th, 1st Air Cavalry. He had somewhat of a "don't give a damn" attitude, which stemmed from the loss of his wife, Barbara, in an auto accident. He had already served time in Vietnam, but after his wife's death, re-enlisted, and volunteered for Vietnam again. Not surprisingly, Rodney's favorite song was "Honey" by Bobby Goldsboro.

July 1969 was about halfway through my tour of duty in Vietnam, and there had already been several friends lost by that time. Now, in combat, as in many stressful situations, the humor that comes out might be considered sick by some, but it's a survival technique. Rodney and I used to joke about things like, "If you die today, can I have your watch?" A possible response would be, "Okay, but only if I can have your socks if you die." Or maybe it went like, "Hey, did you hear we get to change underwear today?" "Oh, really? Good." "Yeah, you get to change with Bill; Sam gets to change with Leon, etc."

I still recall the morning of the day he was killed; he was eating a pork slice "C-Ration" meal for breakfast. We used to kid him about being hard-core, because, in fact, he claimed it was his favorite meal, which was very hard to comprehend; anyone familiar with the old pork slice meal should know what I'm talking about.

Anyway, it was the day after his 21st birthday, and Rodney was saying he thought a man should have his favorite meal before he died. A couple of us were asking him what he was talking about; after all he had just turned twenty-one, and had his whole life ahead of him. Rodney said he didn't feel like living anymore. We tried to get him in a better mood, but he was really quiet, pensive.

A little later our platoon was moving out on patrol, and a Chi-Cong mine was blown which injured a dog handler and his dog who were assigned to our platoon for a few days to help scout the area. Several people gathered around the handler to assist him, and apparently Rodney saw another mine as he hollered for people to take cover, and quickly scrambled toward the mine and threw himself on it, just as it exploded. It killed him instantly. The irony of the whole situation is that Rodney got his wish to die, and saved several lives in the process, for which he, posthumously, received the Medal of Honor.

However, as his body was being carried past, I realized I couldn't cry; there was just a hollow, empty feeling. I also felt guilty about all the joking we had done.

Rodney Evans

Resisting the future
On his 21st birthday, the day after
Declaring he didn't want a
New year ahead, but,
Eventually eating his favorite –
Yuck – Pork slices, C-ration, for breakfast.

Everyone in 3rd platoon on patrol was
Very cautious, but the Viet Cong had set an
Ambush with a Chi-Cong mine.
No one saw but Rodney, who dove on it and died, his wish, and he
Saved our lives – and received the Medal of Honor.

Rodney like A Birthday P/H

Rodney like a birthday rolls around.
He was 21 the day he settled down
To a piece of lifeless clay on a hot Vietnam day;
Yes, Rodney like a birthday rolls around.

I cried over others, but I couldn't over him.
I guess the war had dulled too much by then.
There was just an empty feeling as I watched his body die,
And I knew another friend had been done in.

He'd tasted sorrow deep at an earlier age.
Married young and thought the world of her.
One night, some-time later, she was driving in the rain.
Her wreck and death left Rodney in a constant state of pain.

We'd done a lot of joking, just to keep our sanity,
Like, if you die, I'll take your watch, it should belong to me.
His watch was on his arm as I watched his body die.
I cursed myself for all the jokes, but ached too much to cry.

The play, *Starkle, Starkle, Little Twink*

I mentioned in Chapter Two; Turn It Off, Please, how, during 1982-83, while a graduate student at the University of Kentucky I wrote the play, *Starkle, Starkle, Little Twink* (Appendix B.) The play is roughly autobiographical, which also means there are places where "poetic license" comes into play. For example, Rodney Evans and I were friends, and the details of the day he died and was awarded the Medal of Honor are fairly accurate. However, there are instances and conversations between him and me in the play which did not occur but are there strictly for character development in a dramatic writing that has a theme about overcoming obstacles that are dragging one down through a self-destructive lifestyle.

I also mentioned at the end of Chapter Two that *Starkle, Starkle, Little Twink* was included in *Poetic Healing: A Vietnam Veteran's Journey from a Communication Perspective.*

In late 2008 I received a call from Mark Huglen, co-author, now teaching at the University of Minnesota, Crookston Campus. Mark had used the book as a text in a Humans Relations course and one of his students asked if there was a chance of the University producing the play. The Theatre Department was interested, and Mark asked if I would be able to be there, not only as guest playwright, but also as an actor, to play the role of DAN, the main character, which was roughly based on me.

To shorten a long story (and this appendix), the end of March 2009 found Cora and me traveling to northern Minnesota, the town of Crookston.

You would think since I wrote the play, learning the lines would be easy. However, getting ready for this performance was the most difficult role I have ever prepared for. Winter of 2009 I found myself back almost to where I was originally writing the play; cursing, weeping, praying. I say almost because this time I did not feel the need to drink.

As an actor, to develop a role, you have to dig into the character's lines so you can portray that character on-stage as accurately as possible. In this case, I was dealing with lines that brought back personally some of the things I had needed to "go through a poetic healing" with. Now I had to dig them back up to re-create them in a performance. I am so grateful Cora was in my life by this time, even though 300 miles away, as there were several times on the phone where I had to talk my way through some "down moments." And, I am also grateful she accompanied me on the trip from Kentucky to Minnesota.

After arrival at Crookston, in one heck of a snowstorm, I spent a couple days in rehearsal with a really good and dedicated cast, and then on Friday evening, March 27th, 2009, we presented the play. Later, as "an observer of myself" I was able to evaluate the difference time makes in traumatic events, especially when an emotional healing has taken place. There is life "on the other side," even if you have to revisit the original incident. It was very close to a flash-back situation during the "memorial service" for Rodney onstage, and I had a very hard time keeping the character separate from the actor.

But some things happened after the performance that let me know that taking on the role and all the difficulties experienced while preparing for it were worth it. The cast went out to the lobby to meet those who attended the packed house performance. I met several Vietnam veterans who said they felt a sense of purging as they watched the play. That's what it originally did for me, I've now seen it positively affect others, and, this, also, is **what war wounded, let the healing begin is all about.**

APPENDIX C

A Play.   *Starkle, Starkle, Little Twink (Revised 2013)*

CAST OF CHARACTERS

> DANIEL DELONG: 34, a Vietnam veteran
>
> PAMELA DELONG: 33, Daniel's wife
>
> RICHARD DELONG: 14, Daniels son
>
> PAUL DELONG: 6, Daniel's son
>
> KEVIN DELONG: 31, Daniel's younger brother
>
> DONNA: a neighbor who lives next door to the DeLong's
>
> DR. CHAMBERS: 45, a neighbor of Daniel's who lives next door to Kevin
>
> RODNEY BLEVINS: 20, Daniel's Vietnam buddy
>
> FAT MEDIC: 20, a medic in Daniel's unit in Vietnam
>
> GARY KNOWLES: 23, a soldier in Dan's unit
>
> CAPTAIN RUSHMORE: 28, Daniel's company commander in Vietnam
>
> THREE U.S. SOLDIERS:P about 20, soldiers in Daniel's unit
>
> CHAPLAIN: about 30, assigned to Daniel's unit
>
> NORTH VIETNAMESE ARMY SOLDIER: about 16

SETTING

The action takes place during a weekend of April, 1981, in Daniel De-Long's kitchen in West Orange, Massachusetts. There are flashbacks to 1969 in jungle locations within twenty kilometers of the villages of Quan Loi, Song Be, Phouc Vinh, and Tay Ninh, Vietnam.

> SCENES
>
> Reverberation
> The DeLong's kitchen. Friday about 6 p.m.

Scene i
Later Friday evening about 10 p.m.
Scene ii
Saturday about 8 a.m.
Scene iii
Later Saturday morning
Scene iv
Saturday about 1 p.m.
Scene v
Saturday about 6 p.m.
Scene vi
Saturday about 6:30 p.m.
Resonance
Sunday, a little before 10 a.m.
Reverberation

The lights come up on Dan, Pam, Richard, and Paul DeLong eating at the table. The kitchen depicts a middle class American room, large and homey enough to double as a family room. There is an outdoor exit stage right and another door stage left leading to the rest of the house. Dan looks like he is under some kind of pressure, as though it is difficult for him to totally focus on the situation at hand. Pam is soft-spoken, not easily moved to raise her voice. She is good-natured, but has been under a growing strain from years of trying to cope with something she cannot understand. Richard is extremely perceptive, inquisitive and frank. Paul is a happy-go-lucky child, also very inquisitive, and innocently resilient.

RICHARD: Dad? In my history class we are talking about events that led to American involvement in the Vietnam War. I was wondering if I could go through your slides and maybe take some to class?

DAN: Sure no problem . . .

PAUL: Daddy, do you know that at my Easter program in school I am going to say the poem "Twinkle, Twinkle, Little Star?"

DAN: Yeah, I know. You are learning the poem well, and you know I will be there just as close to the front as possible.

RICHARD: Thanks for letting me do that, Dad.

DAN: Sure, no problem. Tell you what, after supper I will get the slides, and we can look at them together.

PAUL: Oh good!

(PAUL slides off his chair and comes over to crawl up on DAN'S lap)

Tell some funny stories, Daddy. Tell us the one about the guy who thought you were a log when you were sleeping and peed on you.

DAN: You like that one, don't you?

PAM: I still remember when you wrote that to me. I didn't know whether to laugh or cry. I felt like doing both. I think I did.

PAUL: Tell us what you did, Daddy!

DAN: Aw, you've heard that story before.

PAUL: I know, but it's so funny.

DAN: Well, the next morning as we were getting ready to move out, I asked Steve if he had pissed on a log after he got off guard duty. When he said, "Yes," I told him I had been the log. Boy, he was so embarrassed.

PAUL: Why didn't you tell him to stop?

DAN: Couldn't chance it. You learned real quickly in the bush to be quiet, especially at night. I would rather be pissed on than killed. Now you better go back and eat.

PAUL: (Not moving) Who would have killed you, Daddy?

RICHARD: Vietcong. Now go back to your chair and eat.

PAUL: (Obeying) What did Vietcong look like, Daddy?

DAN: (Bothered) People, now be quiet and eat.

PAUL: (Pause) Did you kill any Vietcong, Daddy?

DAN: (Sharply) Paul, I think I said to be quiet and eat.

(Lights fade out)

End Reverberation

Scene i

(It is later Friday evening, about 10 p.m. As the lights come up, the kitchen is empty. DAN enters the kitchen from stage left. He has been drinking, but is not sloppy drunk. He looks out the window at the evening stars.)

DAN: Twinkly, twinkle, litter star. Hi. (He moves to the refrigerator, pulls out a beer, opens it, faces the window, and raises the can in a toast.)

Starkle, starkle, little twink, I ain't what the heck you think. I ain't under the afluence of inkerhol like most steeples pink. (He laughs sadly. RICH-ARD enters stage left during the "poem" and pulls a schoolbook off the table. DAN notices him.)

Oh-ah, hi, Rich. What do you think of my poem? Course it's not mine. I mean I didn't write it, you know. Well, what do you think?

RICHARD: Flunked English, didn't you?

DAN: Come on. Come on. Put `em up. Better back those words with something, Rich.

Come on, I'll take you with one beer tied behind my back. Hey, I'll drink to that one.

(Takes a drink and mellows)

Say, Rich, let me tell you something. If Santa didn't bring the little soldier's suit you asked for at two, then don't let him give it to you sixteen years later.

I made that mistake. Except I was older than eighteen, so I should have been smarter, huh? 'Cept back then I thought I was doing the right thing. (Dan's mood becomes very serious.)

Rich, I have made a lot of mistakes, and I try to correct some as I can. I guess that's why I've tried not to make you feel like that when you are old enough that you ought to go into the military--as your duty.

RICHARD: No. You have not done that.

(Richard takes his cues from his father's actions in a manner he has unconsciously acquired so as not to irritate his father.)

DAN: That damn war changed everything. I lost some good friends, learned that life really don't mean nothin', and that's where this damn ringing in my ears started. (Pause) 1969. Almost thirteen years ago. Thirteen years of listening to this … Maybe it wouldn't have happened if I had been more like Rodney.

(Pause--takes a long drink and then makes a playful jab towards RICHARD)

Course, if I'd been like your uncle Kevin, I'd never gone at all. But I'm not too much like Kevin, am I? Him a Presbyterian pastor, and me a nothaterian truck driver.

RICHARD: Speaking of truck driving, can I go with you on your next trip to Boston?

DAN: Subject changer … Sure, I would like that. I have an evening run in about a week, I think.

RICHARD: But just me, Paul can go another time, ok?

DAN: Sure, what is the matter? Problems with your little brother?

RICHARD: No, no problem, I just don't want him along this time. He wants everybody's attention constantly.

DAN: Well, I guess that is just Paul. You know, I am sorry I couldn't be with you your first year like I was with him. (Pause) But as my good friend Morales used to say, "asi es la vida"--that's life. And you have to start learning that life is no bowl of cherries. Got that?

(Tosses empty beer can into the wastebasket)

Hey, guess I'll let the next one be a coffee.

RICHARD: Got it, should I have not asked to see the slides?

DAN: (His expression is half-startled, half-quizzical.)

That was okay. Why do you ask?

RICHARD: I was just wondering if they made you feel bad?

DAN: Oh, no. Starkle, starkle, little twink--I ain't what the heck you think ... I am not embarrassing you, am I?

RICHARD: No. Just wondering if everything's really okay?

(Dan looks at RICHARD and a strange look crosses his face. Then, it's as if he doesn't see Richard, but instead is perhaps talking to a judge in a courtroom.)

DAN: (Moving downstage left) I was younger then, and besides, what the hell, that's what they paid me to do ... I wouldn't have done it if I'd thought more about it, but they told us not to think ... I thought he was ... well, what else could I do? How long 'til I'm free? Why don't memories let loose ... Why? ... Why? ... Why?

(DAN'S voice is now heard on tape as if in an echo chamber. While the echo effect is taking place, the lights dim, and DAN freezes as a spotlight comes up on him. RICHARD inconspicuously sits at the table, and from there he detachedly observes the remainder of the scene. In actuality the flashback might only be observed by RICHARD as a 10-15 second period of disorientation for DAN. DAN'S echo voice is heard.)

Why? ...Why?'... Why? ...Why?

(The scene shifts to a flashback of a site near Quan Loi, Vietnam, December, 1968. The action of the flashback takes place in DAN'S mind, the details being acted downstage of the kitchen. In the flashback sequence props should be used only if they don't require stagehands to set and/or strike them, and much of the action is pantomimed. Characters in the flashback should get into the kitchen area. The spotlight fades; then as the downstage area is lit, it comes up again on DAN and RODNEY "in wait" on an ambush. RODNEY is a youthful-looking lad of twenty years. The men are lying down stage left center, facing the "kill zone" of the ambush located downstage right.)

RODNEY: Why what?

DAN: I just figured out why in basic training we always had to run to get someplace so we could wait half an hour.

RODNEY: Ah, the good old days of "hurry up and wait" ...Why?

DAN: For this, they were training us for this.

RODNEY: Yeah ...What day is it anyway? (Pauses. Answers himself) Friday, I think.

DAN: It's just a matter of time. But what's the rush; we have nine more months to go. I'd just as soon spend it waiting here rather than go home like Neely did. (Shakes head silently) Son of a bitch!

RODNEY: And for what? (Pause. Reflectively) Always did his job.

DAN: And for his reward he's shot in the head. On what turned out to be a senseless tactical maneuver.
(His voice changes to a mixture of sarcasm, bitterness, and sadness.)

Of course, there's the Silver Star. But comfort to a widow and two kids ...
(Pause) I pity any Vietcong that walks within my range.

RODNEY: But, Dan, don't you hear what you are saying! The inconsistency!

DAN: Ah the hell with inconsistencies! I want to kill a Charlie.

(Pause as he hears something offstage right)

Sh-h-h. Listen! (Whispers) Do you hear that?

RODNEY: Yeah ... Sh-h-h-h.

(The two men "hug the ground" and DAN reaches for the "detonator" to a "claymore mine" set in the "kill zone." A few seconds later a lone North Vietnamese Army SOLDIER warily enters from downstage right and starts moving upstage. DAN "squeezes" the "detonator," and there are sound effects for a mine exploding. The NVA SOLDIER falls with a cry.)

DAN: (Excitedly) I think I got one for Neely!

RODNEY: I guess. Let's go easy in case there are more behind.

(The men slowly arise from their positions and cautiously move toward the body. The NVA SOLDIER starts to move.)

DAN: Look out! He's still alive! Look out!

(DAN'S next action is a combination of a reaction to sudden fear, hatred, bitterness, and the desires for revenge all reaching a peak. At that peak is an instant opportunity to unleash all these emotions.)

You rotten son-of-a-bitch. You have one coming for Neely.

(DAN slowly extends both arms as he "pulls the trigger" on his "M-16," pumping twenty rounds on automatic into the NVA. There are sound effects of the rifle firing. As soon as the firing starts, there are sound effects for an explosion from the body.)

(At this moment a high-pitched ringing tone starts and builds for 5-10 seconds-then suddenly stops. Simultaneously with the explosion and during the ringing, the lights have dimmed and the circular moving spots from a reflecting ball or lighting to achieve the same effect have been employed. When the ringing stops, the lights return to the pre-explosion setting.)

RODNEY: What the hell! Are you okay?

DAN: I guess. What happened? (Shocked) I ... I thought I was dead for a minute.

RODNEY: Take it easy ... I think your friend was carrying hand grenades, and you hit one. (Pause) Why did you do that anyway?

DAN: For Neely, I though. (Pause) But I don't know ... All of a sudden I wonder ... What if his mother could see this or her son? Who gave me the right to ...

(A pause as DAN struggles to justify his actions.)

Ah the hell with it! He wouldn't have worried about me! Just chalk one up for Neely, Rodney. This one was for Neely. (Pause) Hey, all this happened during the ambush, okay? Like I don't want a murder rap in the middle of a friggin' war, you know?

RODNEY: (Pause) Sure. (Pause) Well, let's check him for papers, get our stuff and move out. (Looking around) I don't like it here.

(They search the body for documents.)

DAN: I feel like I am in a never-never land, you know? This all seems so unreal, and my ears, they have been ringing ever since that explosion.

(DAN freezes and the previously heard ringing starts and builds for 5-10 seconds, then suddenly stops. During the ringing the lights "wave" up and down. When the ringing stops, the lights return to the prearranging setting.)

RODNEY: Yeah, ... what are we doing?

DAN: Don't you know? You can't remember?

RODNEY: I'm serious. (Pause) What are we doing?

DAN: I don't know. Guess I'm starting to be an animal, huh? That it? Sure starting to feel like one.

(Pause. DAN shrugs his shoulder with an "oh well" movement, then sniffs towards RODNEY.)

And I know you damn sure are starting to smell like one.

RODNEY: Oh jeez, a man with a little shrapnel in the shoulder, give him a half-decent meal and a shower and ... poof ... one each smart-ass on your hands. Problem is the field manuals forgot to tell us the Army solution.

DAN: Hey, first shower in twenty-eight days. It gets to you, you know.

(By this time they have finished searching the body and are "gathering their patrol gear." From downstage left the company commander, medic, radio-telephone operator (RTO), and two other soldiers enter. CPT. RUSH-MORE is twenty-eight years old, nearly six feet of solid muscle, has close-cut hair, and looks very military. His appearance is a sharp contrast to the other soldiers. FAT MEDIC is twenty years old, of medium height, and has a "rolly-polly cuddly" look. The RTO and the other two SOLDIERS look between seventeen and nineteen years old.)

CPT. RUSHMORE: What happened? Did you get anyone?

FAT MEDIC: You guys okay?

CPT. RUSHMORE: (Sees dead NVA) Ah, good work, men.

(He indicates the locations at the downstage left and right corners to the two INFANTRYMEN with him.)

You two go pull security. (To DAN) Did you get any more?

DAN: Not that we know of, sir. This one may have been an advance point though ... don't know.

CPT. RUSHMORE: Any papers?

RODNEY: No, sir. Searched him thoroughly. Nothing.

FAT MEDIC: (To Dan and Rodney) Are you guys okay? Either of you hurt?

CPT. RUSHMORE: Well, at least we got him. I was hoping for something more like Tuesday though. We got seven of the little bastards then.

DAN: But they got Neely, damn it! And seven of them (Indicates NVA) doesn't equal one of him! And that doesn't even count the sixteen men we had wounded!

CPT. RUSHMORE: Neely was a good man, and he died like a good soldier--one of the finest I've known.

DAN: (Turns away in disgust) Hey, Fat Medic, I don't have any wounds, but I sure as hell have a headache and a ringing in my ears. You have any aspirin?

CPT. RUSHMORE: RTO, give me the horn. Jungle Master Six, this is Day Ranger Six, over ... Jungle Master Six, this is Day Ranger Six. (Pause) This is Ranger Six. (Pause) One of my patrols just conducted an ambush at coordinates Papa Victor, one-three-eight-six, five-niner-seven-eight.

FAT MEDIC: (To Dan) Yes, I'll get them out of my pack. (He starts searching through his aid bag.)

CPT. RUSHMORE: Yes, sir. The cunning little devils were advance for a larger party. The way they were set up, if it wasn't for the quick, professional actions of the ambush team, some people might have been killed. No, no people were injured, but we did get some of those little bastards. We didn't find any documents, but there are five bodies and numerous blood trails. Yes, sir, I'll call back if there are any new developments. Yes sir, and out here.

You did real good work, men; the Old Man's happy, and you know that's the way we like it, right? Come on, RTO, let's get back to base. You men follow when you are ready.

DAN: Got it, sir.

(CPT. RUSHMORE indicates for the two SOLDIERS to follow him and the RTO; they exit downstage left.)

Listen, Fat Medic, what about this ringing in my ears? When will it go away?

FAT MEDIC: Oh, after exposure to loud noises, there often is some ringing for a while, but it's usually temporary. Course, if there's been some nerve damage, then the ringing may be more permanent; you'll just have to wait and see. Guess that is just one of the hazards of being Infantry. Here's your aspirin.

DAN: But what if it keeps on? (Takes aspirin with drink from canteen)

FAT MEDIC: (Putting items into the bag) I don't know much about that particular area, whether the ringing can be treated or not, probably worth some disability money.

RODNEY: In other words, if the ringing keeps on, he may not like the song, but he can be paid for listening to it, huh?

FAT MEDIC: Well, let's hope that never has to be decided. It's probably only a temporary thing.

DAN: Well, I hope so. I don't like the pitch. (Pause) Hey, let's get back to base and leave this sucker here to rot--like I hope all VC do.

RODNEY: I guess that won't take long in this heat.

DAN: Maybe this will be a warning for others to watch out.

(RODNEY and FAT MEDIC stare at the NVA. Then the lights start to fade out as RODNEY and FAT MEDIC leave stage left.)

FAT MEDIC: I wonder if the families are ever notified?

(RODNEY and FAT MEDIC exit. DAN is in the position he froze in as lights come back up in the kitchen.)

DAN: (As though awakening) Yeah, I wonder if his family was ever notified. (Pause) Oh, hell, let me get some coffee.

(Lights down)

End Scene i

Scene ii

Saturday morning. As lights come up, DAN is sitting at the table and PAM is fixing coffee at the stove.

PAM: (Taking a cup of coffee to the table) ... Here is your coffee, Dan. How do you feel today?

DAN: Not bad, considering. Thanks for the coffee. I need it.

(PAM goes back to the counter area and begins placing food items on the table for breakfast. DAN drinks coffee.)

DAN: (Starts to say something two or three times. Stops, ponders, then finally) ... Rich asks some tough questions sometimes, huh?

PAM: (Shrugs. Her mind is occupied with fixing breakfast.) He is straightforward, but I never have had trouble with his questions. What did he ask?

DAN: (Pause) Oh, I guess it was nothing much.

(There is a knock on the door.)

PAM: Would you get that, please?

DAN: Bet it's Kevin. He said he might be over. Hi. Come on in. (Kevin enters. He is well built and has laughing eyes.) I thought it might be you knocking at the door. Did you walk?

KEVIN: Yeah, I get almost a mile of exercise, you know. Kind of early, but I figured you would be up and around. You always are. Used to wake me up when we were kids. (Playfully jabbing.) I guess you couldn't stand to see your younger brother sleep.

DAN: Well, little brothers were made to pester, weren't they?

PAM: Hi, Kevin. Coffee?

KEVIN: Sure, thanks.

DAN: Ain't going to ask me to church are you?

KEVIN: Shoot no. We don't want any bricks falling down.

PAM: (Bringing Kevin's coffee. Teases.) All right, boys.

KEVIN: Thanks. Listen, what I wanted to ask you about is that fishing trip we have been putting off. One of my church members has a cottage on Sunappee Lake, and he has offered to let us use it. I was wondering, how about leaving in a couple weeks on a Thursday afternoon and staying through Saturday. We can go by Brattleboro and see Uncle Karl and Aunt Helen. What do you think?

DAN: Sounds all right. I can get the time off, and I could use the break. Maybe relaxing will take off some of the pressure I have been feeling; the break may let me get my head together.

PAM: (For the first time in this scene, PAM gives her full attention to DAN, her face revealing their lack of past communication.) Pressures? What do you mean?

DAN: Oh, I don't know. Like last night, Paul asked me--I don't know. I just get so tired of this ringing. (Sarcastically) Well, the VA's educated word for it is tinnitus. I about go crazy with it sometimes when Paul and Richard are carrying on. You just don't know.

PAM: (Nonchalantly. She has not heard anything new like she thought she might.) Oh.

DAN: Oh. That's it, and that's about how much you understand tinnitus too.

(Dan stands up and takes his coffee cup to the window.)

PAM: How can I understand something I haven't experienced?

DAN: It's not just the ringing. It is also how the ringing started. (Ringing starts, builds 5-10 seconds and suddenly stops. During the ringing the lights "wave" up and down, and at the end of the ringing the sound goes back to the preringing setting. DAN reacts to this; the others are detached observers.) I live with a constant, daily reminder that I killed, deliberately shot and killed, a wounded man. I would like to put all that in the past, but the reminder is always there. And, I just cannot wish the ringing away.

KEVIN: (He's heard this before and is very frustrated because he feels so helpless.) Kind of like a monkey on your back, and you can't get it off.

PAM: But don't let the monkey kill you--or you knock yourself out trying to kill it. It makes it rough on us too you know.

DAN: Yeah, that's all right. It is easier to present the answers than try to understand. After all, you're not the one caught in a downward cycle.

KEVIN: Dan? I think she is only trying to say that usually the monkeys on our back don't upset us as much as what we tell ourselves about them. (KEVIN is embarrassed about interrupting, about being there.) I am sorry.

I would like to help change the direction of your downward cycle if I can. I don't believe it is hopeless.

DAN: (The lights "wave" up and down as in the ringing sequences. DAN has undergone a personality change. His words now are very hostile, biting, and seem very harsh and illogical for the talk for which they are in response.) Oh yes, I forgot, little brother, everything is beautiful, isn't it? Peace on earth, goodwill towards men, and don't forget to pray every Sunday for the men in service preparing for war. Maybe if you preachers got out of the church and lived in the real world, you would be able to relate to real people.

KEVIN: (Smarting from these words. He never before has seen DAN acting quite like this.) That is not true, and you know it.

DAN: (Like he has gone too far, but feels like he must continue or else admit he is out of line.) Oh bull! You talk about positive philosophies and all that crap, but what do you know about reality, huh? It is a different world out here. (The lights return to the prior setting.)

KEVIN: Well, I am sorry. (Moving toward door) But you know right well that when Ramona and I stood at the gravesite of Lisa Mae last year, we suffered. You are not a unique person in this universe who has squatter's rights on problems. And I hope you wake up to that fact! (Goes out slamming the door--DAN and PAM freeze.)

PAM: (After a pause during which DAN sits down at the table and grips his cup tightly.) Well, you did that up right!

DAN Shut up, will you? Just shut up!

PAM: Why? 'Cause I said something you don't like. It is okay for you to say whatever you want to me. Yes, that's okay, but let me talk that way just once to you and you explode--go through the roof.

DAN: Damn it. I said ...

PAM: No! Now I don't know what your ringing is like, but it is sure not to blame for everything. I think it is you. Sometimes I don't think anyone could live with you. I have thought about it, and it is not me. You are the problem. (PAM is exhausted and grips the counter for support.)

DAN: (Oblivious to Pam's emotions, laughs.) Yup, now that sounds like a nice summary of the situation. It's all my fault. I mean "why even try to understand someone who doesn't fit my little cookie cutter world. They are all wrong anyway ..." Yeah, you definitely got a mindset. Damn!

PAM: Do you always have to use that language?

DAN: There ain't a damn thing wrong with my language!

PAM: Well, I find it offensive.

DAN: So, I find life offensive. What's the big deal?

PAM: That sounds like your problem.

DAN: Hey look. Do you think I really like it? I wish I didn't. Sometimes I wish I didn't hear anything. (Mellowing. He is near tears.) I wish I could somehow explain my feelings. It is like a volcano bubbling inside sometimes. I wish I could explain how it is to have something that the only time it doesn't bother you is when you are asleep. And, even then it wakes you up sometimes. But you don't ... and won't understand.

PAM Oh no you don't ... I told you not to blame me. I have tried, and I have really tried. But you won't help; you don't ... I have been trying ... Why don't you help? Why won't he help me? (On this speech, DAN moves to the last flashback position. Lights dim as DAN freezes.)

PAM'S ECHO VOICE: You help me ... Help me ... Help me. (Pam's voice is now heard on tape as DAN's was earlier, as if in an echo changer. PAM inconspicuously sits at the table, and as Richard did earlier, detachedly observes. Again, in actuality PAM might only observe the flashback as a

10-15 second period of disorientation for DAN. The lights go down. As they come up, the scene has shifted to a location near Song Be, Vietnam, January, 1969. There are sounds of a firefight in the background. DAN is lying down stage left. FAT MEDIC lies wounded downstage right center. Props are used only if they do not require stagehands to set or strike them.)

FAT MEDIC: Help me! Help me! Please come and help me! Oh, God! Oh please help me. (The firing subsides and DAN "moves out of the foxhole" and crawls to FAT MEDIC.)

DAN: Hey, it's me. Were you hit? Are you okay?

FAT MEDIC: Oh, God, my leg. I think I took a round in the thigh. Oh, Jesus, it hurts.

DAN: Yeah, guess so. Doesn't look too serious though. Just messy. (Looking around) Where the hell are your big bandages?

FAT MEDIC: (In pain) Second squad's hole, I think. Give me the small one, and I'll use it to slow the bleeding til you get back. And hurry, damn it! I want to keep my leg you know! (Dan "places a bandage" over FAT MEDIC's wound, and FAT MEDIC then holds the bandage in place.)

DAN: I will be right back. (He lowcrawls to a position center stage left and searches for FAT MEDIC's aid bag. A fresh volley of gunfire opens up. DAN dives for cover, and FAT MEDIC shudders.)

FAT MEDIC: Chaauh ... oh, Gauod, ... uh, uh. (DAN raises head a couple times, but due to close proximity of bullets immediately drops.) Oh God ... oh, help me. Oh Jesus, please. (A cry) Why won't you help me! Help me! Help me! (He shudders slightly--then lies still. DAN continues trying to return, but each attempt is a failure due to gunfire. After a minute or so the gunfire fades, and DAN cautiously raises his head.)

DAN: Oh, God. (He again lowcrawls to FAT MEDIC. Some cries of wounded persons and general confusion are heard in the background.) Oh, God, why did I leave you. Oh, Doc, I am sorry. I am sorry. Oh damn. I

left you alone; I left you, Doc. I am sorry. I am sorry. (Numbly, DAN observes as SOLDIERS come, put FAT MEDIC on a makeshift poncho stretcher, and carry him out. RODNEY enters and goes to DAN putting his arm around him DAN buries his head on RODNEY's shoulder. Lights "wave" up and down for 5-10 seconds.)
He's gone; I can't believe it, Rodney. FAT MEDIC is gone. I left him, like a damn fool. I left him and didn't come back when he needed me.

RODNEY: Dan. You did what you thought was best at the time. Don't blame yourself.

DAN: He is gone, headed for a damn plastic bag. I left him. He was fine, rip in the thigh … I come back. He is dead, bullet in the chest. I left him, Rodney. I left him. (DAN breaks down crying.)

RODNEY: Dan, it wasn't your fault. You didn't know the VC would open up again. It's not your fault. (CPT. RUSHMORE enters with GARY KNOWLES, a six foot, lanky, boyish looking man of twenty-three.)

CPT. RUSHMORE: I'm sorry, men. We lost some good ones. Jose's dead, too. A bullet in the head, it killed him instantly. He never knew what hit him. Look, Battalion sent us a new guy. I guess he's Neely's replacement. I don't know when they will ever get us up to full strength.

DAN: Need to get to the rear, for a day or two, I need to get drunk or something. I can't take this anymore.

RODNEY: Sir? He needs a break.

CPT. RUSHMORE: Hell! You know I can't do that. We're already at too low a level. Damn! Your platoon gets two killed and thirteen wounded, and you're talking about giving a man a break? I don't believe it. You men are professional. Got that? None of us want to be over here, but someone has to be a man and do what those "protest chickens" won't. Dan, you need to get yourself together. You have a job to do. And number one on your list is to break in your new man correctly. Do you understand? This is Gary

Knowles--take care of him. (CPT. RUSHMORE wheels sharply about and exits.)

DAN: Right. All you have to do is to remember who you are, okay?

GARY: Sure, but I, uh, don't know what you mean.

DAN: Look, til you know what's going on, you're just an FNG -- a friggin' new guy. That's the way we all start, and if you're lucky, then you make old-timer, okay? In the meantime, don't count on anything except that war is hell, and combat is one big mother!

RODNEY: Easy, Dan. Don't take your pain out on him.

DAN: He'll learn. He'll learn soon enough.

GARY: I'll do my best. I don't plan on screwing up.

DAN: Well, don't plan on anything over here, and then you won't be surprised. Hey, look; I'm sorry. We just lost two men, and I might could have saved one of them. (DAN is almost overcome again and turns away. He recovers and turns back.) Rodney, take Gary over to meet the rest of the squad. (RODNEY and GARY exit. DAN is in the frozen position as lights come back up in the kitchen.)

PAM: (Concern now in her voice) Dan? (DAN starts at the sound of PAM'S voice, almost pleading.) Dan? Why don't you help me? (Lights down)

   End Scene ii

   Scene iii

(The time is later Saturday morning. As lights come up in the kitchen, PAM is washing dishes and RICHARD is drying them. A neighbor, DONNA is sitting at the kitchen table.)

PAM: I like it when you help me do the dishes, Richard.

RICHARD: I don't mind, Mom, but please don't tell my friends.

DONNA: Don't tell anyone, Richard, but my Ronnie helps me, too.

PAM: (Laughs) And I'll bet he tells you the same thing; don't tell … (Pause, looks out the window) I'm glad it's spring. It's such a pretty time of the year … my favorite. Oh, Richard, I wish you had been told enough to remember the spring we went to Holland when your father was stationed in Germany. It was gorgeous, just beautiful. You were barely three--it was so pretty.

RICHARD: (With a sidelong glance toward Donna) Did, uh, did Dad get upset as easily then as he does now?

PAM: (Deep breath) No, I don't think so . . . I kind of hate to say this, but I don't think so … now … I am not sure why … people change, Richard. Everybody does, because things happen, and we change. I guess the biggest change for your father was between the times before leaving for Vietnam … and … his return. I mean there are things--well, I'd think a certain way about them, and he would get upset. (Pause) Like medals, I mean my father received a Bronze Star in World War II, and he still occasionally mentions it with pride. Your father has two Bronze Stars, and a Silver Star, and if he ever does mention them, somewhere in there he says, "They don't mean nothing." I don't know why. (Pause) I don't know. He never has said much, mentions a friend now and then. Occasionally he says he's not proud of everything he did; and, of course, he's talked about the ringing in his ears.

RICHARD: What about the ringing? It seems like if he hears it all the time, then we should too, you know?

PAM: No. When the VA gave him disability on his ears, they sent some information on it. It says it is subjective, only noticeable to him. I don't know if that means it is all in his head, or what? I just don't know. (Richard responds with a shrug.) Oh, Richard, why don't you run along and let me finish the dishes.

RICHARD: (To Donna) Is Ronnie home?

DONNA: Yes. Why don't you go see him.

RICHARD: Mom?

PAM: Sure. Go along.

(Richard exits)

PAM: I'm glad you're here, Donna.

DONNA: Need to talk?

PAM: Yes ... you know, Donna ... I've been doing a lot of thinking about it lately ... about Dan, and Richard, and Paul.

DONNA: (Laughs) Oh, Paul has no problem. He has his dad wrapped around his little finger, and he knows it.

PAM: Now, Donna, you know that is not ... well ... maybe it is. I don't know. Look, Donna, (PAM continues to dry and put away dishes.) I can't take much more. I just don't know how much longer I can hold on. (Pause) I know about vows 'til death do us part, but ... (Pause) and ... I know that marriage is supposed to be for life, but there has to be room for mistakes. (Pause) I don't see any sense going through my whole life being miserable.

DONNA: Do you think maybe you just need a chance to get away from it all; a good rest?

PAM: (Pause, thinking) I think it's more than just needing a rest. (Pause) No. I guess I've come to realize that I can't be what Dan wants; and ... I don't know what I want ... but ... I intend to find out. (PAM looks at DONNA with guilt.) I am sorry Donna. I guess I shouldn't be talking this way, but ...

DONNA: That's all right, Pam.

PAM: It's just ... I ... I don't know what to ... (Paul bursts into the room.)

PAUL: Hey, Mommy! Do you have my star finished?

PAM: No, Paul; it's on my table. I'll finish it later this morning. Maybe you could help me with it?

PAUL: Sure. I'm going to go get it.

PAM: Could you be polite and say hello to Mrs. Harris first?

PAUL: Sure; hi. (He runs out the doorway.)

PAM: (Smiling.) Him and his star. He'll be cute in the program.

DONNA: Yes. Pam, I wish I knew what to tell you. It seems like answers aren't as simple as I used to think they were.

PAM: No they're not, and that seems to be the only thing I feel like I do know for sure anymore.

(PAUL re-enters holding a large cardboard star.)

PAUL: When are you going to put on the tinfoil, Mommy, so it looks nice?

PAM: I just told you, later this morning. I will do it as soon as the kitchen is clean. And, what about you, Paul? Do you know your part yet? Huh?

PAUL: Oh, yeah. I know most of it. Listen … Twinkle, twinkle, little star … How I wonder what you are … Hmmm … and I don't know the rest yet. (PAUL exits again. PAM and DONNA both laugh.)

PAM: Doesn't know the rest, yet. Guess that's a good description of how I'm feeling.

DONNA: Well, I know one thing for sure.

PAM: What's that?

DONNA: I think we all sometimes ask the same question of the stars; how I wonder what you are, and where do we fit into the picture?

PAM: Yeah, you've got that one right, for sure. (The lights quickly dim.)

End Scene iii

Scene iv

(It is Saturday afternoon, early. As the lights come up in the kitchen, DAN is sitting at the table drinking a cup of coffee. He has a troubled appearance. There is a knock at the door, and DAN answers the door. It is KEVIN.)

DAN: Oh, ah, hi.

KEVIN: Hi, Dan. Can I talk with you?

DAN: (Rather sheepishly) Yeah, come on in ... Pam and the kids went shopping. Can I get you a cup of coffee or something?

KEVIN: Sure, coffee will be fine, thanks. (As DAN gets coffee for KEVIN, there is an awkward pause. KEVIN sits at the table, then breaks the silence.) Dan, ... I came to apologize for this morning. I feel bad about the way I left, and ...

DAN: Oh that's okay. I was ...

KEVIN: No. I have had my problems, but really, they have been different. I think in retrospect that I was starting to sound like a Sunday morning preacher getting ready to spout off a bunch of theological answers. Except, Monday morning is always so different.

DAN: (Sitting down) Well, I was in the wrong, Kevin, and I guess you were just trying to help.

KEVIN: I was trying to help. But the problem I am running into--not only with this morning's situation, but in my congregation, too--the problem I have is how do I help without interfering? It seems like such a fine line to try and walk.

DAN: I guess.

KEVIN: Guess? You remember as well as I do how upset Dad used to get over Haines.

DAN: Haines?! That goat.

KEVIN: Well, before I entered seminary, I vowed I would never be a preacher like him, and then this morning I started ...

DAN: (Lightly punching at KEVIN) Oh, cut it, Kevin. I may have been mad this morning, but it sure wasn't because you reminded me of "The Pain."

KEVIN: Well, but I do care. The problem is that I feel helpless. I guess because I don't know what you are feeling. So, I really don't understand. I want to try to help.

DAN: I wonder if others have felt this way? Do you suppose it changes with any war? I mean throughout history there have been all kinds of causes fought for, and everyone in each war thought they were fighting for the right thing. But when you look back at it, and try to get the whole bloody affair into some kind of perspective, my God it doesn't make any sense.

KEVIN: Yeah, I agree.

DAN: I just don't know, and I don't want to make this a big issue, but I just don't know how to cope sometimes. It seems like such a simple little thing to adjust to, but constantly, I don't know, there is just no break from the ringing. Oh, I get busy and forget it, but never for too long. There is always a drawing back to it, and you don't get used to it. Instead, it seems like I think about it more. It's louder, and I know it's gonna go on and on and on ...

KEVIN: Dan? ... Please ... listen.

We all have obstacles in our paths, and I'm not sure. But I would like to believe that for each one, somehow, there is a constructive way to overcome the ringing, or at least find a way of realistically living with it. (There is silence as DAN gets up with cup in hand and goes to look out the window.)

DAN: Okay, you mentioned Lisa Mae earlier? I don't know if I could hand that situation. You and Ramona seemed to accept her death without bitterness.

KEVIN: There was some bitterness for a while. With a crib death, well, Ramona and I both felt that we were somehow responsible. How, I don't know. But we had that feeling. So anyway, here we needed each other more than ever before in our lives. (Laughs) Pastor Kevin, … "the counselor." Well, you know Dr. Chambers? He has seen several crib deaths and has counseled parents, and he helped Ramona and me realize that we needed to face each other and to kick out at the problem. We had started to face away and kick each other. So quite simply, we saw the need for reconciliation and trying to comfort each other in a way that strengthened us, and I don't know when, but somewhere, Dan, in that process, the bitterness left.

DAN: Pam and I sure need some reconciliation. I know I can't blame everything on the ringing. But there are times when I just get so tired and frustrated. It wakes me up at night, and I can't get back to sleep. I get so irritable. I don't know, Kevin. I just don't know.

KEVIN: Maybe, seeing a counselor would help free up some of those tensions inside.

DAN: (He starts moving downstage, pausing along the way.)
But, how are you freed from . . . guilt? I've told you about the ringing, how it started. Then I was told I might always have it. It was my fault, but I felt so bitter. I hated the VC, all of them. I did stuff I can't change. I can't get rid of … it just burns. (DAN's voice is now heard on tape with the echo change effect. The lights dim, and DAN freezes as the spotlight comes up on him. KEVIN stays at the table as a detached observer. As with the other flashbacks, he would in actuality only observe it as a brief period of disorientation for DAN.)

(DAN's echo voice) Burns, burn, burn ... (The scene shifts to a place near Phouc Vinh, Vietnam, April, 1969. Offstage lights are flickering stage left indicating a fire nearby. Then the downstage area is lit. RODNEY enters, stage left. He has two small packs.)

DAN: Aahh, burn, baby, burn. We grunts ought to make it our theme.

RODNEY: Here is your pack. Dan, we have to talk.

DAN: (Cleaning rifle) About what? What I just did? That ain't nothing to what I would like to do.

RODNEY: Dan, I am your closest friend. What you are doing is self-destructive. My God, what if another patrol had come along?

DAN: (Lightly) Then I would know that their patrol lead could not read a map `cause there ain't supposed to be another one in this area.

RODNEY: (Disgustedly) Dammit, do you have any cigarettes? You don't even hear what I'm saying.

DAN: Let me check. I know what you're saying, but I think you're worried over nothing. Here, bottom of the barrel. Pick your poison, Pall-Malls or Camels?

RODNEY: Pall-Malls. I'm desperate, not crazy. Look, Dan, our orders were to search this hooch, round up any civilians, then burn the places.

DAN: I was close. (Pause) Hey, I thought the lady looked like a Viet Cong, okay? She must have been some kind of guard or something. Here all alone with five hooches. Don't look right. Besides ... (DAN is near tears, but continuous to justify his actions.) That is another one for FAT MEDIC. (DAN immediately throws off the emotion and starts to open a C-ration can from his pack.)

RODNEY: (Shaking his head in disbelief) I don't believe it. You're crazy. Or else I am. Maybe that's it. Maybe it's me. I mean why should it bother me that while I'm pulling security--to cover his rear--my best friend shoots a woman and then sets the hooch she's still in on fire. (Pause.) Then, to top it off, he says it's nothing and goes ahead to fix a meal within smelling range of the burning body. Yeah, maybe it's just me.

DAN: Get off my case, will you? Why don't you think about it, huh? (Sarcastically) Now just go do your duty for Wall Street, live and smell like an animal, but make damn sure you act civilized.

RODNEY: Okay, okay, I get the message. I don't like it any better than you do. (Pause) But I still don't see how you can eat cold pork and beans with that smell of her so close.

DAN: Like you say, I'm a hardcore. Just call me IceMan, cold and hard, . . . and lonely, damn it! I want to get out of here and see my wife, and Richard. (Embarrassed pause) I'm sorry, Rodney, I didn't mean to ...

RODNEY: (Grinds out cigarette and immediately lights another one. Rambles. DAN has heard this before.)

That's okay, I was thinking about Barbara anyway. I guess the smells, and the association with a woman's death gets me thinking about her, she was at her mother's and called me just before she left. Tell me she was on her way, she was going out to celebrate our third month wedding anniversary that night. I told her to be careful because it was raining. Then, the next call came from the State Police; she was going too fast on a corner and hit a small propane gas truck ... closed casket funeral ... had to be. (Pause) She was some woman, crazy broad, one beautiful, lovely, crazy, woman.

DAN: (Very embarrassed) I'm sorry, Rodney. (Disgusted with himself) I didn't think.

RODNEY: It's okay, turned me into a philosopher. Part of why I enlisted for this hole. I thought it would take my mind off her but that's a laugh. (Pause) Barb and I talked about having our own place someday, plant our own trees--watch them grow older along with us. I don't want to grow old anymore.

DAN: (Reflectively) I do. I have some dreams when this mess is over. Our own place, and Richard. Hope he makes out better than I have. Hope the hell he never winds up in some garbage dump of the world. I want him to be something more than a grunt, pounding the ground, counting the days to go home, burning hooches, killing gooks, (Pause) and eating cold beans. (Throws can away offstage left towards the "fire") I want to pick up on some dreams, Rodney. I want to get away from all the shades of gray and find the good life again.

RODNEY: (Sincerely) I hope you can find it, Dan. I really do.

DAN: Me too. (Pause) Now, I guess we'd best just hope to find tomorrow. And, I hope we don't lose anyone else. Hey, Rodney, there is no problem with me shooting that guard, is there?

RODNEY: (Long Pause) No, I guess not. Besides, I don't know what you are talking about. I didn't see anything. (RODNEY exits. DAN is in the position he froze in as lights come up in the kitchen.)

DAN: I still see her. I've carried her with me. Damn, Kevin! I'm glad you stopped by.

> (Lights dim)

> End scene iv

> Scene v

(As the lights come up, DAN, PAM, RICHARD, AND PAUL are at the table eating their evening meal.)

PAM: You say Kevin was here today. Did you have a good visit?

DAN: Yeah. Can you believe this? He wanted to apologize to me.

PAM: Trying to make things better is just like him, isn't it?

DAN: True. (Eating goes on for a few more seconds in silence) I have a headache. Do we have any aspirin?

PAM: Yes. I just bought a new bottle this afternoon. (DAN gets up from the table, goes to one of the cabinets and gets some aspirin.)

PAUL: Daddy, I saw the Easter Bunny at the store today. He gave me a lollipop.

DAN: Now that sounds all right. Did you get one for me? (DAN has returned to the table and takes the aspirin with his drink at the table.)

PAUL: You're too old for lollipops, Daddy.

DAN: Yeah, maybe you're right. Richard, would you please pass the salt?

RICHARD: (Handing DAN the salt) Sure.

PAM: Are you and Kevin still going on that trip?

DAN: I guess so; we didn't talk about it again, but I reckon it's still on the agenda.

PAM: It'll probably be a good break for you.

DAN: Yeah, and he does have some pretty good ideas on life. They're not always so easy to incorporate into the real world, but they're good ideas.

PAM: For crying out loud, Dan, he's only trying to help. Why can't you accept the help?

DAN: Don't start in on me again, do you hear?

PAUL: Mommy, did you get my star done?

PAM: (Her expression is a response to DAN's statement, not PAUL's question.) Yes, it is done.

PAUL: Good. Daddy, do you know that at my Easter program I'm going to say the poem "Twinkle, Twinkle, Little Star?"

DAN: Yeah, I know. You're learning it real good. And you know I'll be there as close to the front as I can get. You want me close to the front, don't you?

PAUL: (Laughing. Pleased) Yeah.

DAN: (To Richard) "Twinkle, twinkle, little star: Kind of reminds you of "Starkle, starkle, little twink," doesn't it?

RICHARD: (Uncomfortably dabbing at the food on his plate) It reminds you, you mean. Your poem, not mine.

DAN: (Immediately defensive) What do you mean? I'm not embarrassing you, am I?

PAM: Dan, leave him alone, will you? You're the one saying you're so bad. Now couldn't we just have a meal in peace?

DAN: (Knowing he should stop, but feeling like things are starting to spin out of control for him) Probably not as long as I'm here, is that what you're trying to say?

PAM: I didn't say that, but since you mentioned it, when you're at work, there are more pleasant meals.

DAN: (In combined tone of self-pity and anger) Well, you bitch.

PAM: (Angrily getting up and heading out of the kitchen) I don't have to put up with that, especially in front of the children. (Exits stage left)

DAN: (Close to breaking, hollering after her) Well, don't then. (Pause) Well, you kids eat. Don't just sit there.

PAUL: (Yelling) Mommy, would you bring out my star?

DAN: Don't holler.

PAUL: I want her to bring out my star.

DAN: All right, but don't holler. It bothers me.

PAUL: (Louder) Mommy?

DAN: (Yelling) I said stop that damn yelling.

PAUL: Okay, Daddy. (Even louder) Mommy?

DAN: (Almost slaps PAUL, but he catches himself. DAN pushes angrily away from the table and slams his fists down on it, which knocks over a glass.) Damn it! Why the hell can't you hear what I'm saying?

PAM: (Re-enters with pocketbook, she has put on a sweater and has jackets for the boys.) Dan! Stop it!

DAN: (Backing to counter) Tell him to stop hollering!

DAN: I have had it! I have to get out of here! I don't know what your problem is, but it includes being nuts, and I will not live here any longer with a crazy person. You are ... I swear ... I have never seen the likes ... You are crazy. (Pause) Come on, children, let's go. We can get our things later.

DAN: (Almost to himself) You're not really leaving are ...

PAM: (Handing RICHARD and PAUL their jackets) I don't know, Dan! I just know I can't take any more of this nonsense. I can't believe that my purpose in life is to stay in a place where I am constantly miserable. (Pause) Now, let's go children.

PAUL: But, I want my star, Mommy.

PAM: It is not important now, Paul, because we can get it later. (PAM half pushes PAUL in the direction of the outside door. PAM, RICHARD, and PAUL exit.)

DAN: I don't believe ... I guess I've known it was coming. I asked for it. (Kicks chair) I wish I could treat them better. I want to treat them better. I want ... damn it, but then like a dumb shit I blow it. (Pause) I don't blame her for leaving. (DAN is overcome with loneliness.) Oh God, I don't think I have felt this bad since Rodney ... huh, Rodney (Pause.) (Dan slowly moves downstage left, pausing along the way.) What a weird damn world. (Pause) I think I would have been better off born dead. No sense to it. Maybe Rodney is better off: least now he doesn't have any problems. (DAN's voice is now on the tape with the echo chamber effect. The lights dim and DAN freezes as the spotlight comes up on him.)

DAN: (DAN's echo voice) Problems, problems, problems, ... (The scene shifts to a jungle location about twenty kilometers southwest of Tay Ninh, Vietnam. It is July, 1969. As the lights come up on the downstage area, RODNEY and GARY are sitting on the "ground" eating C-rations. Three other SOLDIERS are downstage right also eating.)

GARY: Problems ... We have problems, Dan.

DAN: (Sitting down with GARY and RODNEY and reaching for C-ration can) How's that?

GARY: Well, this trail junction we are headed for tomorrow--isn't it that same area where Alpha Company had thirty-one men wounded?

DAN: Yeah, why?

GARY: I was just wondering ... What if the same Charlies hit us?

DAN: (Pause. Joking) Well, only our platoon's going, and there ain't but eighteen now; so at least we won't get thirty-one wounded.

GARY: Somehow that wasn't what I wanted to hear.

DAN: (Lightly) Because you're not an FNG anymore, you should've figured that one out.

GARY: Sure is nice to have graduated from the friggin'-new-guy category.

DAN: Well, you finally stopped smelling funny.

RODNEY: He didn't smell funny--just clean.

DAN: Three more months and out we go, Rodney. Slide into that big old Freedom Bird and head back to "the world."

RODNEY: (Pensively) I guess.

DAN: Guess! What's your case today? You look like you are on a downer instead of on a celebration of your twenty-first birthday.

RODNEY: I don't know. (Pause) I remember looking forward to the day when I would turn twenty-one, but, it doesn't seem to matter now. What's a birthday over here? (Pause) What's there to go home to? Don't mean nothin'.

GARY: Hey, come on! You have pork slices in your "C's" today? What more could you want?

DAN: Yeah, and you know, I picked them out just for you because it's your birthday. Least we can do is give you your favorite C-ration when you turn twenty-one.

RODNEY: (Pause. Somberly) I think a man ought to enjoy his last meal.

DAN: Last meal? What's with you anyway? Aint got no funny ringing in your ears, do you?

RODNEY: (Shrugs) Nah, just a ... a feeling? Acceptance? This patrol? Let's go; it's time, isn't it? (RODNEY starts to put his things in his pack.)

DAN: (Trying to cheer RODNEY) Almost--but clear your head, huh? Rephrase Patton. You ain't here to die for your country--you make those bastards die for theirs.

RODNEY: I'm tired of all this ... killing ... dying (Pause) sometimes living is just as tiring.

DAN: (Pause) Well, maybe. I guess if this damn ringing keeps up for years--I'll eventually get tired of it all, too.

GARY: Yeah, war can get to you, but a person has to think about-- (A single shot rings out. All the men immediately hit the ground--one is hit)

WOUNDED SOLDIER: (Clutching shoulder) Jesus, I'm hit! Oh, Jesus, Jesus, Jesus.

RODNEY: Medic! (The men all gather around the WOUNDED SOL-DIER and some start to administer aid while others scan the area.)

DAN: Check trees for a sniper! Damn bastards are at it again! (GARY has pulled out a small aid pack.)

GARY: Look out. Let me get to him. Looks like it is not a real bad wound. Where is the medic? (To WOUNDED SOLDIER) Not that I can't fix you and all. We just want to add the professional touch.)

DAN: Looks like you might have that old million dollar wound. Just enough to get you to a real bed for a while, decent meals and nurses.

SOLDIER: Through clenched teeth) Oh God. I can think of better ways to …

GARY: Beggars can't be choosy, you know.

SOLDIER: Yeah, I guess . . . (A hand grenade is thrown near the group. RODNEY reacts and dives on top of the grenade. As he lands, there is a an "explosion.")

DAN: (In shock) Oh, God. I don't believe it. (Two SOLDIERS cautiously move offstage right in the direction the grenade was thrown. DAN kneels by RODNEY and rolls him over. Offstage right there is the sound of gunfire for a few seconds.)

OFFSTAGE RIGHT VOICE: Got him! Got the bastard trying to crawl away! We got him!

CPT. RUSHMORE: (Enters stage left) What happened? Did we get anyone?

GARY: (Indicating RODNEY) He's dead, sir.

CPT. RUSHMORE: What hit him!

DAN: Dazedly) Nothing hit him ... He jumped ... grenade landed near us, and he threw himself on the grenade. It would have killed us all if he hadn't. (Shaking his head) I can't believe it. I can't believe it. (The two SOLDIERS return from stage right.)

GARY: Hey, give a hand here! Get a stretcher. (GARY takes a poncho roll from his field belt, unrolls it and covers RODNEY. Simultaneously, the other SOLDIERS leave stage left and return with a stretcher. GARY and two SOLDIERS put RODNEY on the stretcher while CPT RUSH-MORE helps the earlier WOUNED MAN to his feet and assists him out stage left. DAN watches as the other men lift the stretcher and start to carry RODNEY out stage left. When the stretcher comes alongside DAN, he steps to it. The men carrying it stop. DAN lifts the poncho and stares at RODNEY. Then he slowly covers him. The men carrying the stretcher resume walking out stage left.)

CPT. RUSHMORE: (Re-entering) I'm going to write him up for the Medal of Honor.

DAN: He deserves it.

CPT. RUSHMORE: I'll arrange for the Chaplain to hold a memorial service.

DAN: No tears ... just hollow and empty. Hurt. (The lights dim while DAN and CPT. RUSHMORE turn, facing one -quarter right. A SOL-DIER enters from stage left with a bayoneted rifle stuck into a flat wooden crosspiece. He sets it downstage right of DAN and CPT. RUSHMORE and returns to stand with them facing it. GARY enters stage left and brings a steel helmet that he places over the butt of the rifle. As he moves to a position behind DAN and the others, and faces the rifle, he is joined by two other SOLDIERS. Simultaneous with the last entrance, the CHAPLAIN enters stage right and moves to a position stage right facing one-quarter left.)

CHAPLAIN: (Makes sign of cross and the following are said as segments of a longer speech floating through time.) Rodney shared … many times … agonized over man's ability … to treat other men … but Father, aren't we all …? Gentle spirit made him … man of sorrows. (DAN is obviously troubled.) These words sum all we can feel about RODNEY. (Pause) "Greater love hath no man than this, that a man lay down his life for his friends." (All exit except DAN. The lights come up in the kitchen.)

DAN: (Desolately) I killed him. He was dead inside before the grenade, so lonely, so empty. I'm dead too. (DAN moves to stage left door and then changes his mind.) Lonely … a hex … damn plagues cursing me. (Pause) I feel like I want … held … cradled … hmfh . . . stupid … too old (Pause) who'd want to hold a dumb shit? (Pause) Rodney was right. Life can be tiring.
(DAN is stoop-shouldered and moving slowly. He drops into a chair. He sits for a period obviously finalizing something, making a choice. Once he has decided, he goes to the cabinet, opens it, and pulls out the bottle of aspirin. He removes the cap, gets a glass, takes a pitcher of water from the refrigerator, pours a glassful, and starts taking the aspirin four to five at a time, washing each group down with some water. From the moment DAN pulls out the bottle until he sets it down empty on the counter, there is a ringing that increases in intensity and ends simultaneously with putting down the empty bottle. The lights also "wave" up and down. He goes back to the table and sits. Then he stares at the phone. DAN stares at the phone a little longer. Then he moves over slowly to dial.)
Hello . . . Ramona? Dan, Kevin There? Thanks. (Pause) Hi, Kevin. Dan. Look, I'm calling to let you know I can't go on anymore. Pam left with the kids tonight; I don't blame her. I've done nothing but screw up our marriage; I've screwed up since the day I was born. Can't go on, and I'm not going to screw up one more person's life. I've done enough of that already. So, anyway, I've called to let you know that I've pulled my final dumb shit act, so I can stop everyone's headache. Kevin, thanks for trying to understand.

End Scene v

Scene vi

(As the lights come up, DAN is center stage.)

DAN: They might call me weak, but damn it, it's the only way I know to be set free from it all. (Pause) I wonder what's next? Hope I like the answer. (Pause) (DAN moves back to the counter and picks up the empty aspirin bottle, moves downstage to the table.) I never, never thought it would be this peaceful. Like it's all right. (Pause) It might be the best for Richard. (Pause) I don't think I've been too good a father to him, and at least it'll be the last time I embarrass him. (Pause) And Pam? We had something once … gone, best for her, too. My fault, no one could live with me. Paul? I've loved him, but treated him … (DAN's despondency changes to desperation.) Oh, God! I'll mess up his program. I didn't think, oh God. (DAN throws the empty aspirin bottle down so that it bounces behind him upstage.) I'm only making more headaches. Oh, God, I can't believe this. (DAN slumps into a chair, crying. The stage right door bursts open and KEVIN in T-shirt, pants, and slippers rushes through the door followed by DR. CHAMBERS, a forty-five year old kindly looking man.)

KEVIN: Dan, are you all right?

DAN: (Sobbing) Help me, Kevin! Help me!

KEVIN: Doc Chambers is here, Dan.

DR. CHAMBERS: Dan, did you take something? Poison?

DAN: About fifty aspirin … just a few minutes ago, Doc, I don't want to die!

DR. CHAMBERS: Puts his arm around DAN and starts to guide him off stage left.) It's okay, Dan. We can get them out of your system. (DR. CHAMBERS exits with DAN stage left.)

KEVIN: (Notices the empty aspirin bottle, picks it up, and turns it in his hands in frustration. Then he throws it in the wastebasket.)
How stupid of me! I should have realized just how frustrated he was.

What if he hadn't called? And, God, I'd like to thank you that he called. But I'm mad over the stark, raving idiotic conditions that brought him to this point. I know we each make choices that affect our lives, but so many are in ... "damned if you do--damned if you don't" situations. And, I can't believe there are that many damned people around. I'm sorry, but that's what I feel right now. Thanks for listening. (KEVIN crosses to the phone and dials.) Ramona, listen ... It looks like Dan will be okay, but he told me over the phone that Pam took the kids and left. I'm going to stay here tonight and tomorrow morning at least. I'll call when I know more. Listen, one other thing, the service in the morning ... would you take it for me? Just tell them I was called away. Besides they could use the break. Ramona, I really appreciate you. Bye, Hon. (Kevin hangs up the phone, starts clearing off the table, and rather absentmindedly straightens up some of the kitchen area. DR. CHAMBERS returns.)

DR. CHAMBERS: He's already asleep, physically and emotionally exhausted. I'll check in later. I want to call an audiologist friend and get more information on the ringing. There has to be some relief.

KEVIN: I hope so. I know it really bothers him.

DR. CHAMBERS: It's not over yet, but his cry for help is a good factor. (Going to the door.) Hopefully, I can get in touch with Dr. Payson before I come back.

KEVIN: I'll be here. I'll stay at least until tomorrow afternoon. Ramona's taking services. I think I'll try and call Pam, and, and, I don't know. I will see what she wants to do.

DR. CHAMBERS: She has some tough decisions ahead. (Pause) Well, call if you need me before I get back.

KEVIN: Okay, and thanks for coming.

DR. CHAMBERS: Sure. Take care. (Exits stage right. Lights down.)

End Scene vi

Resonance

(It is the next day, Sunday, a little before 10:00am. KEVIN is alone in the kitchen pouring a cup of coffee.)

KEVIN: (Calling offstage left.) Dan? Ready for coffee?

DAN: Yeah, I'm coming. (Enters stage left.)

KEVIN: (Putting coffee on table.) Here. How do you feel?

DAN: (Sitting down) Okay. Well, I feel kind of foolish.

KEVIN: (Getting himself a cup of coffee) Don't. Okay? Dan, I love you.

DAN: Thanks. Hey, it's Sunday. How come you're not in church?

KEVIN: Anyone can preach. It's more rewarding to help your brother. There are things and people in life that are more important to me than a Sunday morning service. Okay?

DAN: (With growing awareness that KEVIN really loves him) Thanks. Hey, I think I discovered something last night. I don't really want to die.

KEVIN: As a pastor, I have noticed that a lot. All over the world about once a week, lots of folks sing like crazy about going to Heaven, but when it gets right down to it … Well, I guess you have to fill a songbook with something.

DAN: Yeah, but seriously, I have to do something different. I feel like I've been on a dead end street. How I got there, I do not know. When Pam and I got married, and then Richard; I had high hopes. (DAN gets up with coffee cup in hand and moves near the kitchen window.)Then after the war … somehow gone, Kevin. Something was lost somewhere. Something died!

KEVIN: Dan, look out that window. See the cycle taking place. Nature dies and comes back to life again. (KEVIN gets up from the table and

moves to DAN.) And we are all part of that cycle. Like the rains are bringing new life, so you can let faith wash over you. We have to keep trying.
And loving. Otherwise, I agree, there is nothing to live for. But I love you,
Dan. And, I believe you love your family, even when you strike out with
frustrations. You would be indifferent if you didn't love them.

DAN: I feel like ... I do ... but then ... Is there any help for this ringing?
Pam ... Rodney?

KEVIN: I know. Seems like so much ... But first of all let me tell you that
Doctor Chambers contacted a colleague of his last night--an audiologist.
There may be a breakthrough soon in drugs that offer relieve, and already
there are hearing aid masker devices that in many cases offer partial or total
relief. We'll need to contact the VA.

DAN: I'm going to check it out. I'd like to believe that there could be some
relief from this ringing. Sometimes at night it'll wake me up, and it takes
forever to get back to sleep. I h've taken aspirin for it if I have a headache,
but that doesn't help much.

KEVIN: (Searching for the right words. Wondering if DAN will take
advantage of the ironic humor) Yeah, I, ah, Dan, another thing Doctor
Chambers said is that ... ah ... too much aspirin often causes temporary
ringing in the ears. (DAN sharply turns to look directly at KEVIN, then
laughs.)

DAN: Aspirin; ringing - I don't know. (Pause) And then there is Rodney.
He died saving my life, but I didn't deserve it.

KEVIN: Yeah, lots of people struggle with that. But if we can't change it,
somehow, we have to accept the circumstances and keep living.

DAN: And, Pam's gone.

KEVIN: (He watches DAN closely for his reaction, hoping he has done
the right thing in DAN's eyes.) Maybe not. I called her last night. She
agreed to come over this morning around ten. That's why I called you.

DAN: (Looking at clock) well, it's almost ten. She should be here anytime. I wonder what will happen. (DAN sits back down.)

KEVIN: Maybe repair some broken bridges; might build some new ones.

DAN: Maybe. (The stage right door opens, and PAM is standing there. PAUL pushes past her and rushes to DAN throwing himself onto him.)

PAUL: Daddy! (PAUL crawls on DAN's lap.)

DAN: Hi, Paul. (Pause) Pam. Richard. (PAM and RICHARD enter.)

PAM: You boys run along to your rooms. (PAUL and RICHARD exit stage left.)

KEVIN: Do you want me to stay? (DAN and PAM look at each other and quickly nod. They all sit at the table. KEVIN sits in the middle.) Can't promise to be through by noon. I guess maybe we should start with the realization that we ought to, ah, not count on any quick answers. Most of the instant miracles I know are from the books. The rest take time and work. First, Dan, maybe your could try to tell us how you were feeeling last night.

DAN: Well, different that today. I am embarrassed now, but last night I felt like I'd come to the end of my rope. That I couldn't go on anymore. (DAN gets up and goes to the window.) I felt like I needed help, but didn't know how to get any. (Pause) I, uh, guess I felt a lot of self-pity, too. Like no one understood me, like no one cared. I think maybe I was wrong, but I didn't feel that way last night. (Pause. All are somewhat self-conscious.)

KEVIN: One thing that does enter into this situation, very strongly is the ringing. Doctor Chambers said that he found out that severe tinnitus is medically considered to be in the top three of afflictions. The first is severe, constant pain; the second sever, constant dizziness; and, the third is this severe constant ringing in the ears. The ringing is quite a handicap. A major problem is that it is a disability that is not visible to others. This form of hiddeen wounding is another handicap in itself.

PAM: (Slowly) Maybe I should have tried harder to understand you, Dan. (Gaining courage) But, I would get so frustrated because there were times where I felt bad. I was physically tired, and felt bad, too. And maybe you did feel that way all the time, but you didn't want to allow me to feel that way ever. Well, I did, and I do!

DAN: (He is making a real effort to listen and understand.) I know. I know. I have been angry over the past, and angry because I didn't feel like you loved me, and bet I guess that since the war, I have not really given you too much to love. I had certain dreams about what we would become together. The way things would be, I remember thinking how it would be when I came home. But in Boston as I walked to a bus station in uniform `cause that's the way I'd arrive on the plane, a group of protesters followed me a screaming, "Babykiller, babykiller" and a bunch of others garbage. I felt then that I wished they'd been Viet Cong so I could waste them, and I think I carried that home.

PAM: (She stands up and moves toward DAN, obviously feeling the first small ray of hope in a long time.) I remember. I remember the minute you walked through the door feeling afraid of you, (DAN and PAM reach for each other and embrace.) and I didn't know why. I wanted to ask why, but I was afraid. And, I hugged you and asked if you were all right, and you . . . (PAUL bursts in carrying her completed star. RICHARD follows)

PAUL: Daddy! Have you seen this since Mommy finished it?

RICHARD: Paul, we are supposed to ...

PAM: It's okay, Richard.

DAN: It looks real nice, Paul.

PAUL: Daddy, would you like to hear my poem for the program?

DAN: Sure, Paul.

PAUL: (He speaks very fast and excited. The poem is just words, his emotion coming from the fact that he knows all of it. There is no pause between the ending of the poem and the question to DAN. It is all said in the same breath.)

> Twinkle, twinkle, little star,
> How I wonder what you are.
> Up above the earth so high,
> Like a diamond in the sky.
> Do you like the poem, Daddy?

(By the time PAUL finishes, everyone including RICHARD has the hint of a facial smile.)

DAN: Yes ... (deliberately) Yes, I really like the poem.

PAM: (Softly) Me, too, Paul. Me too.

(CURTAIN)

Alphabetized Index of Poems

Adobe Jenson Pro on LSI 50# Créme White
Type and Design by Karen Paul Stone

About the Author

Basil Clark is a retired Associate Professor of Speech and Theatre from the University of Pikeville in Kentucky where he taught public speaking; theatre; oral interpretation; and interpersonal, political and health communication courses.

His interests lie in writing, gardening, hiking, art, photography, and enjoying all activities with his wife Cora, and their eleven grandchildren.

In 1983, he won grand prize in the Performing Arts Repertory Theatre, now TheatreWorks, USA (NY), for his play *Change of Exchanges*. In 2001, his story "The Town Drunk" was included in *The World's Best Shortest Stories* published by Quality Paperback Book Club (NY), and in 2005 he coauthored *Poetic Healing: A Communication Journey from a Vietnam Veteran's Perspective*. (Parlor Press, Anderson, SC)

He served fourteen months as an Infantryman with the 1st Air Cavalry Division in Vietnam where he received the Silver Star, two Bronze Stars (one for Valor) and a Purple Heart.

In 2007, 2008 he wrote a DVD script for use by 4th grade teachers, *Mars Invasion: Coal Camp to Space Camp*. The curriculum is approved by the KY Department of Education and coordinates with the Mars Invasion program at the Challenger Learning Center of Hazard, KY.

Also, Basil has developed and performs several character monologues ranging from 20 to 40 minutes in length:

Presidents: Abraham Lincoln, U. S. Grant, James A. Garfield.

Biblical: Adam, Moses, Jepthah, Naaman, Job, Jonah, Mordecai, Micah, King Solomon, Nebuchadnezzar, Barabbas, Peter, and Paul.

Historical: Dr. Thomas Walker (early Kentucky Explorer.)

Other: Cpt'n B (Pirate.)

To contact the Author for speaking engagements, visit:
CLARKS-COVE.COM
or write Basil B. Clark, P.O. Box 71, Ooltewah, TN 37363

www.ingramcontent.com/pod-product-compliance
Lightning Source LLC
Chambersburg PA
CBHW031230090426

42742CB00007B/138